Testing the Limits of Foster Care
Fostering as an alternative to secure accommodation

British Association for Adoption & Fostering
(BAAF)
Skyline House
200 Union Street
London SE1 0LX
www.baaf.org.uk

Charity registration 275689

British Library Cataloguing in Publication Data
A catalogue record for this book is available
from the British Library

ISBN 1 903699 18 5

Cover photographs by John Birdsall
Photography, posed by models
Designed by Andrew Haig & Associates
Typeset by Avon DataSet, Bidford on Avon
Printed by Russell Press Ltd (TU), Nottingham

BAAF Adoption & Fostering is the leading
UK-wide membership organisation for all those
concerned with adoption, fostering and child
care issues.

Testing the Limits of Foster Care

Fostering as an alternative to secure accommodation

Moira Walker, Malcolm Hill
and John Triseliotis

BAAF
ADOPTION
& FOSTERING

Contents

Chapter 4: The young people in the study: their characteristics and circumstances

Chapter 5: Needs and expectations

Chapter 6: Young people's overall experience and outcomes

Acknowledgements

A study of this kind can only be carried out with the co-operation of many people and we would like to thank all of those who have contributed. The research was made possible through the willingness of the project managers and staff to open this new and challenging project to scrutiny. Despite being fully occupied with setting up and running the Community Alternative Placement Scheme (CAPS), the manager, Pauline McHugh, senior practitioners and administrative staff took an active interest in the research and generously made time for interviews, meetings and various requests for information. We are also grateful to other representatives of NCH and the CAPS Fostering Panel, who were interviewed as stakeholders. However, it was carers who bore the brunt of our demands for interviews, diaries and form filling. We learned so much from what they told us and are extremely grateful to them for sharing their experience and wisdom. Meetings with the young people themselves were always a pleasure. We relied on them to gain an understanding of what living in a CAPS placement had entailed and we were frequently impressed by their thoughtful comments. We would wish to thank all of them for their essential contribution to the study.

While focusing primarily on CAPS, the research also followed the fortunes of some young people who had been placed in secure care. Again we were impressed with the young people's willingness to contribute and their thoughtful insights. We are very grateful to them and to secure accommodation staff who helped arrange our meetings.

Managers and social workers from a range of local authorities contributed through helping recruit young people to the research, being interviewed in respect of individual placements and providing an overview of their authority's use of the service. The local authority perspective was crucial to the evaluation and we very much appreciate that busy people made time to co-operate.

We are grateful to the Scottish Executive for funding the study and to the members of the study's Advisory Group for ongoing advice and support. From our own Centre, Lynn Hilley did an excellent job in transcribing the taped interviews.

Particular mention is warranted of one young man who took part in the study. Derek Munro was an enthusiastic participant who was keen to share his care experiences for the benefit of others. He was good with words and graphically described how much he valued his experience of living with CAPS carers. Sadly Derek died before the field work had been completed.

Moira Walker, Malcolm Hill and John Triseliotis
August 2002

Note about the authors

Moira Walker is Senior Research Fellow (Children and Young People) in the Social Work Research Centre at Stirling University. Previously she worked at the Centre for the Child & Society, University of Glasgow where this research was carried out.

Malcolm Hill is Director of the Centre for the Child & Society, University of Glasgow. He also edits BAAF's journal *Adoption and Fostering*.

John Triseliotis is Emeritus Professor, University of Edinburgh and Visiting Professor at Strathclyde University. He has published extensively on adoption and fostering.

1 Background and context

Introduction

Any evaluation of a new service promises valuable opportunities to learn from innovative practice and organisational change. When the then Scottish Office decided to fund an evaluation of the Community Alternative Placement Scheme (CAPS) set up by NCH Action for Children Scotland, there were good reasons for anticipating that this innovative project would provide more learning than most. This was because the scheme was established to offer foster care for a group of young people who hitherto had been placed in secure residential care and who were thought to present too great difficulties for family placements to be appropriate and hence were beyond the existing limits of foster care. CAPS was set up in response to the Social Work Services Inspectorate report, *A Secure Remedy* (SWSI, 1996), which recommended that community alternatives to secure care should be developed. The project[1] set out to break new ground in two major respects. The first was to place in foster care young people who would otherwise be in secure care; the second to pay foster carers the equivalent of a full-time salary, while also according them the status of fellow professionals. The scheme was aiming not just to develop good practice but to create a quite new and distinctive service.

Though innovative, CAPS clearly built on wider developments, notably the emergence of professional or specialist fostering and the growth of the independent sector. In some ways CAPS might be viewed as very much a product of British child welfare policy at the turn of the century. As the research progressed, it became increasingly clear that many of the challenges CAPS faced reflected, even highlighted, more general tensions in child welfare provision. Consequently the "limits of foster care" could not be understood or tested simply by examining work within the project.

---

[1]The terms "project" and "scheme" are used interchangeably to refer to CAPS. Though "scheme" is more consistent with its formal title, in conversation CAPS was commonly referred to as a "project".

In addition, it was necessary to consider the ways in which this was shaped by the wider context.

The Community Alternative Placement Scheme opened its doors in the spring of 1997. The evaluation started in October of the same year and lasted three years. This book describes the research and its findings.

Plan of the book

This introductory chapter describes the context in which the scheme was introduced, first by summarising background information on specialist fostering and secure care, then in relation to the current social and welfare climate, with a particular focus on how risk operates and is responded to in contemporary society. The chapter ends with brief details of the study's aims and design. Chapters 2 and 3 report on the development of the project, while Chapters 4 to 7 describe the young people who took part in the research and how they fared over the study period. Chapter 8 provides information on costs and how the project was appraised by key stakeholders, with Chapter 9 providing a conclusion which draws together salient issues and highlights the implications for future policy and practice. In order to preserve anonymity, identifying details were occasionally altered. Closed brackets within quotations indicate that some text has been omitted.

Developments in specialist fostering

Specialist or professional fostering (also known in North America as treatment foster care) originated in the 1970s and grew rapidly during the 1980s (Galaway, 1990; Nutter *et al*, 1995). Among the original components were payments to foster carers (in addition to the normal allowance), greater than usual preparation, training and support and focusing on a particular group of children. In the UK, the earliest specialist schemes catered for adolescents, though later on services for disabled children grew in importance, some offering "respite" (Shaw and Hipgrave, 1983, 1989). Similar trends occurred in other countries like Australia, sometimes with the support from a multi-disciplinary team as in the Netherlands and Canada (Colton and Williams, 1997).

Two key ideas characterised specialist fostering which remain significant for CAPS. The first was the idea that foster carers can be recruited and retained to look after children with more than average difficulties, provided that the carers are properly rewarded, supported and recognised. The second was that young people who were typically placed in institutions could and should be looked after in the community by foster families (Triseliotis *et al*, 1995).

One of the best known early fostering schemes in the UK was the Kent Families Project targeted at serious young offenders. Carers were specifically recruited to look after challenging young people on the basis of a negotiated agreement. Extended preparation was provided for carers (Hazel, 1991). This project adopted a contractual and behavioural approach. Many North American schemes also espouse a specific treatment orientation, but this has been less common in the UK (Hill *et al*, 1993). When agencies adopt a single specific approach, use of cognitive-behavioural principles has been most popular, but other orientations include ecological (Pine and Jacobs, 1989), attachment (Downes, 1992), strengths and life domain-based (Clark *et al*, 1994) and solution-focused therapy (Houston, 2000). Aldgate *et al* (1989) suggested that the main role of fostering for adolescents was to help them make successful transitions to adulthood, which might encompass but was not confined to dealing with difficult behaviour.

The 1990s saw both extensions to specialist fostering and a blurring of the distinction between it and "traditional" fostering. A number of local authorities "mainstreamed" the notions of higher pay, more intensive support and careful contracting, so that in theory at any rate all their foster carers became "special" (Lowe, 1990; Hill *et al*, 1993). This stemmed in part from dislike of a two-tier system and resentment by non-specialist foster carers, who were often caring for difficult children anyway (McKenzie, 1994; Triseliotis *et al*, 2000). Although it appears that the majority of social work and foster carer opinion has swung in favour of professionalisation, a significant minority are concerned that this detracts from informal, altruistic and unconditional ideals of fostering (Testa and Rolock, 1999; Triseliotis *et al*, 2000).

Remand fostering for older adolescents has become quite common in England, while others have helped young adults prepare for independent living (Field, 1992; Graham *et al*, 1992; Kosonen, 1993). For example, CARE Remand Fostering (CRF) was established in Berkshire in 1998 aiming to divert young people from the criminal justice system, challenge thoughts, attitudes, values and behaviour, and give an opportunity for positive development. Partly as a result of schemes catering for those on the threshold of adulthood, a comparative study carried out in the early 1990s showed that young people aged 15+ made up a higher proportion of users of British specialist fostering schemes (42 per cent) than was the case in North America (28 per cent). This may in part account for the somewhat higher breakdown rate for British schemes. The UK also had more schemes for disabled children (Hill *et al*, 1993).

A major trend in UK fostering during the last decade has been the proliferation of independent fostering organisations. Although many are small (fewer than 25 carers), some are large. In a survey of 55 such agencies, Sellick and Connolly (2001) found that 14 (about one-quarter) had 50 or more carers. Most independent agencies appear to provide "conventional" fostering (emergency, short-term and long-term place-ments), but a minority provide specialist or task-centred services. However, all give round-the-clock support and most provide additional services, such as therapy and an educational liaison worker. The growth of independent schemes has not always been welcomed, with critics claiming that they attract foster carers from local authorities and then charge much higher rates for the same service (Millar, 2000).

Outcomes of specialist fostering

A number of schemes, especially in North America, have been subject to systematic evaluation, some using a comparison or control group, which strengthens the value of the findings in attributing change to the particular project (Gabor and Charles, 1994). The studies comparing young people with similar characteristics and levels of difficulty have normally shown that they do better in special schemes, compared with standard foster care (e.g. Almeida *et al*, 1989; Chamberlain, 1990; Clark *et al*, 1994; Testa and Rolock, 1999). A detailed study of programme characteristics and outcomes by Nutter *et al* (1995) found that there was no simple relation-ship between the type and cost of a scheme and treatment goals met or post-placement living situations. Reddy and Pfeiffer (1997) under-took a meta-analysis of 40 outcome studies. This provided evidence of interesting and differentiated impacts, depending on the criteria used. They identified large positive effects by treatment foster care on subsequent placement stability and on children's social skills. More moderate though still positive impact was identified for children's behaviour, the restrictiveness of post-discharge placement (i.e. avoidance of custodial and residential placements) and psychological adjustment.

British evidence has been less clear cut. This reflects the use of different criteria and normally the absence of matched comparison groups. Berridge and Cleaver (1987) subsumed specialist fostering within "intermediate fostering". They found that on the whole the breakdown rates and other aspects of the placement (e.g. birth parent and social worker involvement) were better than for other types of placement, though the differences were not significant. The Kent scheme was shown to produce improvements for many young people (Yelloly, 1979; Smith, 1986; Hazel, 1990), with experienced foster carers doing particularly well. Young people with combined school and behaviour problems did least well (Fenyo et al, 1989). However, according to Triseliotis et al (1995) similar success has not been repeated elsewhere. The study by Rowe et al (1989) covering six local authorities found that slightly over half the specialist fostering placements ended sooner than either planned or needed, though more than half were seen as helpful. A report on Barnardo's Family Placement Services in Scotland (2001) reported a 12 per cent disruption rate for 138 foster placements of children with special needs (average age = 13 years).

Based on a review of the literature, Curtis and colleagues (2001) reported on studies comparing therapeutic foster care and residential group care in the USA. These have shown that:

- the young people usually have similar levels of difficulty;
- the foster programmes tend to cater for a younger age group on average and for more children with a history of serious abuse;
- foster care provides greater time input from supervising adults and less time with delinquent peers.

Two studies (one American, the other British by Colton) with small samples found no difference in problem reduction between foster and residential programmes. Studies by Chamberlain and colleagues of a programme for young offenders to which young people were randomly allocated has found that the foster programme produced better results than the residential alternative with respect to completing the programme and running away during the placement, and known re-offending and incarceration one and two years later (Chamberlain 1998; Chamberlain and Weinrott, 1990). The foster carers were trained to use specific behavioural techniques, so that their approach to the young people was more structured, monitored and controlled than is normally the case in family-based care.

Illustrating the view that foster care is not able to cater for the most challenging and difficult young people, Curtis and colleagues cite Dore as follows:

> ... children who are highly aggressive, consistently impulsive, hostile or defiant, who threaten violence to themselves or who engage in delinquent acts which threaten community safety and elicit negative community reactions towards a foster family, whose education needs exceed community resources, and who have a very limited ability to engage with or empathize with others, are unsuitable for even the most specialized family foster home ... (Dore, 1994, p 3)

In some respects CAPS set out to challenge this position. The scheme incorporated the key features of successful specialist fostering projects (pay, training, 24-hour support), but in addition made the fees higher than has hitherto been typical in British schemes and made respite standard. Its target group corresponded to some extent with previous projects for young offenders, but with added dimensions. Young people heading for secure accommodation are not necessarily offenders and their crucial characteristic is that their behaviour either puts themselves at severe risk (e.g. through running, sleeping rough, substance misuse, self-harming) or their behaviour is a serious threat to others.

Secure accommodation

Secure accommodation in Scotland occupies a distinctive position among resources for children and young people. While firmly located within residential child care provision, it operates at the interface with the criminal justice system. Approximately two-thirds of young people in secure accommodation are placed there on the authority of a Children's Panel.[2] The remainder are subject to a court order, either serving a sentence for a serious crime or on remand. For some in the latter category a supervision requirement from the Children's Panel continues to be in force and is reviewed annually. This reflects the predominant welfare focus which underpins the Children's Hearing system. Some young people held in secure provision have serious mental health difficulties and, in some circumstances, might also be considered for admission to psychiatric hospital.

Locking up children is clearly a serious step to take. The UN Convention on the Rights of the Child states that secure accommodation should only be used 'as a measure of last resort and for the shortest appropriate period of time'. However, in practice, secure accommodation tends to be used when no other viable alternative is available to care for young people seen as putting themselves or others at risk (Harris and Timms, 1993a, b). A Scottish inspection-based report on secure provision described the optimum position as one in which all young people who require secure care are admitted, while all who can be accommodated elsewhere are catered for in alternative resources. The report concluded that this position had not yet been reached. Instead, young people found themselves in secure care because other services had failed them, either immediately before their admission or at an earlier point in their childhood (SWSI, 1996). It was in this context that the report's authors suggested community alternatives should be developed.

In recent years, between 200 and 250 young people have been admitted to secure care in Scotland each year, with about 90 in placement at any one time. A majority are boys but girls typically account for more than a quarter. A survey undertaken on behalf of SWSI in 1998 reported that girls were more likely to be admitted for welfare reasons rather than offending. Only one of the 21 girls included in the survey was on a court order, the remainder having been placed by a Children's Panel. Running

---

2 Children and young people subject to secure authorisation by the Children's Panel need not be placed in secure accommodation if the head of the secure establishment and the chief social work officer consider this is unnecessary.

away and the risk of sexual harm or prostitution were the most common concerns (SWSI, 2000).

Based on research in England, O'Neill also found that girls were more likely to be held because of concerns about their safety. Even though they were told that the placement was for their own care and protection, all the young people in the study by O'Neill (2001) experienced it as a punishment. O'Neill found that the young people received relatively little therapeutic intervention. Social workers and young people evaluated the 29 secure placements and only nine (less than a third) were seen as "beneficial". Most of those who benefited were boys and offenders. The prospects for all those admitted on a welfare basis were seen as poor or very poor. Social workers were dissatisfied that the secure units provided little more than containment.

In a Scottish context, Kelly (1992) found that staff sought to provide personal help to young residents in secure accommodation, but for the most part lacked the relevant skills and training. The Scottish survey referred to on page 7 also found that care staff were ill-equipped to provide the diverse and intensive service young people required, while specialist services such as counselling and psychology were not consistently available and sometimes poorly integrated with the work of the unit. However, in some instances young people had made good progress when specialists and care staff worked effectively together (SWSI, 2000).

The same Scottish survey confirmed evidence from other sources that most young people in secure accommodation have complex and overlapping problems (Harris and Timms, 1993a, b). Admission to secure care usually followed persistent offending, aggressive behaviour, absconding, self-harming and on occasions heavy dependence on drugs. These behaviours reflected complex and in some cases long-standing needs. Around half the young people had shown some sort of problematic behaviour before reaching the age of eight, in which case their difficulties were generally serious and entrenched. At the other end of the spectrum, approximately one in five had first come to the attention of social work professionals in their teens. Typically their problems were less severe, though a higher proportion had committed a serious offence and been sentenced by the court.

Young people in secure care therefore have diverse needs, while their difficulties vary in intensity. However, most require emotional support and to be helped to change certain aspects of their behaviour, so that looking after them involves a combination of care and control.

Theories, concepts and principles

The main theoretical perspectives which underpin specialist foster care reflect this care/control duality. Attachment theory emphasises the importance of establishing caring relationships which foster emotional development, while cognitive, task-based models are geared primarily to facilitating behavioural change and a sense of responsibility for one's own actions. Traditionally foster care has incorporated elements of both, though, as noted previously, the original specialist schemes favoured a cognitive approach.

In principle a combined approach is consistent with ordinary parenting and is not obviously problematic. However, within a foster care service the theoretical underpinning also reflects how young people and the caring task are constituted. This is particularly relevant in relation to teenagers at risk of secure accommodation. Are they damaged young people who need care and support to develop and overcome previous adversity and trauma? Or are they independent, autonomous individuals on the verge of adulthood who need to learn to take responsibility for their actions and make choices about how they want to live their lives? If the former perspective prevails, foster placements would be expected to last for years rather than months and to concentrate on developing trust, self-confidence and the capacity to make and sustain relationships. The second model typically involves shorter-term, contract-based interventions with clear practical aims. Evidently these distinctions strongly influence expectations of carers, how services are organised, and service agreements with local authorities.

It might also be argued that they represent different models of social work practice. Howe (1996) differentiates between *depth* and *surface* social work. While depth social work is concerned with *why* people have difficulties and addresses underlying issues, surface social work is concerned only with alleviating visible problems. Howe argues that social work practice operates increasingly on the surface, with this in turn reflecting fundamental changes in expectations and attitudes towards individuals who require social work support. Post-war optimism that individuals in need should and could be helped through personal support has been replaced by a fear of welfare dependency and an emphasis on each individual's responsibility to take up and make use of services on offer, or suffer the consequences. Changes in criminal justice social work clearly demonstrate this shift in emphasis. It can also be detected within child welfare services, though less so, since children are evidently dependent on adults and the local authorities are duty bound to safeguard them and promote their welfare throughout their childhood.

This analysis highlights that, in providing placements for young people who might otherwise be in secure accommodation, CAPS was required not only to achieve a balance between care and control but also to potentially straddle two different models of social welfare. The inevitable tensions were manifested in key aspects of the scheme's development and are highlighted in subsequent chapters.

Whatever the theoretical orientation, foster care is underpinned by the provisions of the UN Convention on the Rights of the Child, which has guided relevant UK legislation and policy. The key requirements are that young people's views are taken seriously, their safety ensured and steps taken to maximise their life opportunities, both in the present and the future. Given the overall requirement to be guided by young people's best interests, it can be difficult to achieve the appropriate balance between taking account of young people's views and wishes and keeping them safe (Marshall, 1997). Drawing on attachment theory, Bell has highlighted the importance of adult relationships in enabling young people to exercise their rights (Bell, 2002). She argues that relationships based on supportive and companionable interactions with adults are more able to empower children than those based on domination and control, since young people will only feel secure enough to get in touch with and express their feelings in the context of a relationship based on trust. However, other researchers have pointed out that young people typically have little choice over the options available to them, so that the rhetoric of rights can mask continuing disadvantage and disempowerment (Furlong and Cartmel, 1997; Dalrymple, 2001).

In recent years, the concept of resilience has gained ground as a means of helping understand how some young people exposed to adverse life experiences fare better than others. There has been interest both in identifying the characteristics of resilient children and exploring how resilience can be fostered in specific groups, for example, those looked after and accommodated by local authorities: (Fonaghy *et al*, 1994; Gilligan, 1997, 1999). A host of factors have been identified as associated with resilience. These can be grouped as follows:

- individual characteristics such as good self-esteem, higher intelligence and an easy temperament;
- good social and problem-solving skills;
- presence of at least one strong supportive and trusting relationship;
- positive social and educational experiences;
- higher socio-economic status.

Thus some of the characteristics associated with resilient children are inherited, others reflect social and economic structures, and a few can be developed with appropriate support. Foster care can potentially provide that support, so that the concept of resilience is useful in assessing the potential but also the limitations of foster care.

This brief review of relevant theoretical and conceptual frameworks lends support to the view that a project such as CAPS should be evaluated not just in terms of how carers respond to individual young people, but in broader terms which take account of the wider social and policy context. In practical terms this means taking into consideration the structures in which young people live their lives and how social work services are developed and delivered. Houston (2001) proposes a theoretical framework based on critical realism as potentially useful in child welfare, since it views social phenomena as created by social interactions, which in turn are both constrained and facilitated by underlying structures and dynamics. These are often invisible and seldom within the immediate control of the social actors. We would propose that this is also a helpful framework within which to examine the development of CAPS and that, in the present context, the operation and management of risk merits particular consideration.

Foster care in the risk society

In setting out to cater for young people thought to require secure care and paying carers the equivalent of a full-time salary, CAPS was building on recent developments in foster care but also considerably extending them. In principle, the project adhered to the widely held view that, with appropriate support and financial rewards, foster carers can look after virtually any child. It could be argued that the carers, project staff and referring agencies were in fact setting out to test the limits of foster care in the present context. They would also be taking on young people likely to test their coping and caring capacities to the limit.

It soon became evident that the achievements of the scheme would also be strongly influenced by factors well beyond the scope of staff and carers. In reporting the study we give due emphasis to these wider considerations, partly because this provides a more complete evaluation of the work of the scheme, but also to enhance the book's relevance to wider debates about the potential and limitations of foster care. Aspects of the social, policy and service provision context did not simply constitute a backdrop against which the scheme operated but also impinged directly on each aspect of its work, including the recruitment of carers, the referral and acceptance of young people, the nature of the care provided, and the young people's future prospects. Understanding the interface between the day-to-day operation of the scheme and the key dimensions of the wider social context proved crucial to appreciating the challenges the scheme faced.

While it is acknowledged that all social work services are shaped by external influences, CAPS' situation was distinctive, notably because risk considerations were inherent in each aspect of its operation. Criteria for secure placement are that a young person presents a danger to self or others, or that (s)he has repeatedly absconded and is likely to do so again. Thus in catering for young people who met these criteria, one of the scheme's key objectives was to manage risk in a community setting. Placements entailed a level of risk for young people and carers alike, with NCH Action for Children responsible for monitoring and managing any potentially or actually dangerous situations. In addition, launching the scheme involved considerable financial risk for the organisation.

Parton (1996) has convincingly argued that risk considerations have become central to all child welfare services. This can in part be attributed to the effects of a series of child abuse inquiries in the 1980s, each set up after a child had died at the hand of a parent or step-parent (Hill, 1990; Parton, 1996). These both heightened public awareness of children's vulnerability and created the expectation that social workers would be able to keep children safe, as long as they became skilled at detecting which children were at risk (Parton, 1985). In practice there is no certain means of predicting which children will be abused, so social workers and their organisations have had to find ways of managing the tension between what is expected of them and what is possible (Parton et al, 1997). The development of multi-agency child protection systems sought to ensure that professionals would prioritise child protection over other aspects of their work, share information with each other, and make decisions within a uniform framework of case conferences and reviews. Social workers know that they will be severely censured if they fail to protect a child, so the child protection system has become a way of managing risks to professionals and children alike (Tunstill, 1996; Parton, 1997).

> Child protection has been no less a priority within care settings. Revelations that large numbers of children had been abused in institutions prompted far greater vigilance in the recruitment and monitoring of staff. In addition the importance of listening to young people was emphasised, with a range of provisions introduced to give them a say in how the homes were run and ensure that any complaints were taken seriously.
>
> (The Scottish Office, 1992; Scottish Executive, 2002)

Detecting and managing potential danger has thus become a central preoccupation across child welfare services. These developments within child welfare have not occurred in isolation from wider developments. Rather they reflect heightened awareness of risk in society (Beck, 1992) and parallel changes in how responsibility for risk is allocated in welfare policy (Parton, 1997; Culpitt, 1999).

As we hope to demonstrate throughout this book, the setting up of the CAPS scheme was very much in line with, even made possible by several key aspects of the current social and policy climate, even though these also constrained what the project could achieve. These enabling and constraining effects were evident in both the overall development of the project and in the day-to-day experiences of young people and carers in placement. Yet it would not do justice to the scheme to portray it as completely at the mercy of outside influences. As they grappled with a host of issues and tensions in their daily work, project staff and carers also challenged prevailing attitudes and practices. Risk considerations were operating in many of these interactive processes, even if these were not always made explicit.

Relevant connections are highlighted briefly throughout the book and considered in more detail in the final chapter. However, here the term risk is examined, followed by a summary of some relevant sociological and social policy analyses and a broad overview of the implications for CAPS.

Meanings of risk in child welfare

Douglas (1992) points out that, whereas early uses of the word risk referred to the mathematically calculated likelihood of a positive or negative event occurring, it is now generally unquantified and almost synonymous with the term "danger". Within social work, risk taking is sometimes viewed positively, as a means of achieving personal development. However, in the context of child welfare, the term risk is more often associated with danger or impairment. Indeed the terms "risk" and "danger" are often used interchangeably.

Brearley was one of the first writers to write about risk in social work and to differentiate the components (Brearley, 1982). He defines risk as 'the relative variation in possible outcomes' and identifies two distinct elements in assessing risk:

- estimation: considering how likely it is that a particular event will occur;
- evaluation: assessing the value attached to the outcome or how serious any adverse consequences of a particular event are likely to be.

In addition, Brearley defines "hazards" as factors which increase the possibility of a negative outcome, "dangers" as the feared consequences, and "strengths" as protective factors which reduce the likelihood of a negative outcome. The process of weighing up "hazards" and "strengths" is central to risk assessment in child welfare, with increasing recognition that social and cultural considerations need to be taken into account as well as the characteristics and circumstances of the child and immediate family (Department of Health, 2000; Gabarino and Sherman, 1980).

Hazards in foster care

As Kendrick has pointed out, there is surprisingly little research evidence on abuse in foster care, though the information available indicates that it occurs often enough to merit more detailed study (Kendrick, 1997). The issue has been studied more widely in North America than in Britain. In a study of abuse in residential and foster care placements, Rosenthal and colleagues reported that just under a third of reported incidents (102 of 290) had occurred in family foster homes and two-thirds in residential care (Rosenthal et al, 1991). Foster carers were identified in 45 cases of physical abuse, 34 of neglect and 20 of sexual abuse. Foster siblings were identified in seven cases of physical abuse, nine of neglect and 15 of sexual abuse. Thus the research highlighted the risks adolescent foster siblings might pose.

Evidence from the UK is less systematic, primarily coming from research on related topics. In a study of children referred to the sexual abuse unit of a London hospital over a three-year period, La Fontaine reported that four per cent of the perpetrators abusing girls and three per cent of those abusing boys were classified as a foster father or brother. In comparison only one child had been abused by a residential worker (La Fontaine, 1990, p 320). A study of calls to ChildLine identified 24 children who reported having been abused in foster care, with older foster siblings accounting for almost half the reported incidents (Morris and Wheatley, 1994). In addition, 20 children reported being physically abused, most commonly by foster fathers. NFCA (now Fostering Network) and the University of Birmingham carried out a study of how local authority departments in England responded to allegations of abuse (NFCA, 1996; Nixon and Verity, 1996). They reported that an allegation had been made against a member of approximately four per cent of foster families (305 reports). Just over a fifth of the reports were substantiated and in a further fifth it was not possible to establish whether abuse had occurred or not. The foster carers' own child was the alleged perpetrator in 44 cases, 12 of which were substantiated, and in 12 cases there was no resolution of whether abuse had occurred or not.

Thus foster care does present a risk to children, with foster carers' sons and daughters forming part of that risk. As with risk at home or in residential care, it is suggested that a range of factors contribute to abuse in foster care (McFadden and Ryan, 1991; Rosenthal *et al*, 1991). These include the isolation of a family home for vulnerable children, over burdening carers with too many children, pressure to place ever more challenging children in community-based placements, and lack of support to carers and their families. It would be surprising if other factors identified in relation to institutional abuse did not also make children vulnerable in foster families, notably the low status of children in public care, especially those with disabilities or from a minority ethnic group, and an acceptance of male domination (Colton, 2002; Green and Masson, 2002).

The risks foster children may pose to others has also been acknowledged. In a study of 250 looked after children, Farmer and Pollock (1998) highlighted a number of concerns about both the risk of sexual abuse from other young people and how these risks were managed. Children who had been abused or had abused others emerged as a particularly disadvantaged and problematic group. They also posed a threat to other young people, with half of those who had been abused themselves going on to abuse others. The authors described a care system ill-equipped either to protect and cater for the needs of young people themselves or to protect other children they might harm.

While acknowledging that foster home safety is the priority, over the last decade the National Foster Care Association has also drawn to attention to foster carers' vulnerability to the risk of being falsely accused (Hicks and Nixon, 1991; NFCA, 1996). We consider the implications for CAPS carers in more detail in Chapter 3.

Risk assessment

In terms of foster care, risk assessment usually relates to identifying any potential risks to the child or risks the child may pose to others in placement. Different approaches to risk assessment reflect the contested nature of risk itself (Lupton, 1999). From the objectivist perspective, risk is viewed as an objective reality which can be reliably assessed and measured. Actuarially based approaches to risk assessment are consistent with this approach. These compare the characteristics of a particular child or family with those known to be associated with dangerous behaviour, based on statistical analysis of relevant child populations or expert opinion.

However, even with the use of sophisticated statistical techniques, actuarial approaches are unable to assess how different factors interact or judge the significance of specific hazards or strengths in a particular situation (Wald and Woolverton, 1990; Gambrill and Schlonsky, 2000). For the latter, clinical or professional judgement is required, together with detailed knowledge of a child's individual characteristics and circumstances. This approach is more consistent with subjectivist approaches which view risk as comprehensible only in terms of the meanings actors accord to particular events or situations (Houston and Griffiths, 2000).

There is evidence that the reliability of assessments is improved when actuarial assessment and professional judgement are combined (Cash, 2001). Nevertheless, risk assessment is not an exact science and cannot accurately predict all potential dangers or their likely effect on specific children (Kemshall, 1996; Macdonald and Macdonald, 1999). Despite its predictive limitations, risk assessment has been proposed as a useful means of systematically examining potential dangers in a wide range of situations, including the assessment of prospective foster carers and placement planning (Byrne, 1997; Farmer and Pollock, 1998).

While the term "risk assessment" is most commonly used in the context of preventing a child being deliberately harmed, other sorts of assessment are concerned with a wider range of risks, notably the likelihood of impairment or vulnerability to social exclusion. The Assessment and Action Records which form part of the Department of Health's Looking After Children Materials and the Department of Health's Framework for the Assessment of Children in Need are both means of systematically identifying obstacles to present and future well-being, with a view to offering appropriate supports to overcome them (Ward, 1995). These are not concerned with predicting future events but with anticipating and ameliorating adverse consequences which are likely to result from a child's present circumstances. These assessments are couched in the language of need, with risk being viewed as resulting from needs not being met.

Risk and need

With the introduction of the Children Act (1989) and corresponding legislation in other UK jurisdictions – in Scotland, the Children (Scotland) Act 1995 applies – the aim has been to reframe the majority of child welfare interventions in terms of responding to need rather than risk. In practice this would mean developing family support, reserving the child protection system for more serious cases where children are considered at risk of "significant harm". The provisions of the legislation reflected events in Cleveland and Orkney which had raised fears that social workers were able to remove children too readily, against their own or parents' wishes (Cleveland, 1988; Clyde, 1992). They were also influenced by research findings which had indicated that, although the multi-agency child protection system usually worked well for the relatively small number of children at risk of serious injury, it was often unhelpful for the majority who come within its scope because of less serious concerns. The focus on investigating abuse could alienate and undermine parents and children, while drawing resources away from other support services (Cleaver and Freeman, 1995; Dartington, 1995).

The shift from a child protection system to family support has proved more difficult than had originally been anticipated, with resources continuing to be channelled into child protection services (Audit Commission, 1994; Colton et al, 1995). In addition there is evidence that, even when the language of need is used, risk considerations are still crucial in determining priority access to services (Audit Commission, 1994; Colton et al, 1995) and how social workers respond to families in difficulties (Spratt, 2001). From research and theoretical analysis there are strong indications that this reflects the centrality of risk in the social and policy context and the structures within which social work operates.

The risk society

Beck has coined the term "risk society" to describe current social life (Beck, 1992). According to his analysis, life has become characterised by increased uncertainty and fluidity as growing technology results in an unprecedented level of change and risk. Individuals can no longer expect a job for life, but rather live with the expectation of periods of unemployment, part-time work and retraining for both men and women. Alongside this, traditional forms of family life have been replaced by a range of more fluid and varied arrangements. Life thus becomes more stressful and less predictable.

Beck also argues that, though making life more precarious, the loosening of traditional structures and expectations opens up unprecedented opportunities, for example, through increased access to further education and life-style choice. While acknowledging that class and gender still constrain individual options, Beck argues that there is more scope for social mobility as individuals are no longer expected to travel through life along a predefined path. Beck claims that, through a process of individuation, people are able, indeed required, to "create their own biographies". This, he argues, is a calculative process in which individuals assess options, taking into account the potential risks and opportunities (Beck, 1992).

This analysis has a number of implications for foster care. As patterns of work and family life become more diverse, opportunities may open up for individuals to take up fostering at different points in their lives. Foster care will be one option among others and prospective carers can be expected to weigh up what it offers alongside what it demands. In the risk society, life is a project, and in this entrepreneurial spirit, people from all sorts of backgrounds can be expected to give it a try. However, life is also more stressful, so that fewer individuals and families may feel able to take on the extra demands of fostering, unless they have considerable encouragement and support.

Similarly, the Beck analysis has positive and negative implications for young people: while life is more stressful, there is the possibility of more life-style choice and opportunity to escape disadvantage through training and education. However, Furlong and Cartmel provide convincing evidence that, despite increased choice and diversity, young people's routes through life can still be predicted on the basis of class, gender, race and disability (Furlong and Cartmel, 1997). The same authors claim that the illusion of control over their lives adds to life's stress because individuals hold themselves responsible for any perceived failure, even if opportunities, for example, in terms of employment, are in fact largely determined by structural factors beyond their control.

A somewhat different analysis of how risk operates in modern society was provided by Foucault. His focus is on governmentality and the ways in which notions of risk allow certain objectives to be met. Identifying groups as "at risk" or presenting a risk to others legitimates state intervention in their lives, ostensibly to help them but also to reinforce their adherence to accepted values and behaviour. However, in most instances direct government intervention is unnecessary since notions of potential risks and what is required to overcome them are subtly conveyed through a myriad of practices and organisations. In relation to child welfare these include health visiting, schools and welfare services through which powerful ideals are conveyed about what constitutes the good, responsible family (Rose, 1989; Dean, 1999). This analysis is consistent with Parton's evidence that assessments of risk to children are based not on technical calculations of likely harm, but rather on judgements about whether parents, primarily mothers, are conforming to accepted standards of behaviour (Parton *et al*, 1997). Similar considerations would no doubt explain the fact that more young women than men are placed in secure accommodation for their own protection (SWSI, 2000). From this perspective on risk, social work's social control functions are highlighted.

Since foster families operate both as a family and as a form of social service provision, this analysis also highlights the social control aspects of fostering. These are inevitably enhanced when the young people placed are formally identified as "at risk" or presenting a risk to others. While fostering always involves balancing elements of care and control, carers have traditionally been motivated by a sense of altruism and a wish to promote the interests of individual young people, rather than the wider public. Some tensions can therefore be anticipated as the controlling aspects of the foster care role are enhanced, as when providing an alternative to secure care.

Risk in social policy

Inevitably the impact of wider sociological changes on foster care are mediated through the social welfare climate in which foster care operates. Within the UK, changes in how responsibility for risk is allocated have underpinned significant developments in policy. In terms of ideology, the early welfare state's principles of universal welfare provision and pooling risk have been replaced by an ethos which emphasises individual responsibility (Culpitt, 1992; Holman, 1998; Culpitt, 1999). Under the policies of the Thatcher Government, individuals were increasingly held responsible for their own or their children's welfare, the withdrawal of benefits to 16–18-year-olds being but one example of this trend. Welfare services were only to be provided for the few who could not be self-sufficient and would be at risk without additional support.

At the same time individual service users were in principle given more power and choice, as welfare services were increasingly provided by a range of voluntary and private providers, and market principles of competition and value for money were introduced to the public sector. On the positive side this increased opportunities for voluntary organisations such as NCH Action for Children to further their long-standing tradition of developing innovative and potentially "risky" services such as CAPS. On the other hand, to be financially viable the services they offered had to accord with local authority priorities and be perceived as good value. Through these various changes, Parton argues state action to manage and distribute risk was weakened, instead relying on the calculating choices of individuals and organisations (Parton, 1996).

Since 1997, the Labour Government has taken a more proactive stance towards tackling the accumulation of risk and disadvantage in certain areas and communities. Tackling social exclusion has been high on the Government's agenda, with a predominant focus on getting people back into work or training and regenerating communities where risks, such as poverty, drug use and crime, had accumulated (Social Exclusion Unit, 1999, 2001). Reducing child poverty is a central policy objective (Scottish Executive, 2001). However, the Government's approach to social exclusion does not represent a return to the collective responsibility of the past. While respecting rights to employment and opportunity, policies also emphasise individuals' responsibilities to be as self-sufficient as possible and contribute to the community. At the same time, the trend towards marketisation, privatisation and competition continues. This has afforded more diversity in services, but there is also evidence that in some contexts, for example education, it undermines inclusion and the possibility of achieving better opportunities for all (Power, 1999; Blyth, 2001). The present climate is therefore in some respects favourable for disadvantaged young people but in other ways quite difficult and harsh.

Williams (1998) argues that, by focusing primarily on individual behaviours and reintegration into normative society, the present Government's approach to social exclusion is concerned not simply with widening opportunity but also with fears about an excluded "underclass" which threatens society's values and safety. Services are provided to help people back into mainstream society, but these are offered alongside harsher penalties for those who remain on the margins.

This dual approach to social inclusion has special relevance for children and young people. Jenks (1996) argues that in the dislocated, unpredictable post-modern world, children serve an important function for adults in that they link an idealised image of their past with hopes for a better future. Investment in children is a key element of social inclusion programmes. Initiatives such as Sure Start and Community Schools have been set up to tackle disadvantage through ensuring that all children engage with the education system and so are equipped to take up future employment. On the other hand children who step out of line, for example by truanting or committing crimes, are feared and harshly treated. It is widely acknowledged that the murder of James Bulger prompted "moral panic" that the threat posed by certain children was indicative of society's moral decline (Earle and Newburn, 2002). In England and Wales such attitudes have resulted in harsher treatment for young people within the youth justice system, for example, by being held in secure treatment centres (Muncie, 2002a, 2002b). Goldson has argued that young people in trouble are increasingly viewed as offenders rather than children "in need" (Goldson, 2000). Though to date these particular developments have been less pronounced in Scotland, other measures, such as the introduction of child curfews in some areas, reveal a similar willingness to restrict, control and blame young people (Waiton, 2001).

This emphasis on self-sufficiency and control of anti-social behaviour has had significant implications for social work. Statutory social workers now spend much of their time assessing risk, both in order to manage dangerous behaviour and to gauge entitlement to scarce resources (Jones, 2001; Jordan, 2001). The service social workers offer is now largely circumscribed by procedures and managerial priorities. According to Howe's classification referred to earlier, most statutory provision would constitute "surface" rather than "depth" social work (Howe, 1996).

Implications for foster care and CAPS

From this perspective, it is evident that several aspects of the social, policy and child welfare context are directly relevant to the work of CAPS, impacting on the overall organisation, the carers and the young people placed. We have argued that preoccupation with risk is a critical dimension of the current context and that the ramifications of this inevitably shaped how CAPS operated and what it could achieve.

The basis on which CAPS was set up was very much consistent with market-based economies of welfare. The scheme was devised in response to a central government report and recommendation, but was not government funded. Instead NCH Action for Children took the initiative, a step which involved both financial and professional risk. To be financially viable, CAPS had to provide what local authorities would pay for, so was inevitably constrained by their priorities. In professional terms, the scheme had to demonstrate that young people identified as presenting a risk to others could be cared for safely in well-supported community placements.

Despite the nature of the proposed client population, within the project the foster care task was not viewed as primarily about managing risk. Instead the approach was explicitly needs-led. On the face of it this welfare ethos seems somewhat at odds with other aspects of the present risk dominated climate.

In other respects, too, the development of CAPS was apparently inconsistent with current trends. While concerns about child safety have resulted in residential care being more closely regulated and field work more proceduralised and subject to managerial scrutiny, the care offered within foster homes is not governed by care standards or subject to inspection. In addition their quasi self-employed status and the home-based nature of their work means foster carers retain considerable discretion over how they look after the young people in their care, albeit within a clear ethical framework and explicit expectations. The high level of trust accorded to foster carers is also consistent with the paucity of research on how safe foster placements are.

From these perspectives CAPS might be viewed as anomalous, but it can also be understood as exemplifying some key aspects of the current context. As noted above, the family is viewed as a key site for socialising children, with parents held responsible for their children's welfare and "good parenting" essential to producing a well-ordered and safe society. At the same time, young people are viewed as having *choices* about how to live their lives. Together, belief in the power of "good" parenting and young people's potential for change make foster care an attractive option. In addition, it costs less than residential care, especially if changes can be brought about within a relatively short timescale. According to original plans for CAPS, the average length of placement was to be six months, though in practice a number of placements lasted much longer. Foster care is also consistent with a rights-based approach which seeks to limit the time young people spend in locked accommodation.

Thus the scheme was very much of its time but also challenged some current trends, such as the demonising of troublesome and troubled young people. Arguably it is foster care's strong identification with a needs, welfare-based approach which makes it acceptable as a form of community care for young people considered to present a risk. It might be argued that being placed in foster care in itself defines young people as "children in need". CAPS evidently faced the challenge of identifying and responding to risks appropriately, without losing a predominant focus on young people's welfare. Managing this tension inevitably permeated the project's work.

Though the placements were focusing on needs, risk was the key criterion for admission to the scheme. Since it is risk which accords priority to resources within the child welfare system, this raised questions about whether local authorities would continue to fund placements, once the level of risk lowered. Arguably the short-termism favoured in present policy in order to reduce welfare dependency also mitigated against prolonging placements. Yet it is known that many young people facing secure care have serious and entrenched difficulties and so require long-term skilled support to become self-sufficient. CAPS' role in providing this and in what circumstances local authorities would be prepared to fund it was initially unclear.

Risk-related aspects of the wider context thus shaped which young people would be placed with carers and for how long they would remain there. At a more practical level, carers were called upon to manage a range of risks within the context of a family home in a community not necessarily sympathetic to troubled and troublesome young people. Given the preoccupation with risk within child welfare and the wider community, carers could expect their practice to be severely scrutinised, should the young person be harmed or harm someone else. They could also expect to be subject to a detailed investigation if a young person made an allegation of abuse. The likelihood of such an allegation being made is heightened in a situation where young people know that social work services respond most readily to child protection concerns. Inevitably then an integral part of the foster carers' tasks would be to anticipate and reduce risks to themselves, young people and others.

Though potentially benefiting them, foster care also involves some risks for young people. As noted previously, some young people are abused in foster care. However, the most likely risk is that the placement will not work out, so that young people will be exposed to further upheaval, rejection and a sense of having failed. In light of the foregoing analysis of how risks are distributed, there is also a danger that, although the placement apparently offers young people a potential route out of disadvantage, their future quality of life will be largely shaped by factors outwith their or their carers' control, such as access to employment and housing and the level of support they can expect from family, friends or formal services. However, young people are unlikely to identify these underpinning dynamics, but instead blame themselves (Furlong and Cartmel, 1997). It remained to be seen how the potential benefits and risks to young people would balance out and be managed in practice.

The research sought to examine some of the issues and provide at least partial answers to some of the questions they raise.

The study's aims, design and methods

The research aimed to assess the extent to which the project met its own goals and evaluate the impact of its work on the young people placed. The purpose was to develop evidence-based understanding of professional foster care's potential to provide a community alternative to secure placement. The study's design included several key elements:

- It was *longitudinal*, so that changes were charted in the project's development and the first 20 young people placed with the project were followed for two years after their placement started.

- It involved *process evaluation*. This meant identifying how the implementation of the project corresponded to its goals and exploring the ways in which distinctive aspects of the project (such as pay and support) affected the fostering role and tasks.

- It included *evaluation of outcomes* for the young people and gathering of limited cost data.

- It had a *"quasi-experimental" aspect*, through following a comparison sample of young people in secure care over a similar period.

As others have pointed out, the seemingly straightforward question of whether a placement has worked or not, and has had a positive outcome or not, is usually far from simple to answer (Rowe *et al*, 1989; Triseliotis *et al*, 1995; Hill *et al*, 1996). The same placement may be judged as positive, mixed or negative by different participants, the outcome may be quite different on one dimension compared with another, and the picture may change rapidly from one point in time to another. This complexity of impact was always likely to be great with an innovatory project seeking to improve the lives of very vulnerable and damaged young people in a relatively short time. In order to gain as full as possible an understanding of their experience and outcomes, young people's progress was assessed by both qualitative and quantitative means.

A series of semi-structured interviews with key participants held at three key stages of the research were central to charting the development of the project and individual young people's progress. The first was held as soon as possible after the young person joined the placement, the second and third at intervals of six to nine months. The current social worker was interviewed at each stage, the carer up to the point when the young person left the placement, and the young person as long as he or she was willing to be interviewed and could be contacted. In addition, CAPS staff were interviewed in relation to each placement at the initial stage, while at the second round, four parents were interviewed who had been closely involved with the project.

A parallel set of interviews was carried out with a sample of young people who had recently been admitted to secure care or been made subject to a secure order but placed elsewhere. Interviews were held with the social worker and young people at the first stage but resources allowed for follow-up with only the social worker.

Young people's inclusion in the study was dependent on them agreeing to participate, having been given information about the purpose of the study and what taking part would entail. However, two of the young people in the secure sample were later reluctant to be interviewed, while remaining keen that their social worker should participate on their behalf.

Interviews with both samples focused primarily on identified needs and progress in relation to: education; health; family relationships; offending, and self-harming behaviour. In addition, at each stage a standard measure was used to assess self-esteem (Rosenberg scale, Rosenberg, 1979) and emotional well-being (Goodman's Strengths and Difficulties Questionnaire, Goodman, 1994). Background and biographical details were obtained from records.

Carers' views were sought not only on young people's progress but also on aspects of the social work task and their experience of working for CAPS. In the final year of the study an additional interview was held with all carers. This focused on the development of the project, the nature of their work, and the impact on them and other family members of being a CAPS carer.

Most information on the development of the project was gained through interviews with the project manager and key stakeholders. In addition, CAPS' records were the basis of three surveys of referrals and placements. Their purpose was to ascertain whether the characteristics of young people being placed by the project were changing with time.

The overall costs of individual placements to local authorities were identified through information obtained from social workers, supplemented by telephone contact with a range of professional and administrative staff working in social work and education services. The key elements included charges made by CAPS and additional costs, such as those for a child's travel between foster and family home and education support.

In terms of analysis, quantitative data were coded and analysed using SPSS, while transcripts of the first round interviews were coded and analysed using the NUDist software package. This facilitated systematic identification of key themes which were developed in the later stages of the research.

Summary

- CAPS was set up in response to a Scottish Office report which recommended that community alternatives to secure accommodation should be developed.
- The project was building on developments in specialist fostering, but also setting out to extend foster care's capacity to cater for very challenging young people through providing carers with a high level of remuneration and appropriate training and support.
- Outcome research on specialist foster care is relatively scarce but positive results have been reported for some British and American schemes. Most of those evaluated have adopted a cognitive approach, but within the literature it is argued that attachment theory, focusing on relationships and emotional development, is equally relevant. Some critics argue that foster care is not a suitable option for seriously challenging and damaged young people.
- Between 200 and 250 young people are admitted to secure accommodation in Scotland each year, with about 90 in placement at any one time. Approximately two-thirds of young people in secure accommodation are placed there on the authority of a Children's Panel, the remainder being subject to a court order. Approximately a quarter are girls, most of whom are there for welfare reasons, rather than as a result of offending. Many young people in secure accommodation have long-standing and complex difficulties.
- The research examined several aspects of the project's development

and practice. In addition, it considered the impact of key dimensions of the current social and welfare climate, notably in relation to the operation and management of risk.

- The term "risk society" has been applied to contemporary society. The claim is that more diversity in family structures and patterns of employment open up opportunities for individuals, while also making life more hazardous and unpredictable.

- Whereas post-war social policy emphasised shared responsibility for the welfare and social risks of the nation, individuals are now expected to be self-sufficient, with welfare services reserved for the few who are in need or at special risk. Social exclusion programmes aim to support people towards becoming self-sufficient, primarily through education and work. However, under the previous and present government, those who cannot be self-sufficient or who threaten social values can expect to be harshly treated.

- These developments have influenced social work services in a number of ways. There is a predominant focus on child protection within community-based services and care settings, with resources now allocated primarily on the basis of risk. The preference is for short-term interventions which enable people to become self-sufficient.

- The work of CAPS was profoundly influenced by these developments. NCH Action for Children bore the financial risk of setting up the project, so had to provide a service which corresponded with local authorities' priorities. The project constituted an expensive, scarce resource, so local authorities assessed eligibility for funding on the basis of risk. This corresponded with the project's own criteria for admission.

- Managing risk was not viewed as necessarily central to the fostering task, though it was an important component and carers were required to undertake training in managing challenging behaviour.

- Carers could expect to be closely scrutinised if a child placed with them was harmed or harmed others. Within a risk-based system they were vulnerable to false allegations.

- For young people, CAPS involved the risk of further rejection or upheaval. There was also the possibility that they would blame themselves if they were not able to achieve or sustain significant change.

- The project adhered strongly to a needs-based, welfare approach and in this respect could be viewed as out of step with current trends towards harsher treatment for troublesome young people. In a highly regulated climate, it might also be viewed as somewhat anomalous that young people who presented a risk to themselves or others were trusted to a family home. However, CAPS also fitted with three tenets of contemporary society: a preference for the private rather than public sphere, a belief in the power of "good" parenting, and the notion that people can shape their own lives, so that, given the opportunity, young people can find a way out of disadvantage. In addition, it was expected that foster placements would prove less expensive than secure care.

2 Development of the scheme

Introduction

This chapter focuses on the main ways in which CAPS developed during the first three years of operation. While this was broadly in accordance with initial plans, the partnership arrangements with local authorities, geographical spread and timescale of placements diverged from what was originally envisaged. This chapter outlines how the project developed in terms of partnership arrangements with local authorities and the scope of its work. Developments in staffing and carer recruitment are described and an overview of referrals and placements provided. Practice and policy developments are summarised here and developed in Chapter 3.

Arrangements with local authorities

When the idea of the project was first conceived it was envisaged that it would service all authorities in central Scotland. However, the particular interest of two local authorities resulted in a decision to establish a partnership arrangement whereby the two together would take up and pay for 18 out of the 20 placements that were planned. This was the position when the project opened, but the situation rapidly changed.

The Education Department's reluctance to fund education costs outwith their own area meant that one of the two authorities withdrew, while financial considerations led the other to halve the number of placements it wished to reserve. Faced with this sudden loss of business, the scheme decided to accept referrals from across Scotland. Many authorities were experiencing difficulties in placing young people whom they considered relevant, so within nine months the number of referring authorities had risen to 20 out of 32. In total around two-thirds of Scottish authorities expressed an interest in working with the scheme within the first three years, while at any one time the project typically had placements funded by about 12 authorities. The two original partner authorities no longer had a distinctive role within the scheme except that the project's fostering panel continued to be registered with one of them.

In addition to working with referring departments, effective operation of the project required close collaboration with the local authorities where carers lived, especially with respect to schooling. CAPS' staff were in contact with 12 "receiving" authorities as service providers.

Enlargement of the project's role

The geographical spread of the project's work was accompanied by diversification of referrals, as regards type of young person, age and placement duration, with CAPS being asked to cater for gaps in current service provision. The project initially set out to provide planned, time-limited placements for young people "close to secure" aged 12–16. One of the original partner agencies had encouraged the project to include young people inappropriately placed in residential care, but not necessarily at immediate or indeed any risk of secure care. The widening range of referring authorities led to further diversity in requests. The project was asked to accommodate several young people below the age of 12 and others at the point of leaving care aged 16–17. Requests were received to accommodate young people on an emergency basis, and to consider some who needed longer-term family placement with carers.

The project sought to keep its focus on young people with exceptional emotional and behavioural difficulties, but a number of referrals were accepted outside the original criteria (see below for details). In part, this reflected the fact that the intention to have tight regular screening meetings with just two authorities became impractical when referrals came from far and wide.

The modifications in purpose and clientele made more complicated the task of evaluating the scheme's role as an alternative to secure accommodation. Yet it might be argued that, through responding to the requirements of local authorities, CAPS developed a more responsive needs-led service.

In response to demand, CAPS also grew larger than planned. In the first three years its placement capacity expanded to cater for 36 young people, almost twice the original target. Inevitably this also involved recruiting additional staff and carers.

Staffing

The project manager took up post early in 1997 and three senior practitioners and an administrator were appointed a few months later. Further appointments were made to increase the staff complement. By August 2000 the staff group comprised:

- 1 project leader and 1 practice team manager;
- 5 senior practitioners;
- 2 administrative/secretarial staff.

Each senior practitioner acts as link worker to six or seven carers, while also being responsible for the assessment and preparation of new carers, delivering training and tracking the progress of young people on referral.

The growth in staff and the decision to appoint a practice manager made possible the management and support of more carers. Staff supervision, chairing of review meetings, and development tasks came to be shared between the Project Leader and Practice Manager. However, a significant gap has been the absence of an education worker. One of the two initial partnership agencies had wished to provide such a post, but in the event was unable to.

The depute director of NCH Action for Children in Scotland has overall management responsibility for CAPS. An external consultant has provided professional input since before the scheme was operational. It was originally intended to set up a management group including external professionals but this has not been established.

The carers

The original target was that by the end of 1998 the scheme would have recruited 18 carers who between them would provide placements for around 20 young people. In response to the developments just noted, the number of main carers in fact reached 28, offering placements for a maximum of 36 young people. After the initial expansion, the project committed itself not to increase the number of carer households beyond 28, so that carers would know each other and have a sense of belonging and cohesion. No carers left the scheme in the first three years of its operation.

Most of the original carers found out about the project through information distributed by the then National Foster Care Association, now Fostering Network. Thereafter, applicants learned about the project by word of mouth or from newspaper articles. A newspaper advertisement placed in the summer of 1998 attracted approximately 30 replies and six people proceeded with an application.

The recruitment philosophy was to give full information about what being a CAPS carer entailed and to work together with applicants to identify whether their personal attributes and family circumstances corresponded to the demands of the task. During the research period no applicants had been turned down, though several had withdrawn, either because of illness or because the demands of the scheme did not suit them.

All the carers live in central Scotland. Since the referring agencies are more widely spread, a number of placements have been over 100 miles from the child's home.

Of the 28 carer households in August 2000, 23 were couples and five were single women. The project required that one carer in each household should work for the project on a full-time basis, i.e. not have other paid employment. Among the couples, 17 operated on the basis of the woman being the CAPS carer, while six men were main carers. These men had previously worked in a variety of jobs, including a fisherman, a builder, a joiner and a residential carer. More of the female carers had relevant experience, for example, in residential care or as a social work assistant.

When approved, both female and male carers ranged in age from early 20s to late 50s, half being in their 40s. All carers apart from two had children of their own, when joining CAPS:

14 grown up children all living away from home;
4 youngest child at home aged 16+;
5 youngest child at home aged 10–16;
3 youngest child at home aged under 10 years old.

Less than half of the CAPS carers (12) had previously fostered for a local authority, their length of service ranging from three to 18 years. In addition, four carers had provided Supported Lodgings or Throughcare to young people leaving care.

Thus the scheme succeeded in attracting new people to foster care by tapping into sections of the community who would not have considered traditional fostering but were interested in the fact that this could be undertaken as a job. Some had experience in residential work with children, but a number had previously been self-employed, running a wide range of businesses, including shops, joinery and pet grooming. It is the project's policy to recruit and work with a diversity of backgrounds rather than to try to mould carers into specific ways of dealing with young people.

Referrals and placements

The changes in relationships with local authorities noted above were accompanied by a diversification in types of referral. Here the evidence is presented on the extent to which, during the period covered by the research, the project reconciled its original aims with the pressures to admit young people in a much wider range of circumstances.

The referral process

The original partnership plan envisaged a tight joint screening process, with the Project Manager attending the local authority admissions groups. Most referrals from one authority still came from their screening group dealing with admissions to secure or residential schools, but the CAPS manager no longer attended these meetings. With other authorities, most discussion about potential referrals were between the young person's social worker and a CAPS senior practitioner. However, the principle remained that a formal referral was only made after CAPS *and* local authority staff had both agreed it was appropriate.

Ideally and usually several stages followed a formal referral:

- convening a referral meeting to identify the young person's requirements;
- circulating papers on the young person to possible carers;
- matching the young person with carers or await a suitable match.

When a vacancy arose, carers were sent papers on several young people who seemed suited to them. They and the senior practitioner then met to decide which young person was most appropriate and/or could be offered most from the placement.

In some instances young people were admitted on an emergency basis usually because they had nowhere else to go or it was important to respond quickly in order to prevent further deterioration or admission to secure care. In these circumstances, full assessment of their requirements and the suitability of the carers proceeded during the course of the placement.

No formal waiting list was kept. Instead, senior practitioners checked periodically the situation of children held "on referral". To be financially viable, a minimum of 29 young people needed to be placed at any one time, so staff planned ahead to avoid carers having unnecessary vacancies, while also seeking to ensure they were not overloaded.

The nature of enquiries

Information provided by the project indicated that until August 2000, enquiries had been received in relation to 272 young people. The number of enquiries had risen from ten per quarter near the start to around 20–30 per quarter. An analysis of enquiries and referrals was carried out after the project had been in operation for 18 months, followed by two less detailed surveys of referrals and placements at yearly intervals thereafter.

The analysis of enquiries and referrals during the first 18 months of the project revealed that there had been 128 enquiries, of which 48 resulted in a formal referral. Where the enquiry did not proceed to referral, this usually reflected decision-making by local authority staff. Only on a few occasions did CAPS staff take the view that an enquiry should not be pursued, usually since the need for a placement was urgent and no suitable carers were immediately available.

All 48 young people who were formally referred in the first 18 months were white and none had a significant disability. There were 14 girls and 34 boys. The age range of referrals was 9–17. All but one-sixth of referrals were within the age criteria set by the project, over half being aged 15. Young people outwith the age range were usually accepted because they met the main criteria of being close to secure care. For instance, one ten-year-old was living in secure accommodation when referred and another would probably have been placed there without the CAPS placement. Similarly both 17-year-olds were placed from or facing custody.

At the time of the survey, 21 of the young people referred were currently with carers, while six had been linked with a family but had not yet moved in with them. For nine there had been an introduction to potential carers but the proposed placement had not gone ahead, while for 12 young people, no carers had yet been identified. At this stage, girls stood a better chance of being linked with a carer than boys. Whereas 12 of the 14 (86 per cent) girls referred had been linked with a carer, this applied to only two-thirds of the boys (n = 22 of 34).

Information on where young people were living when referred indicated that they came primarily from residential care. Details are outlined in Table 2.1.

Table 2.1

Placements of young people referred and linked with a carer during the project's first 18 months

Placement at referral	Total number referred	Number linked with a carer
Residential school	21	15
Children's home	11	10
Secure care	11	8
Parents' care	5	3
Total	**48**	**36**

Residential schools were the most common placement at the time of referral, but a lower proportion of young people from residential school than from children's homes had been linked with carers.

There were no indications that CAPS was selecting the less difficult young people from among the referrals. Where possible, young people in secure care were given priority, though in two instances it had not been possible to identify suitable carers.

Subsequent surveys revealed a substantial increase in the number of young people

a) on whom initial information had been sent but a formal referral not (yet) made and

b) whose formal referral had been accepted.

	Initial information sent	*Accepted and awaiting placement*
September 1999	13	15
August 2000	30	24

In 1999 more girls were awaiting placement, but the following year two-thirds of those waiting were males. Similarly there was a shift in the age distribution towards more young people in the 12–13 years group awaiting placement. Broadly the pattern of pre-referral placement stayed the same. Of those awaiting placement in August 2000, all three in secure care were boys aged 15. Among the eight in children's homes, one 13-year-old boy was subject to a secure care order and a 13-year-old girl was on the verge of a secure admission. The boy had already been considered unsuitable by three carers. The girl had been on referral for two months and was currently the top priority case for CAPS.

Length of time awaiting placement

The surveys showed that most young people were placed within three months of referral, but between the summers of 1999 and 2000 the number who had been waiting for six months or more rose from one to seven. Some were considered and turned down by a number of carers, before being eventually placed.

Young people placed with CAPS

Information was made available from agency records on all placements which had ended by the beginning of August 2000. This indicated that approximately 45 placements had started and ended in the three-and-a-half years since the project had started. At the time of the survey there were 30 current open placements, so that around 75 young people had spent some time within CAPS.

An analysis was made of all new placements that were current at the three survey points. These comprised:

1st survey   20 of the first 21 placements (i.e. the main sample for this study).

2nd survey   20 new placements current at September 1999.
3rd survey   15 new placements current at August 2000.

The main points arising from this analysis were:

- At each of the survey stages 12 local authorities had young people in placement.
- About half the young people were placed within a month of referral, but some were placed after six months or more of waiting.
- An original gender balance changed to girls outnumbering boys in the new placements of 2000.
- Correspondingly, boys were the majority of those waiting for placement.
- In each year only a few new placements had been outside the target range of 12–16, but that number did increase over the two years
- The age range of those in placement in the summer of 2000 was nine to 18 years.
- Over 90 per cent of the new placements in 1998 followed on from secure care or residential placements, but this was true for only one-third in 2000. The numbers placed from residential schools and children's homes declined sharply from 14 out of 20 in 1998 to two out of 15 in 2000. By then, more placements were being made from family, foster care, hostels and bed and breakfast.
- A small number of young adults were being catered for who had been in secure care and had major addiction, offending and accommodation difficulties.
- The proportion of young people placed who were attending mainstream education had increased, though many of these did need additional support.

Comparison of referral and placement data showed that on the whole the circumstances of young people placed corresponded with referral patterns, except that a significant number of young people of school age in open residential care had been referred but not placed. In each case their behaviour was deteriorating or very difficult in their current placement.

Length of placements

At the outset it was planned that placements would last six months but this was soon increased to 12 months. Of all 26 young people with carers in August 2000, over a third (ten) had been with the project for over one year, including four who had been placed for more than two years. At the other end of the spectrum, only one placement had started in the last three months. It seemed that the project was responding to the fact that these young people were not ready to move on as soon as had been originally envisaged. One consequence was that vacancies did not arise frequently. Since a vacancy was sometimes filled by an emergency admission, this slow turnover accounts for the longer waits noted above.

Those placed during the first year (the main study sample) provided a longitudinal perspective on how long placements lasted. Of those first placements, three had lasted less than three months and two more between three and six months. At the other end of the spectrum seven lasted over a year, though two of these had been part-time for 6–9 months, with the young person attending residential school during the week. The remaining eight lasted 6–12 months.

It emerged that boys tended to stay in placements longer than girls. As a result there were slightly more boys than girls in placement in August 2000 (14 to 13), despite the fact that twice as many girls as boys had joined the project in the preceding year.

Did the placements constitute an alternative to secure care?

The referral and placement data provided several indications on the extent to which CAPS was serving as an alternative to secure care. Young people actually in secure care accounted for about one in six of those on referral (15). One-fifth of the new placements analysed were for young people leaving secure accommodation (11). Thus the project has enabled some young people to move on from secure care. A few in secure accommodation had been on referral for a number of months, having been considered but not accepted by several carers.

For the rest, the imminence of secure placement was explicitly referred to in only a few application forms, but many young people were engaging in behaviours that could have this result. Serious alcohol and drug misuse, aggression and self-harming were common behaviours, while several of the young women were regularly absconding and putting themselves at risk. For some of the older teenagers, prison would have been a likely alternative.

CAPS also appeared to be catering for "adolescent erupters" whose difficulties become apparent or accelerate quickly during the early teens (Bullock *et al*, 1998). A survey carried out by SWSI in 1998 showed that the majority of girls in secure care were in this category, some having reached secure care within a year of coming to the attention of social work services (SWSI, 2000). Typical behaviours included alcohol and drug use, self-harming, absconding and putting themselves at risk. However, many of the girls had had a good experience at primary school and were strong educationally. This profile fitted some of the females admitted to CAPS.

Education

The importance attached to education was evident in the initial plan to appoint an educational support worker, though with the breakdown of the partnership plan this post did not in fact materialise. The need for such a post continued to be recognised, and various steps were proposed or taken to try and secure funding for this and to equip a room in the CAPS offices so that young people not in school could be temporarily offered a few sessions a week.

Carers had a key role in contacting local schools, but many head teachers were reluctant to accept children requiring additional support without a full assessment and approval from their education authority. With placements commonly in a different authority from the one responsible for the child, the receiving authorities generally had qualms about resourcing young people from elsewhere. Hence a more formalised system was developed with the educational psychologist in the placing authority required to carry out a full assessment and plan. Any additional costs were then met by the *placing* authority. This meant schools had more detailed guidance about the young person's needs, but setting up schooling in this way was slower than reliance on the carers' direct approach.

Somewhat different issues arose in relation to specialist education. A number of young people made lengthy and expensive daily round trips by taxi, so that they could stay in appropriate day placements in residential schools at a distance from their foster homes. For some young people it proved impossible to find suitable specialist provision, while others had to wait for up to nine months for this. In these cases young people have had no teaching at all or only the minimum of a few hours each week from a home tutor. Not surprisingly, the resulting lack of structured time put great responsibility and strain onto carers and young people alike.

Policy and practice developments

The scheme began with a set of clear policy documents, but the unexpectedly fast growth in the number of carers and placements meant that it was not always possible for policies and procedures to keep pace. For example, at the time the research fieldwork ended, it had been recognised that the content and format of carers' and senior practitioners' recording should be standardised. Up to that point carers had been asked to keep a daily diary, but some did not manage this and others produced details in a format that could not be transferred to agency files for future reference.

The project encouraged carers to meet regularly as a group. By the time the research ended there were several forums where carers and staff could meet to discuss policy, some led by the carers group and its representatives, others organised by staff. A series of working groups had been established to review a number of issues identified as priorities by staff and carers alike. These were: managing allegations by young people against carers; the referral process; education; and Throughcare.

That these particular issues had come to the fore is consistent with our contention that the work of the project was shaped by the social welfare climate and in particular by the ways in which risk operates and is managed. Carers' vulnerability to false allegations is self-evidently about managing risk. Risk considerations also predominated in discussions of the referral process, with a number of carers expressing concern that they would be asked to care for young people who presented too much of a danger to themselves and the community. In terms of service provision, the difficulties in securing education outwith a young person's home area are unsurprising in a climate where specialist resources are scarce and are predominantly allocated on the basis of risk to the child or the local authority. Thus, for the receiving authorities, local children would inevitably have priority, since specialist day education is often key to avoiding the future expense of residential placement. In a similar vein, carers' concerns about Throughcare highlighted their primary focus on young people's longer-term needs, which could be in conflict with local authorities' wish to keep down costs once the immediate risks which had prompted the CAPS placement no longer applied.

Carers' and staff views varied widely on whether or not the project was still focusing primarily on providing an alternative to secure care and whether it should. What mattered most to carers was that the young people who came into the scheme were able to benefit from being there. All were committed to keeping young people in the community wherever possible. However, there was also a widespread view that some young people may need to be in secure care, so that a rigid focus on keeping them out may serve the interests of local authorities more than the young people themselves.

Summary

Like any new project, CAPS has evolved to take account of experience and changes in the external environment. The original idea of a limited partnership with two local authorities soon gave way to offering a service for children across much of Scotland, though all the CAPS carers reside in central Scotland. By the end of three years and in response to demand, the placement capacity had risen to 36, twice the initial target. CAPS was able to recruit a significant numbers of carers (28 households in August 2000), including some who had not fostered before. Pressures quickly built up for the scheme to accept referrals outside its core criterion (young people at imminent risk of admission to secure care or otherwise unable to leave secure accommodation). Some widening was apparent in the range of characteristics of those accepted, but on the whole a focus on high-risk groups within the relevant age spread has been maintained.

Certain modifications were identified in the kinds of young people admitted to the scheme. An increase occurred in the proportions of girls, of young people in their early teens and those aged 16+. In the early stages of the scheme, nearly all young people were admitted directly from a residential placement, whereas by August 2000, two-thirds were coming from "the community", i.e. birth family, foster care or homeless accommodation.

By August 2000, 75 young people had spent time within the scheme, including 45 whose placement had ended. The intention had been for CAPS placements to be relatively short-term (around six months), but in practice up to a third of ongoing placements have lasted over a year. Plans to appoint an education support worker and for a partnership arrangement including education services have not been fulfilled. Hence schooling has had to be organised on a case by case basis, sometimes leading to major difficulties.

3   Creating a service

Introduction

So far the project's progress has been outlined and a description provided of the structure that was in place at the time the fieldwork ended in August 2000. However, the research was charged not only with charting the project's development but examining *how* it operated. The aim was to understand the nature of the service being evaluated, while also providing an insight that would inform the development of similar projects. This chapter describes how central elements of the service developed, seeking to understand this as a process through which key principles were implemented and new concepts defined or refined. It provides a framework within which to explore the nature of the work with individual young people in later chapters.

In addition to further exploring the development of the project, this chapter begins to consider the nature of the professional fostering task in this context. NCH set out to accord foster carers full professional status, recruiting carers from previously untapped sections of the community and providing family care for young people who would previously have been considered too disturbed or demanding for this kind of provision. The project was breaking new ground on several fronts. In this context it was hardly surprising to find traditional perceptions of foster care being stretched and challenged.

As the research progressed it became evident that, though core elements of the task could be identified, three broad models of professional foster care were developing. Some carers took the view that professional foster care should operate broadly in the same way as traditional foster care but with added support and scope to fully utilise their expertise in caring for and understanding children. For them the CAPS senior practitioner was primarily viewed as a source of support. They valued keeping contact with them friendly and informal. A second approach recognised that becoming a full-time carer conferred different obligations and changed the nature of the service that carers were expected to provide. Adherents of this model expected professional carers to have a wide range of skills and undertake tasks traditionally undertaken by social workers, for example, report writing and assessment. They were comfortable with the language of work, seeing the senior practitioner primarily as a line manager and quite happy for their meetings to become supervision sessions. According to the third perspective, professional fostering involved a range of skills, central to which was caring for children. Carers were seen as having quite distinct expertise and understanding from social workers and it was considered important that their particular views were incorporated in service development. Carers were considered central to the service, with link workers viewed as colleagues who provided administrative and professional back-up, but did not have greater authority than the carers themselves. These three approaches and corresponding expectations of the CAPS senior practitioner might be categorised as follows:

	Professional foster carer	*Link worker role*
Supported, skilled foster carer	Providing high-quality care with appropriate support and recognition	Informed supporter, adviser
Multi-skilled worker	Widening scope to include some tasks previously undertaken by social workers	Supervisor, line manager
Expert carer	Expertise in caring clearly differentiated from social work skills	Partner, colleague

By the third year of the project, all staff adopted the second view which was also predominant among carers. However, a significant minority of carers adhered to the perspectives at each end of the spectrum, highlighting that the professional foster care task could be understood and defined in different ways. For all carers the task involved combining work and family life in a new and challenging situation.

The foregoing summary of the various meanings and strands of professional foster care provides a context in which key aspects of the project's operation can be examined. This chapter begins by outlining the CAPS service in relation to:

- assessment/preparation;
- training;
- support; and
- care planning.

Thereafter there is briefer consideration of four dimensions of the interface between family life and work:

- matching young people and carers;
- defining and managing acceptable risk;
- rights and responsibilities; and
- combining work and family life.

Assessment/preparation

The project's approach to assessing and preparing carers was based on the premise that the most appropriate method was to help prospective carers understand what the job entailed and ask them to consider rigorously how they and their family would be able to provide this. This basic approach had applied from the start of the project, though the format for implementing it was developed over time.

Preparation for the initial group of ten carers had been solely through individual meetings with a CAPS worker. Since all but one of those in the original group were experienced foster carers, it was considered that this would suffice. During 1998 the recruitment/preparation process was widened to include an information meeting and a two-day training session. Both focused primarily on the work of the project and understanding adolescent behaviour in terms of reflecting trauma, loss and deprivation (i.e. an attachment theory model). In addition, at some point before the formal assessment began, carers were asked to complete a written exercise about how they and their family would meet the demands of working for CAPS. The home-study remained the main forum in which prospective carers had an opportunity to explore in detail the needs and likely behaviours of children requiring placement and the likely impact on their family. Dependent and adult children were interviewed at least once. On this basis carers completed a more detailed self-assessment which formed the basis of their application to the project.

The project expects that carers should have the potential of reaching Level 3 in the Fostering Network payment for skills framework. Both carers and senior practitioners recognised, however, that it was only when carers started to work with young people that their particular strengths and weaknesses would emerge. During 1999 senior practitioners carried out a Skills Audit with each carer, based on which individual development plans were devised. These identify aspects of practice the carer is currently developing, thus providing a framework for discussion and appraisal, both in meetings with the senior practitioner and at the formal annual review.

Training

Irrespective of their previous experience or level of skill, within the first year of being approved all main carers were expected to complete two core training programmes. The first was Level 1 of the Consortium of Scottish Counselling Associations (COSCA) approved Certificate in Counselling. This was offered by non-NCH staff on one day a week for 12 weeks. By the third year of the project some carers had progressed to the Level 2 counselling course which is also funded by the project. The second core training was on managing and defusing challenging behaviour and included the safe use of restraint. Originally independent trainers delivered the standard TCI (Therapeutic Crisis Intervention) programme but during 1999 NCH trainers began to provide "Code of Conduct" training, based on TCI principles. Both were offered over a three-day course.

Until the second half of 1999 these core elements accounted for most of the training. Thereafter, when most of the compulsory training had been delivered, more specialised sessions were arranged on topics such as awareness of child sexual abuse, understanding and managing sexualised behaviour, and assessment and report writing (using LAC forms).

In terms of formal qualifications, in time all carers were expected to complete SVQ: Caring for Children and Young People at Level 3. The first group of eight carers embarked on this in the summer of the year 2000. In addition carers and staff had access to relevant training organised by NCH Action for Children for agency staff.

Alongside the more formal training, some carers who lived close to each other arranged for a local policeman to brief them on the use and effects of a range of illegal drugs in current use. The carers group also arranged an information session on Tax Assessment and Allowances for self-employed people.

The majority of carers found most of the training useful. There was particular praise for the counselling course. In part this helped carers recognise and name skills they already had. Carers also found it enhanced listening skills, enabling them not just to hear what people said but to tune into the feelings and unspoken communication behind the words. The TCI/Code of Conduct training was valued for what it taught in relation to defusing tense and potentially violent situations but only a few carers considered that it would be appropriate to use restraint in the relative isolation of a family home.

Additional topics on which carers would have liked training included: children and carers' rights and how these should be interpreted; health and safety within the home; information on different types of illegal drugs and their effects; and self-defence so that carers could keep themselves and their family safe when young people became physically threatening or violent. In general, carers preferred training which focused primarily on the practicalities of the task. It is also striking that all of these topics related in some way to managing and responding responsibly to risks.

Many carers were unreservedly positive about training, seeing this as helping them do the job more effectively, while also enhancing their own skills. However, a few worried that undertaking training, especially SVQs, reduced the time available for young people. A related concern was that as carers broadened their skills, for example, to include report writing, the central importance of caring or nurturing would be lost. A few expressed reservations that some training was mandatory, taking the view that professional carers should be able to decide for themselves what training they required. For some former local authority foster carers, increased autonomy was an important component of professional status. This was less of an issue for carers who had previously been employed, most of whom accepted training requirements as usual or to be welcomed. Attitudes to training thus to some extent corresponded with the three models of professional foster care referred to earlier.

Carer support

Central to the rationale of this project was the belief that if carers were well paid and supported they would be able to provide a service qualitatively different from traditional and even existing specialist fostering. In the initial interviews with carers, they fully endorsed this position as they talked about the importance of the "support package" which would accompany each placement. The promise of a support package had not only attracted them to join CAPS but was seen as a means through which they could do a rewarding and effective job. The main components of the package CAPS offered were:

- substantial remuneration;
- a 24-hour on call system staffed by project staff who knew the carers and young people placed;
- regular meetings with a senior practitioner to review carer issues;
- eight weeks respite in a year and additional respite as necessary in times of crisis or when young people made particularly severe demands.

There was also an expectation that other carers would provide peer support, though, unlike those listed above, this was not seen as essential.

In addition, it was expected that the CAPS placement would be part of a care package, put together in conjunction with the placing social work department. Central to this was the provision of schooling and a suitable subsequent placement, when the young person was ready to leave CAPS. Effective input from the child's social worker was also expected.

Remuneration

From the start it was recognised that treating carers as professionals included paying them at a level comparable with other professional staff. Full-time carers received £440 per week for caring for one young person and £220 for a second placement. Those who offered only respite were paid pro-rata. This was two to three times what most other foster care schemes paid at the time and equated approximately to a senior residential worker's salary. The payments were made continuously, whether or not the carer had a current placement. Carers recruited in the first 18 months were paid from the date the panel approved them. However, from

September 1998, only the lower rate was paid until the first young person was placed. Thereafter, fees were paid at the higher rate, even during gaps in placements.

Most carers readily acknowledged that the level of reward had contributed to their decision to join CAPS. For some carers coming into the scheme meant giving up another job or working self-employed, so receiving a regular income was a prerequisite to even considering joining the scheme. People in this category found it quite unremarkable that they were paid a reasonable rate for doing a difficult and demanding job.

In contrast those who had come from traditional foster care tended to feel they had to justify leaving the service of their local authority. Most were at pains to point out that the financial reward was only one aspect of the CAPS package which had attracted them: the promise of professional support and recognition for their skills had been equally important. Being paid on an equal footing with social workers was considered an important dimension in defining their new status and more autonomous role. As placements progressed and hit difficulties, several carers also acknowledged that being well paid played a part in encouraging them to keep working at finding ways to manage the problems, rather than giving up.

Some former local authority carers also felt that these advantages had their downside. It was suggested that some social workers resented that carers were paid at a level above themselves and consequently expected carers to take on work which was a social work responsibility. In the final interviews some carers had also found that CAPS staff referred to carers' receipt of a "professional fee" to justify encouraging them to take on or stick with difficulties they were finding very tough. Thus some carers had found that receiving a high payment brought with it expectations that they had not anticipated and, in certain instances, were reluctant to respond to. This revealed a gap between CAPS staff and some carers in their understandings about the obligations of being a professional foster carer. Commonly the difference of opinion was about level of risk and disruption to family life to be tolerated, a topic we return to later in the chapter.

Despite general satisfaction with arrangements for paying carers, reservations were expressed. Some found it unfair that a reduced rate was paid for second placements, even where CAPS acknowledged that two full-time carers were required to manage both placements simultaneously.

Similarly it was suggested that, when especially demanding young people were placed, for example, those requiring constant supervision, the additional work should be recognised through the payment of a higher fee. Experienced carers who were regularly asked to take on particularly challenging young people did not always feel that the reward they received was high enough to merit the demands on them personally. In addition, some resented the fact that their level of pay was public knowledge and discussed with interest in fostering circles. While there was a general acceptance among staff that carers were well paid, carers frequently pointed out that, given the hours they "worked", the hourly rate was not particularly high. Carers had no set hours of work but, apart from when they were formally on respite, they could be called on at any time of the day or night.

Carers worked on a self-employed basis and so were liable for tax and National Insurance on the payments they received. This meant each had to engage the services of an accountant to complete the tax return. When asked in the final interviews whether they would prefer to be salaried, about half the carers said they would, partly because they would not have to complete the tax return but also because full employment status would put them on a par with other CAPS employees. However, other carers valued the degree of independence which being self-employed conferred.

We were not able to rigorously assess whether or not the level of remuneration impacted on the quality of care provided. Some carers pointed out that having a more secure and generous income allowed them to devote more emotional energy to the placement and also financed extras such as going out for meals which added to the young person's positive experience in placement. It was not unusual for young people to tell carers in anger that their sole motivation was financial, but this had also happened when carers had worked for local authorities. The young people interviewed did not express any strong views about carers being paid, though a few did refer to carers paying for treats or presents with their "own money" as a sign that they cared about the young person more than their work required.

Out-of-hours support

When asked what aspects of support they most valued, all carers cited the provision of 24-hour support. Knowing the service was available was valuable in itself and carers appreciated that they were encouraged to use the system whenever they thought it would be helpful. Use of the service included informing the duty worker of incidents or developments, checking out planned action or asking for advice, and requesting someone to visit or take other action to help resolve a particularly difficult situation.

At each point in the study carers reported that the CAPS duty system virtually always worked well, with staff being accessible and providing the level of involvement carers requested. In the very few instances when carers had been less satisfied, this was because the member of staff who responded had not known them or the young person. Staff also reported that carers used the service appropriately, with frequency of calls declining as carers developed confidence and/or placements became more settled. The result was that potentially difficult situations could often be managed without undue crisis. When a crisis did occur, for example, if a carer was assaulted or a young person harmed, prompt visits and offers of practical help from senior practitioners and the project manager were much appreciated.

Ongoing support and development

However important 24-hour support was, the main means through which carers had an opportunity to discuss and develop their practice was through regular meetings with the senior practitioner. Each senior practitioner was responsible for six or seven carers with whom they aimed to meet on an individual basis every two weeks. This was in addition to phone contact and other meetings regarding the young person. As the work of the project developed, it became difficult at some points for senior practitioners to maintain this frequency of contact with everyone. However, all carers were satisfied with the level of contact they had.

From the start of the project individual support was seen by senior practitioners as encompassing advice and encouragement, as well as an opportunity to review carers' practice and development and talk over how they and their families were managing the inevitable stresses. These are the traditional components of the link worker role, which most mainstream carers value highly, despite their general criticisms of local authority practice (see Triseliotis et al, 2000).

Initially CAPS carers' expectations of the senior practitioners were also fairly traditional, though they did emphasise notions of partnership and equality of status. All expected them to be colleagues who would act as sounding boards and talk over progress or difficulties in the placements. Approximately half thought senior practitioners would take on a development or educating role and the same people said they considered the senior practitioner to be their line manager. Only a few anticipated that helping carers manage the emotional implications of the placements would be a significant part of the senior practitioner's role, though half expected that this would apply to some extent when particular difficulties arose. Despite the emphasis on parity of status, senior practitioners were seen as responsible for ensuring that children were well cared for and the standard of service was high.

These expectations highlighted a degree of ambiguity about the senior practitioner's role. They were to have equal status with carers, yet monitor and be responsible for standards of care. Again this reflected tensions between different dimensions of what it means for foster care to become professional and in turn what kind of support professional foster carers require.

On the one hand, treating foster carers as professionals meant that their skills and experience would be acknowledged as of equal value to that of a social worker. Within CAPS the commitment to carers and staff having equal status was evident in the comparable level of their remuneration, as well as the fact that they undertook joint training and operated within a flat organisational structure, with the project manager overseeing all the project's work. However, carers were also being paid to work as part of an organisation and mechanisms were needed through which the organisation could ensure that the service it provided met its obligations to young people placed, local authorities, carers, staff and the wider community. While it was just about feasible for the project manager to take on this role as long as the project remained small, once it started to grow, a more formalised system of supervision and support was needed.

The initial ambiguity in the senior practitioner's role had resulted in some variation in how they approached supporting carers. Notably, some staff saw it as their responsibility to help carers review and develop their practice. An alternative view, also put forward by some carers, was that professional foster carers should be responsible for their own development, the main role of the organisation being to give them enough scope to exercise their own judgement. Another difference was the extent to which carers' own level of stress and patterns of engaging with young people would be examined when carers and senior practitioners met. Of course such a diverse group of carers required different kinds of support, but it was in time acknowledged, by staff and carers alike, that it would have been helpful to have greater clarity from the start about the senior practitioner's role and responsibilities in supporting carers.

As the work of the project developed and with changes and additions to the staff team, the expectations of senior practitioners were gradually clarified. One important factor was the introduction in 1999 of development plans for carers. This helped create a structure within which carers' practice could be recognised, reviewed and developed. Of course individual carers and senior practitioners continued to devise ways of working which suited them both but the structure and expectations were clearer.

By the time the final round of interviews were carried out, staff were beginning to refer to their meetings with carers as "supervision" and there were plans to devise a pro forma to further clarify and standardise expectations. The supervision model clearly belongs to the language of work which accorded with the fact that, by this stage, all senior practitioners saw themselves as the carers' line manager. There was also general agreement that a key element in supervision was to monitor how carers were managing the stress associated with placements and help them talk through and process anxieties or tensions. This was the kind of support and supervision which is accepted as essential in situations where people are exposed to strong emotions and need to maintain their capacity to work with them productively. From this perspective, effective supervision was part of safe caring for young people and carers alike.

The line manager model was also seen as an essential element of locating responsibility for risk within the organisation. Some senior practitioners pointed out that, in situations where carers were managing significant risk, the organisation had a duty to provide a clear structure through which that risk would be shared. The key elements of this were to ensure that carers were operating in accordance with agency expectations and to provide a forum where risks could be voiced, noted and responsibility for them held at an appropriate level within the organisation. The move to a line management model was not at all seen as devaluing the carers but recognising that the organisation had a duty to provide an effective system for supervision and support.

Carers' views on individual support and the role of the senior practitioner

In the final interviews with carers, most described their relationship with the senior practitioner in ways which accorded with the senior practitioners' perceptions. Approximately four-fifths said they saw the senior practitioner as their line manager, with responsibility for ensuring the quality of their work and also helping out when a particularly difficult problem arose. They saw the senior practitioners as deriving authority from their position in the organisation and from the fact that they had undertaken professional training. However, carers still felt that they had considerable authority in their own home. The general understanding was that senior practitioners would advise, and that was usually helpful, but on most issues, carers expected to have the final say about whether to act in accordance with their suggestions or not. Few carers had found that senior practitioners expected otherwise.

Just under a fifth of the carers still did not see senior practitioners as their line manager, viewing the project managers as having this role. Some believed NCH senior managers continued to endorse this model. They argued that a senior practitioner could not line manage carers for two reasons. Firstly, because this would be in breach of the project's principle of equality between carers and social workers and secondly, because senior practitioners had less expertise in fostering than carers. They understood the carers to be the central players, with the senior practitioner's tasks being primarily to process referrals and ensure that resources such as respite were in place to enable carers to do their job. People who adopted this perspective also tended to emphasise the importance of carer autonomy and personal responsibility.

Despite a degree of variation in what was expected from senior practitioners, virtually all carers spoke highly of the service they received. Most believed they had established a sound and productive working relationship with their senior practitioner whom they generally found to be accessible, well informed, and committed to fully supporting the placements. Carers liked to be given acknowledgement for their good work but also to be told when they were on the wrong track and helped find ways around problems rather than be overwhelmed by them.

Although carers and staff provided similar descriptions of the content of their meetings, no carers used the terminology of supervision and some specifically said that they liked to keep the meetings informal. Most carers felt they were able to set the agenda and tone of the meetings and found them useful. Some said they preferred to seek advice or emotional support from a partner or other carers, looking to senior practitioners for help with matters which related more specifically to the agency, for example, arranging respite or ensuring social work departments delivered the required resources.

While senior practitioners were seen as very supportive by most carers, a number of them believed that senior practitioners would encourage them to continue to work with children who were very challenging, even when this was causing the carer considerable stress. In these instances, senior practitioners were seen as having responsibilities to CAPS and their local authority customers as well as to young people and carers. For some carers this introduced a business element into the relationship which was not necessarily consistent with being open about feelings and vulnerabilities. Evidently this is an example of how the market-driven context impacts on carers' experience of support, a key element which, it is understood, affects their capacity to care.

The effectiveness of support to carers by the project was borne out not just by carers' direct feedback but also by the evidence that the project had been able to cater for very challenging young people, while none of the carers had chosen to leave.

Group support

Alongside formalising the arrangements for individual support, in 1999 it was decided to introduce a system of group supervision and support in "cluster groups". This involved each senior practitioner arranging a group meeting with all the carers they managed approximately every six weeks. The idea was to provide an opportunity for regular updating on project developments, exchange of experiences and ideas among carers, and training/discussion on specific topics. Attendance at these meetings was compulsory for carers, though initially they had the option of attending any group, should they not be free when their own was convened.

Most carers and senior practitioners thought the cluster groups worked reasonably well in their first year of operation. However, it proved difficult to get everyone together, with the result that they happened less frequently than had originally been planned and some were poorly attended. The arrangement of allowing carers to attend groups other than their own made it difficult for each group to develop a sense of cohesion and identity. It was therefore subsequently decided that the option of attending any groups would apply only to the information session, with the development and supervision element restricted to core group members. The research ended soon afterwards, so we cannot report whether these new arrangements resulted in increased attendance. However, it was evident from interviews with carers that participation in group meetings was one of many demands on their time and was not necessarily accorded priority.

Respite

Respite became an essential part of the support package. Even where placements were relatively settled, carers were clear that they needed some time to themselves to recharge. For those which were more stressful, providing timely respite could help prevent a crisis or placement ending. While most respite involved young people being cared for elsewhere over a period of days, in some instances, usually when the young person needed constant supervision or was out of school, some daytime respite had also been built in to the support package.

Project planning included the provision of eight weeks' planned respite for carers each year. In addition it was recognised that extra respite would be needed from time to time, either to avert a crisis or because caring for some young people was particularly stressful. Respite primarily involved the young person moving in temporarily with another CAPS family, though in time approximately half the carers arranged for someone from among their extended family to provide at least some of the respite for the children in their care. In most instances it was adult sons and daughters who helped out, but carers' parents, brothers and sisters and friends have also been approved as respite carers. The usual arrangement has been for family-based respite to start over a weekend or short break and gradually build up to meeting all or most of the main carers' respite requirements.

Main carers found keeping respite within the family had several advantages. From the young person's point of view, it made them feel part of an extended family and involved far less disruption, as they usually remained in their local area, often in the main carers' own home. It also allowed the carers to arrange breaks at a time which suited them and to be reassured that the young person would be with carers in whom they had confidence.

Despite the availability of some family-based respite, meeting the demand for respite within the scheme proved quite a challenge for project staff. It was not simply a matter of finding a bed but making sure the respite placement was suitable in terms of location, the carers' skill and experience, and the impact on other young people in placement. As young people gained experience of different carers' styles, some of them also set conditions about where they would or would not want to go. Sometimes the difficulty in finding respite meant that young people could not be told in advance where the placement would be, while carers were not always able to have a break exactly when they wanted it. Inevitably respite resources have been particularly stretched during the summer months.

The provision of regular respite was perhaps the clearest indication to young people that looking after them was the carer's job. This was helpful in that it was an honest reflection of the status of the placement and most young people said they understood this and appreciated that carers needed a break. However, a few social workers highlighted that for young people desperate to be accepted, respite could be difficult:

> I mean you think you are somewhere, you think you have a certain level of importance and then suddenly they are going on their holiday and they want a break from you. I think that's when it becomes a reality that you are there and this is kind of like a job. There's a big difference if you see yourself as a part of it all.

Where arrangements for respite afforded some continuity, either within the extended family or with another carer they got to know well, most young people seemed to adapt to the arrangements. Indeed one boy sometimes asked to "go on respite" when he recognised that the main placement was getting into difficulty. However, respite could also be quite disruptive for young people who were placed with a series of carers or found themselves in an unfamiliar part of the country, from where it was difficult to reach their school, work and/or friends. Social workers were reluctant to be critical of respite in principle, but a few did acknowledge that it resulted in care for some young people being somewhat fragmented:

> *Well, I think you see I have a problem with the fact that respite, well it's not a problem, it is just that it seemed to me that we used so many of the different carers and it must have been difficult for him.*

Quite a number of crises or placement breakdowns occurred during respite, presumably in part reflecting the added stress this entailed for the young person. However, most carers were well aware of the potential impact on young people and it was accepted practice, as far as possible, to take respite at a time which would cause them minimum disruption.

Before leaving this topic, the term "respite" itself merits some comment. "Respite" does have certain negative connotations, implying that caring for young people is a trial from which carers desperately need a break. While in some instances this corresponded to how carers felt, such negative terminology was somewhat out of step with the project's positive and child-centred approach. It was not unusual for young people to pick up on the word, sometimes humorously suggesting they needed "respite" from the carers.

During the first year of the project, the carers' group questioned whether "respite" was an appropriate term for professional carers, in that other professionals' breaks were called "holidays". In this context one of the issues to be clarified was whether carers were entitled to breaks irrespective of whether a young person was placed with them. As a result of this debate it was confirmed that breaks had to be "earned" so that significant gaps in placement would count as respite. To reflect this, the term "earned respite" was coined, later replaced with "earned leave". The latter combined an acknowledgement that breaks were dependent on having had a placement, with terminology applicable in a work setting.

Support from other carers

Informal support

Providing respite for each other was one formal means through which carers supported each other. Otherwise peer support was available through informal contact and through the carers' group. Most carers felt they had access to the level of informal support from carers which suited themselves. Some had known other carers before they joined the project and others quickly got to know colleagues who shared a similar approach. In a few instances carers who lived in the same area arranged to meet every so often, while for some regular telephone contact with other carers became an important part of their work. However, for others, close contact with fellow carers was not that important. Some individuals preferred to rely primarily on their partners and the support of their senior practitioner.

Carers' group

Within the group organised by carers themselves, there were competing views about the purpose and format of the meetings. While some carers wanted to focus on their conditions of service, others preferred to use the meeting for peer support. These aims are not necessarily incompatible but they do reflect a certain tension between a traditional approach and one which emphasises carer autonomy and rights.

The arrival of new carers during 1999 prompted a review of how the carers' group should operate. The result was to adopt a more business-like approach encompassing elements such as negotiating on behalf of carers with CAPS management and providing advice on insurance and tax matters. Not all carers were in agreement that this was an appropriate role for the carers' group. About a quarter preferred the more traditional format of mutual support and advice, so chose not to attend meetings. Much of the carers' group time was taken up with writing a Carers' Handbook which was nearing completion by the time the research ended. The intention was that this would outline project policy and expectations of carers.

The wider support package

As noted at the start of this chapter, in the initial interviews several carers anticipated that their work with young people would be part of a wider "support package" from local authorities. By this they meant that services such as education would be in place and the social work department would make sure that another placement would be available by the time the young person was ready to move on.

In general local authorities had not been able to meet these expectations, an issue which will be explored in more detail in relation to practice with individual young people. While several carers felt let down by this, most attributed the problem to lack of resources rather than poor co-operation or commitment from individual social workers.

Carers valued their equal status with social workers, so in most instances did not look to them to provide professional or emotional support for themselves. Rather they expected them to make every effort to ensure that the wider support package was in place and to get to know the young person as an individual. The support expected from social workers comprised three key elements:

- providing full and accurate information prior to placement;
- attending the four-weekly meetings to review the placement and carrying out any tasks they were allocated in that context;
- maintaining a productive relationship with the young person.

Although inevitably there was variation, on the whole carers found social workers provided a good service. Some social workers had to put up a strong argument to have young people admitted to CAPS in the first place, so they were perhaps more committed from the start. The input from social workers is discussed in more detail when work with individual young people is considered in later chapters.

Care planning

Effective co-operation with local authorities was an essential element in care planning. For each young person planning operated at two levels: in terms of the overall plan agreed in statutory reviews and in relation to the more detailed day-to-day work which was planned and reviewed in four-weekly meetings.

The overall care plan

At the broader level, two difficulties frequently arose. First, local authorities would not guarantee for how long individual placements would be funded, and second, they were unable to identify appropriate subsequent placements when young people were ready to move on.

The question of guaranteeing ongoing funding applied particularly in situations where key players agreed that it was in the young person's best interests to remain with the CAPS family until he or she was able to become independent. Few local authorities would guarantee continuous funding, usually framing their commitment in terms of continuing to fund the placement for as long as the young person met the project's criteria, that is, continued to be at risk of secure care. This raises questions of whether risk was, or should be, an admission criteria only, in which case decisions about discharge from the project would be need- not risk-based. The local authority perspective, in principle and partly on cost grounds, was that risk should also be a criterion for continuing in the scheme. This potentially created a situation where young people could be penalised for making progress, but no examples were given during the study where this had in fact applied, perhaps because in practice concern for young people's welfare did take precedence. A more common problem was that young people and carers lived with a degree of uncertainty about the long-term future of the placement.

In most instances it was considered appropriate for placements to become quasi permanent only if young people were already in their teenage years. A difficult situation had arisen in relation to a few children of primary school age who had come into the scheme because of particularly challenging behaviour but in fact required longer-term families. Local authorities had not been able to place any of them, reflecting that it is particularly difficult to find families for children of this age, especially if they also have significant difficulties and may present a risk to other children. By the time the research ended, two remained in the scheme and one had moved to a residential school.

A dearth of suitable provision for young people moving on to independent living had also resulted in some young people remaining much longer with the project than had originally been planned. In some instances, carers had advocated strongly against young people being moved too soon into unsupported situations where they were likely to fail. On the other hand, some carers took the view that progress could be undermined if young people stayed too long and that it was better for them to move on once the "work" of the placement had been completed.

Day-to-day planning

The four-weekly meetings attended by all key players emerged as an important means of ensuring that day-to-day placement planning was effective. These were informal meetings, chaired by the senior practitioner and attended by the carer, social worker, young person and parent, if appropriate, and others closely involved in the placement. There was unanimous agreement that the four-weekly meetings were helpful. They made sure that all key players had an opportunity to share concerns and developments and reinforce agreed goals, while also being a forum where progress could be acknowledged.

The focus of these meetings was primarily on the everyday practicalities of the placement, while also ensuring that any necessary steps were taken to progress wider issues, such as identifying school or other resources. Tasks were allocated to workers or the young person and progress reviewed at the next meeting. It was part of CAPS' contract with social workers that they would contribute to these meetings and most attended regularly. The meetings were thus a key means through which partnership operated in practice.

Beginning and ending placements

Over the period of the research, the approach to beginning placements changed. Whereas initially it was usual for placements to begin gradually, sometimes over a period of several weeks, during which time the young person gradually increased the time they spent in the carers' home, by the time the research ended, carers reported that introductions were seldom lasting more than seven to ten days. In addition, more young people were joining the project on an emergency basis, in which case they might not have met the carers before joining the placement.

Several carers expressed some concerns about very short introductions, since this allowed them little scope to assess whether the young person was likely to work with them. In particular some carers said that they liked to feel they had established a degree of authority and respect with the young person before they joined them. They believed that without this, the level of risk to carers and their families increased. However, long introductions meant it could be difficult for young people to manage, over an extended period, the mixed emotions associated with leaving a familiar placement. In some cases the young person's ambivalence seemed to be played out, so the old and new carers could find themselves in conflict. In addition, long introductions were expensive for local authorities since they had to meet the cost of two placements at once.

Placement agreements stated that the placing authority or CAPS would give at least 28 days notice of their intention to end the placement. In principle this allowed time for an alternative placement to be sought and prevented young people from being moved without due planning. In practice, where placements had been in crisis, young people sometimes moved to other carers to serve the period of notice or insisted on returning to a parent or other relative as soon as this plan was agreed. In one such instance the local authority agreed to pay to keep the placement open for six weeks in case the return home quickly broke down. In contrast, other young people were reluctant to leave the placement and several kept in touch with carers for several months after the placement had formally ended. At least five local authorities had agreed to fund part-time after-care arrangements, either one or two days a week or through carers providing respite after a young person had moved to a secure or other residential setting.

Within the project no formal meeting was held to review what had contributed to placements ending, though carers, social workers and young people were later asked by CAPS to complete evaluation forms on each placement. Every effort was made to make the ending positive and to minimise young people's feelings of rejection or failure. Where the leaving had been particularly traumatic, as when the young person had assaulted a carer, the carer, senior practitioner or social worker tried to help the young person address and make sense of what had happened.

The four dimensions of the project considered so far have been primarily organisational, concerned with key aspects of the supportive framework. Attention now turns to four dimensions more closely associated with practice and processes within placements:

- matching young people and carers;
- defining and managing acceptable risk;
- rights and responsibilities; and
- combining work and family life.

Matching

As noted in the previous chapter, young people could only be accommodated within the project if suitable carers were available. Matching was therefore a crucial process.

Before being approved, carers were asked to identify whether there were specific types of young people or behaviours they would not be able or willing to accommodate. At this stage, half of them indicated that they would not be willing to work with young people whose sexual behaviour posed a threat to others. This was usually because carers had children of their own or other children frequently visited their home. While some carers indicated that they would be prepared to reduce or closely monitor other children's visits to their home, others considered this an unacceptable risk and intrusion.

When asked to consider specific young people, carers said they tried to envisage from reports what the young person would be like to live with and to honestly assess whether they and their family would be able to cater for any specific needs or behaviours. Virtually all carers found that the information they received on young people prior to placement was comprehensive and honest. However, sometimes concerns about a young person were genuinely vague, for example, an allegation about inappropriate sexual behaviour had been made but no conclusive evidence uncovered. In these instances, the nature of young people's difficulties might only come to light after they had joined the family.

Several carers pointed out that a key part of the process was to meet the young person and see whether it was possible to establish rapport. Where young people were known to be aggressive, some carers would only accept them into their home after they were confident they had established enough authority to be able to manage challenging behaviour. In most instances there was a prior meeting but this was not always possible when placements were made on an emergency basis. In these situations carers initially relied on senior practitioners' judgements of the placement's suitability, then assessed the young person for themselves once he or she joined them.

The senior practitioners' role in matching was to make an initial decision about which young people might be suitable for individual carers, then to discuss with carers what caring for them might entail. The decision to proceed towards linking was taken by carer and senior practitioner. We were not aware of instances where the young person or social worker had the opportunity to choose between carers.

Main criteria for matching

The main criteria senior practitioners took into account included whether carers:

- took only girls or boys;
- had an active, outdoor or home-based lifestyle;
- operated firm boundaries or were more flexible;
- were primarily nurturing or task-centred;
- shared an interest with the young person;
- had particularly relevant skills or experience.

In addition consideration was given to where carers lived. This might be important in terms of allowing young people to retain links with their home area or be close to the current or other appropriate schools. The nature of the local community could also be a factor in that some young people found it particularly difficult to keep out of trouble in a council scheme. Another consideration might be that if the previously placed young person had caused trouble with carers' neighbours, a quieter young person would be placed next.

As well as considering the nature of the carers and their surroundings, senior practitioners also took into account the needs of other young people in placement. Approximately half the carers were willing to work with two young people simultaneously and instances were reported where this has worked well. However, there was broad agreement among carers and senior practitioners that the young people had to be well matched, otherwise the established placement could be undermined. Indeed some carers were unwilling to have more than one young person in placement, believing young people with such extensive needs required individual attention.

While all these factors were considered important, some senior practitioners also emphasised the importance of the intangibles which drew carers to a particular child. It was suggested that, if a match was to work well, carers had to have an intuitive confidence that they and the young person would get on. A carer who believed he or she could work with a young person would be keen to see the positives and stick with a young person when difficulties emerged.

Young people's preferences

The young person's wishes were also considered by senior practitioners identifying potential carers. Some young people did not specify what kind of carers they would like, but others indicated a number of preferences, for example, where they would like to stay, the age of the carers, whether they wanted to share the placement with other young people and whether they wanted animals. While young people's preferences could not always be met, it was clear that senior practitioners and carers took them seriously. Indeed one of the concerns carers expressed about the trend towards emergency placements was that young people had little or no opportunity to actively choose CAPS and consider the type of placement they would prefer.

Extending carers' capacity

The project operated on the principle that carers should feel confident in their ability to manage any young person placed, so the carers' agreement was essential. The view of CAPS staff was that no carers would be forced to take on a placement against their will. They also pointed out that the diversity of carers' preferences and skills meant that there was no need to require carers to work with types of young people with whom they were uncomfortable. The formal position was that, should carers refuse to accept three or more young people without good reason, their contract could be terminated. By the time the research ended, no one had been in that position.

However, as carers gained experience, some had been asked to extend the range of young people they were willing to work with. For example, some had successfully cared for young people whose sexual behaviour presented a risk to others, having originally felt unable to manage this. This progression followed due consideration of the specific risks an individual child presented and how these could be safely managed. Initially these placements were all time limited. They required considerable vigilance on the part of carers and, for some, significant changes to their usual family life. The carers concerned felt that they had gained very valuable experience, though some regretted the consequent limitations on contact with child relatives.

In the final round of interviews it was evident that there were different understandings among carers about the extent to which concerns about visiting children would be accepted as a reason for not working with young people who may present a risk. This was in contrast to carers' confidence in initial interviews that they would not be asked to work with sexually aggressive young people if they had said they were unwilling to do so. By the time the research ended, some carers still adhered to this point of view:

> We cannot work with a young person who is an abuser because we have grandchildren that come about the house and there are lots of kids in this area that we do take in – they do come in and out the house – and although we work to a safe care plan as far as possible, I don't think it would work with a known abuser.

However, others emphasised that doing a job that meant that they could not simply refuse a particular type of placement, because other children regularly visited their home:

> I think it's important that you can say no but they also say you need to have a really good reason for saying no to a file . . . because we're supposed to be professional people, we're getting a professional wage and, even though you're working from home and you're working with your own family members around you, you've got to be professional about it.

As the above carer understood it, keeping grandchildren safe would involve close supervision and/or restricting their visits, while working with this level of risk and disruption was part of being a professional carer.

Matching considerations in these situations included carers' skill and experience, whether other children lived in or regularly visited the house, and whether the carer would be able to provide supervised outings and activities. The young person's acknowledgement that their behaviour was problematic and willingness to work at managing it was also a key factor.

Defining and managing acceptable risk

Despite staff and managers' reassurances that no carer would be asked to work with a young person who would place them or their family at risk, from the initial interviews carers raised concerns and sought clarification about the level of challenging behaviour they would be expected to manage:

> We already told them when we started that there was no way we would take violent children, under no circumstances . . . so they agreed to that. But I have noticed that they have said that to other couples and it's not turned out that way. So we're a bit kind of wary at the moment.

Carers consistently differentiated between the young people they would work with and those whose behaviour was so extremely aggressive or unmanageable that they needed a more secure form of care. Some specified that people who had murdered, raped or committed serious assaults were unsuitable for family placement:

> A lot of the carers were thinking that some of these kids we were getting should not be coming into the scheme, like kids who are arsonists and kids who are very, very violent who are attacking residential workers and other kids . . . So we felt, no, there should be work done with these kids to a point where they can be moved to us.

> I think they [CAPS] need to watch what kids they're taking in and whether they're going to be helped within CAPS . . . Alright, we would all like to give these kids a chance but you've got to keep yourself and your own family safe as well.

Several carers referred to the responsibility they felt for the safety of their community, as well as that of their own family:

> It's not just for ourselves, we have to think of other people around here.

If we bring in someone and somebody gets stabbed or hurt, how would we feel? We couldn't face folk . . . we'd have to move away.

Thus carers also recognised that the potential repercussions for them and their family were considerable.

However, attitudes to physical aggression varied. While some carers said they would consider a placement no longer viable if a child assaulted them, others viewed a degree of aggression as an inevitable part of working with vulnerable and angry young people and were prepared to continue caring for a young person following an assault. It proved difficult to get an accurate picture of the level and frequency of physical aggression from young people in placement, partly because reports of violent incidents were not collated centrally but within individual carers' files.

The CAPS' formal position was that no specific behaviour should make young people ineligible for the project. Instead, the project was committed to considering each individual referral and only placing the young person if carers with appropriate experience and skills could be identified. It is important to emphasise that, despite the concerns expressed above, most carers were confident that they themselves would be able to resist taking a young person with whom they felt unsafe. However, a significant minority took the view that an agreed threshold should be set for the project, rather than negotiating such matters on an individual basis.

It might be argued that both the above positions assume a greater potential for predicting future danger than is merited. As Macdonald points out, a certain level of uncertainty is inherent in risk assessment, so that decisions about "acceptable" levels of risk involve an element of value judgement (Macdonald and Macdonald, 1999). This ethical dimension was acknowledged by one of the placing social workers:

I think that's the biggest problem for me because you are effectively putting young people who are potentially at risk or a risk to the community and violent, into a family setting and that's a big thing to ask if a family's safety is threatened. I mean you'd always wish to be able to separate the behaviour from the person but it's not always as easy as that. If there's a history of violence it's a big consideration.

Among CAPS staff it was considered inevitable that a project which set out to provide an alternative to secure care would accommodate young people who might behave aggressively in some situations. The challenge was to find ways of caring for these young people as safely as possible. Ways of managing the risk included:

- giving the young person a clear message that violence was unacceptable;
- helping young people learn alternative ways of managing anger;
- training carers in de-escalating and restraint techniques;
- providing support, including additional respite when tensions were high.

Some CAPS carers also thought they should be offered training in self-defence techniques. However, these measures were not expected to completely eliminate the risk.

Anticipating and managing risk from young people's sexual behaviour raised somewhat different issues. Whereas the boundary between acceptable and unacceptable physical aggression was somewhat unclear, there was universal agreement that no sexually abusive behaviour should be tolerated. Thus the threat of sexual abuse was taken very seriously. This meant there was an agreed plan for the supervision of young people known to present a threat, so carers felt they were actively managing the danger, usually with the support of other professionals. Correspondingly, sexually abusive behaviour was seen as resulting from particular difficulties for which the young people needed specialist help, whereas physical aggression could be attributed to bad temper or the effects of alcohol or drugs. Perhaps most importantly, carers had generally known about the risks before agreeing they would work with the young person. Carers were aware that other young people not identified as abusers might also pose a threat and adopted safe care practices within the home accordingly.

False allegations

When asked in final interviews to identify the predominant risk for CAPS carers, staff and carers most commonly referred to false allegations. Approximately ten carers had been accused of ill-treating the young person or sexually inappropriate behaviour. The relative isolation of foster care potentially places carers in a vulnerable position when allegations are made against them. The stress caused was intense, especially when the allegations became known in their local area :

> *It's against us already, there are people that are aware that the boy went out, he did make the allegation, and he never came back – 'It must be true!' We feel we're sticking out a mile, like everybody in the street will be watching us.*

In this situation carers anticipated that the next child placed was likely to be informed by local children 'the first time he or she goes out to play'.

The National Foster Care Association (NFCA, now Fostering Network) has identified four circumstances in which young people may make false allegations:

- when they have misinterpreted an innocent action such as non-sexual touching;
- as a way of drawing attention to previous abuse for the first time because the carer is trusted;
- as a way for them to exercise some sort of control over their life;
- to try and end a foster placement without losing face.   (NFCA, 1994)

Within CAPS false allegations were usually understood in terms of power and control, prompted by young people trying to hit back at carers who were setting limits, wanting to be moved to another placement, or as a protest at being placed with respite carers. Young people knew that making an allegation would get a response. Several carers and staff believed that, for some young people, making allegations had become a means of avoiding difficult and uncomfortable issues, since it resulted in attention being focused on investigating their claims and probably being moved from the family. In their view this could undermine months of work and have negative long-term consequences, especially if the young person needed boundaries and emotional containment but resisted both.

Nevertheless, in principle, the majority of carers accepted that, in the interests of children's rights and safety, the requirement to fully investigate all allegations could not be relaxed. However, a few carers pointed out that this approach did not necessarily serve young people well, since it resulted in false allegations becoming so frequent that genuine reports of abuse might be discounted. It was also suggested that young people who habitually made allegations should not remain in the scheme:

I think if a kid's made allegations about even two of the carers, it should be thought about whether they should be going to another carer.

Though distressing for carers, a few pointed out that a thorough investigation potentially provided a means through which they or their family could be vindicated. On the other hand, some took the view that 'mud sticks' whatever the outcome, while some carers who had been through the process expressed doubts that they could tolerate allegations repeatedly:

We're actually looking at ourselves at the moment and seeing just can we afford another one? We have to be very careful what we are going to take in.

The point of view of CAPS staff was that carers have to accept the risk of allegations as an occupational hazard. Carers were advised to adopt safe caring procedures, for example, by keeping detailed notes of everyday events and ensuring a male member of the family is never alone with a young woman who has made allegations in the past. In some instances this latter practice placed considerable restrictions on the female carer who could not go out on her own without arranging for someone else to be in the house. One carer who had been subject to allegations also questioned the protection afforded by keeping notes, since no one had wanted to see the diary during an ensuing investigation.

Reflecting the experiences of local authority foster carers, CAPS carers talked of feeling very much on their own when faced with an allegation. At the time the research ended, CAPS was examining how they might improve the level of support available to carers in this situation. This was likely to involve developing joint guidelines with social work departments on how allegations should be managed and arranging for support to be offered to carers from an independent agency. Some carers had already contacted NFCA for support and advice on what to expect from CAPS and the investigating local authority. In addition to the personal distress, carers who had experienced allegations said it had undermined their sense of being a valued part of a professional team:

The main thing is the helplessness of it, the situation, never to have your chance to speak to a group of so-called professionals and we all listen and reason. Yes, if there was something to hide that would be found but the way it is you're guilty until proven innocent . . . We start seeing ourselves as, we're not part of a team – there's definitely not a team thing there.

While making false allegations can be understood in terms of the child-based explanations put forward by NFCA and within CAPS, it might also be argued that the power of allegations derives from their cultural signifi-cance and the responses they elicit. Consequently, it might be expected that false allegations will be more powerful within the UK, where risk considerations predominate and child protection services are highly proceduralised (Parton, 1996, 1998), than would be the case in some European countries which adopt a predominantly welfare/needs-based approach and allow professionals scope for more differentiated responses to risk, at least in the short term (Cooper and Hetherington, 1999). The latter approach is arguably more consistent with how carers worked in that they focused predominantly on young people's needs and used considerable discretion to manage a range of risks on a day-to-day basis. This potentially highlights a tension between how carers are expected to professionally manage risk and how they themselves are treated when they are suspected of constituting a risk to others.

Several carers expressed the view that their vulnerability to false allegations was a constant fear and that carers themselves needed more protection and "rights". Rights were thus seen as potentially offering protection to both children and carers.

Rights and responsibilities

We noted in Chapter 1 that CAPS carers faced the challenge of effectively managing risk within an essentially needs-based service. Underpinning these two perspectives was a rights-based ethos which in principle provided a means of linking risk and need but in practice also introduced further tensions. Children and young people may be seen as having several types of rights, especially to:

- safety and protection;
- proper development;
- appropriate service provision;
- express their views on matters which affect them;
- influence decisions.

For carers the first three were largely uncontroversial but rights to self-determination were viewed as more problematic, primarily as they might be interpreted as young people doing what they wanted, regardless of the consequences. There were particular reservations about the appropriateness of a rights-based approach within a family setting, with a majority of carers citing at least one aspect of "children's rights" which they found unhelpful. Some carers also believed that adopting a children's rights approach was a means of allowing adults to avoid their responsibilities for young people. The following comment from one carer was echoed by several:

> I would say that's the thing I find most difficult – the kids are too aware of their rights.

Children's rights within the family

Adopting a children's rights approach was commonly seen by carers as limiting the extent to which they could treat foster children as "ordinary". While some viewed this as inevitable, acknowledging that young people placed outwith their own families needed the explicit entitlements and protection that formal rights conferred, others believed the rights perspective detracted from carers' capacity to provide sound parenting. Typically the first group saw themselves as working within an essentially sound child care system. In contrast, those adhering to the second perspective tended to view the system as failing young people, out of touch with realities of their lives and setting them apart from their peers, through according them rights not enjoyed by children living with their parents. For these carers, fostering was about providing, as far as possible, "ordinary" family life and children's rights were formal, not "ordinary":

> I mean it's all very well being guided by rights, setting a children's charter up, guided by human rights, EEC human rights and things like that. That may work in a care home where everything is straight down the line but it can't work in an ordinary household.

One of the most frequently mentioned issues was that pocket money and clothing money were higher than most children would expect and were available to young people as a right, rather than having to be earned. Some carers took the view that the generosity of the payments raised expectations of a quality of life which was unlikely to be sustained in the longer term, while at the same time accentuating young people's own family's poverty:

It's very difficult because your own kids don't get half what a kid in care gets.

My own kids would have to earn their pocket money, there's no two doubts about that, but I don't feel strongly about her (foster child) getting it for nothing – firstly because I'm not handing it out.

I honestly feel that the system as it stands is setting these kids up to fail . . . I mean I don't know any youngster who gets £15 a week pocket money without having to do something to earn that. I don't know any young people that get £68 a month for clothing. I feel they're setting them up with false expectations about what life's really about.

What happens is that Christine goes over there and they start calling her names because they don't possess the material things and because she is in care she gets the material things and plus. I must say, you know, there's the pluses as well – the family tend to call her names . . . there's a wee bit of jealousy you know.

Some carers also felt that the principle of entitlement prevented them from withholding money as a means of discipline or control. However, others found their scope to time when money was handed over allowed them to retain a level of parental authority and avoid rewarding unacceptable behaviour :

[At certain times] they don't come and ask because they know they'll not get it. I'm certainly not going to be doling out money to somebody who's been mouthing off or whatever. . . I very rarely keep it off them. I've very occasionally kept some of it and put it to their clothing allowance but they don't just get handed it, you know.

Rights, risk and responsibilities

According children rights is generally accepted as a means of protecting them, by giving them a say about how they are cared for and ensuring that any complaints or allegations are taken seriously. However, some carers considered that focusing on children's rights could in some situations place them at risk. The most frequently cited example was that carers were not allowed to physically prevent young people from leaving the home, even with children as young as ten, and when carers strongly expected that the child would be in danger. In these circumstances most carers thought it would have been helpful to take away a young person's shoes, lock a door, or resort to any measure they would have used with their own children. With physical options curtailed, some carers had found ways of persuading young people to stay put, but others had been unable to keep young people safe and the placement eventually ended.

A few carers had encountered similar issues in medical settings, with one young person refusing treatment when severely under the influence of drugs. Another, who had a history of overdosing, was prescribed medication in confidence, which made it hard for the carers to help her.

More generally some carers felt that an unthinking emphasis on children's rights could add to children's stress. For example, some young people had been encouraged to attend meetings where they had to listen to embarrassing and painful details of their parents' lives being openly discussed. Again it was proposed that, modelling competent parents, carers should have the authority to protect children from such bruising experiences.

In each of the situations described above, carers argued that broad principles based on children's rights to be self-determining were being applied in particular situations where children and young people's welfare necessitated more adult control and care. Whereas social workers or medical staff were operating within general systems and guidelines, carers were seeking practical solutions to protect individual children. A few carers reported that, on voicing their concerns for the safety of a child who was likely to abscond, the social worker had reassured them that they would not be held responsible. Each of these carers reported being shocked by this response, since their immediate concern was not for themselves but to avoid the young person coming to harm. Some even suggested that talk of children's rights to self-determination allowed adult professionals to avoid the difficult task of containing very angry and volatile young people:

> *There's nobody held responsible, because that's the out for them, the corporate parents can't be held responsible because they gave the child this right 'There you are, that's a right – now you can do that because it lets me opt out.' Instead of us being responsible and saying 'No, you're not going and we'll take the consequences of what happens'.*

Thus, for some carers there was a real tension between operating as part of an impersonal care system and caring deeply about an individual young person.

These issues involving rights, risk and responsibility thus highlight the tightrope carers walked between the culture of professional care provision and committed family care. Many carers advocated strongly on behalf of the young people in their care or supported them to make representations on their own behalf for better service provision. In these external, quasi-legal situations, all parties were comfortable with a rights perspective which emphasised young people's self-determination and competence. However, many carers were less comfortable applying this perspective within the foster home. Some felt it compromised their authority and capacity to provide "ordinary" family life, while potentially placing young people who required more adult control at risk. While concern for the individual child's welfare should underpin a rights approach, many carers had come to see some aspects of the rights agenda as obstacles to effective work with young people.

Combining work and family life

It was important to all carers that, for as long as young people were living with them, they would be treated as part of their family. Yet at the same time being a CAPS carer was very much a job. It was therefore of interest to understand how carers combined these family and work dimensions but also managed the boundary between them. Carers were asked about four key aspects:

- the role of and implications for the wider family;
- the impact on family life;
- differentiating between work and family life;
- sharing private space.

Role and implications for the wider family

Working for CAPS was seen as a family commitment, though the main carer had responsibility for specific tasks such as attending meetings and writing reports. In some situations couples shared responsibility equally, despite the fact that only one was named as the main carer.

The role of carers' children varied according to their age. Compared with younger children, adolescents potentially had more involvement with the young person placed. Whereas some carers encouraged their sons and daughters to befriend the young person, others sought to protect their own children's privacy. There were few indications that one approach was preferable to the other. Approximately a third of the carers had arranged for adult sons or daughters to care for the young person during respite.

Inevitably there were times when carers' responsibilities to their own children, other relatives and young people in placement were in conflict. Most carers were confident that they managed these demands effectively, but a few had become worn out from trying to cater for everyone's needs. The formal CAPS view was that, unless carers were on respite, the needs of the foster child should be accorded priority. For carers whose own children were young, it was considered important that they had good support networks, so that the children could stay with local relatives or friends for brief periods when the difficulties of the young person in placement made it unsafe or too stressful to remain at home. However, while some carers accepted that in some situations it might be best for their own children to be temporarily cared for elsewhere, others did not:

> I feel this is my home and we've got to come first. If I couldn't see to my own family, how could I see to anyone else's? If I don't put them first, how can I take anybody else in and treat them with the same kind of commitment that I give to my own family?

The extent to which other relatives and friends contributed to the placement varied depending on a number of factors including the expected length of the placement, whether the young person spent a lot of time with their own family, and the foster family's life-style.

The impact on family life

Not surprisingly, the extent to which carers thought working with CAPS had changed their family life reflected both what they had been doing beforehand and the circumstances of the specific young people placed with them. The biggest adjustment was for people who had not previously cared for others within their home and for those who found themselves caring for young people who required constant supervision. This might arise if the young person had no schooling and was at home all day, or in situations where sexual behaviour presented a threat to others. For a few women, the risk of allegations meant that they were unable to leave a young girl alone with their husband or other male relatives. In some instances this very much restricted their scope for going out alone. A number of carers found they had much less free time because of requirements to attend meetings and training.

For some carers it was necessary to adjust to the life stage of the young person placed. For example, carers who had younger children or none could find themselves having to adapt family outings in order to accommodate teenagers' interests.

Differentiating between work and family life

Most carers emphasised that caring for the young person was an integral part of their life, so that on a day-to-day basis they did not distinguish between being on and off duty. It was only when carers were formally on respite that they considered themselves "off duty". Even when young people were with a member of their own family at weekends, carers could be called at any time, if problems arose or the young person decided they wanted to come home. Nevertheless, most carers indicated carving out some time for themselves on a day-to-day basis was an important means of coping with the strain.

Some carers were willing to take young people on holiday with them but others felt that they needed a complete break. Inevitably this to some extent reflected the extent to which the young person was seen as part of the family. Thus proposing to take young people on holiday was imbued with meaning and needed considerable thought. Some young people felt unable to live up to the affirmation and acceptance implied by joining a family holiday and responded by creating havoc before and/or during the planned holiday. On the other hand, being excluded from a family holiday could be difficult for young people who were very keen to be claimed by the family. Both having respite and separate holidays emphasised that looking after the young people was carers' work.

The informal and formal roles of carers were highlighted in terms of how they kept in touch with young people after a placement had ended. While a number of carers had young people dropping in on an informal basis, a few were paid by local authorities to provide regular after-care support. This part of the service was therefore to some extent becoming formalised, prompting questions about whether carers, as a paid expensive resource, could continue to offer informal contact free of charge. Most carers felt that they would retain the right to keep up contact with young people if they wished to do so but some did acknowledge that current placements would have to take priority.

Sharing private space

Carers' homes had also become their place of work where some unpleasant incidents and battles occurred. In addition, some had made changes to their home, for example, adding locks to bedroom doors, while others had had to have extensive damage repaired. However, asked whether they felt differently about their homes now compared with before they started fostering or when the young person was not there, most carers said they did not. Living and working in the same place did not seem to be an issue for most carers.

Most carers played down the extent to which being CAPS carers had impacted on their family life and their home. Yet by most standards, arranging to have own sons and daughters cared for elsewhere in times of stress, ensuring male family members are not alone with certain young women, and adding locks to bedroom doors are significant changes. Their normalisation to accommodate risk in fostering is therefore in itself worthy of note.

Summary

The project developed a co-ordinated programme of assessment, preparation and training geared to professional fostering. In addition CAPS offered high levels of financial reward and support. Key elements were: a good salary; frequent routine support; access to 24-hour crisis support; and entitlement to respite care.

Carers and staff agreed that the service CAPS offered was qualitatively different from conventional foster care. On a day-to-day basis, carers exercised considerable professional judgement and took on more responsibility than other foster carers. They were also encouraged to develop a range of skills, for example, in formal assessment and report writing. Three perspectives on the professional foster care task were identified: skilled supported foster carer; multi-skilled care worker; and expert carer.

Carers were virtually unanimous in their praise for the support received from project staff. In time senior practitioners took on a line manager role with carers.

On the whole, collaboration with local authority social workers has been good. Four-weekly meetings were central to effective partnership and co-operation among the key people involved. However, other elements of the "support package" were not readily available, notably educational provision and suitable placements for young people to move on to. Local authorities' reluctance to guarantee funding on a long-term basis made care planning somewhat uncertain.

This chapter also reviewed complex issues related to matching, managing dangerous behaviour, rights and responsibilities and combining work with family life. These topics had particular implications within the context of developing professional family-based care for young people who require security, both in terms of containment and emotional support, yet often resist it.

4   The young people in the study:
Their characteristics and circumstances

Introduction

In this and the following three chapters the focus is on the nature of CAPS' work with individual young people. Here are introduced the first 20 young people placed with the project. These formed the study sample, alongside 20 young secure care residents who constituted the comparison sample. Their characteristics and circumstances, as described at the first research stage, are outlined. This provides baseline data, while also giving an indication of the extent to which the young people placed with CAPS resembled their counterparts in secure care.

Characteristics of the young people

Placing authority, age and gender

With the exception of one early placement, the first 20 young people placed with the project's carers formed the "CAPS" sample. They came from nine local authorities. The sample comprised ten girls and ten boys. Young people were recruited for the secure sample from four authorities. Thirteen boys and seven girls formed the secure care sample.

In terms of age, the CAPS sample ranged from nine to 17, half being 15 years old. Half the secure sample were also aged 15, the range being 13 to 17. No young people were aged 11–12.

Table 4.1
Ages of young people taking part in the study

Age group	CAPS sample	Secure sample
9–10	3	0
13–14	5	6
15	10	11
16–17	2	3

In terms of age, both samples were broadly representative of that within the secure population as a whole. According to the Social Work Services Inspectorate (SWSI) census carried out in 1998, the age range was 10 to 19, with the majority (81 per cent) between 14 and 16 years old. However, comparison with the SWSI results indicates that girls are over-represented in the study. While they accounted for only 26 per cent of the overall secure population, 35 per cent of the study's secure sample and half of the young people placed with CAPS were girls.

CAPS sample: the young people's experience of secure care

Only four young people placed with CAPS had previously been in secure accommodation, but several more were behaving in ways which social workers thought could merit secure authorisation either now or in the near future. On the basis of their current behaviour and circumstances, the secure status of the young people placed with CAPS was assessed as follows:

Table 4:2

CAPS Sample's secure care status in relation to age and gender

Secure care status	Gender and ages	Total
1. Placed from secure care	2 girls (aged 13 and 14)	
	2 boys (aged 9 and 15)	4
2. Secure authorisation sought/ alternative to prison	4 girls (aged 13–17)	4
3. Behaviour potentially warrants secure care	2 girls (aged 14)	5
	3 boys (aged 10–15)	
4. Not close to secure care	2 girls (aged 15)	7
	5 boys (aged 9–16)	

1. The four young people placed from secure care comprised two girls aged 13 and 14 and two boys aged 9 and 15. For the first nine months of his placement, the nine-year-old was concurrently placed in a residential school, spending weekends and holidays with the carers. Both boys placed from secure care had been involved in offending,

and there were also serious concerns about the nine-year-old's safety during periods of absconding. One girl frequently went missing, while the other repeatedly harmed herself. The length of time they had spent in secure ranged from 4–12 months. A CAPS placement was made available for each of these young people as soon the referral process was complete. However, reluctance to start the placement on the part of parents, Children's Panel members or the young person meant that three were delayed for six to eight weeks.

2. At the point when they were placed with CAPS, a further three girls were either subject to secure authorisation or their local admissions group had agreed they were close to requiring secure care. In addition, a 17-year-old was facing custody following assault charges. Two of these young women were placed from residential school, two from a children's home. They ranged in age from 13 to 17. Though their individual circumstances varied, all were seen as highly vulnerable. Concerns included drug use, involvement in prostitution, self-harm and offending.

3. In addition, five young people were considered at risk of secure care, either because their absconding or behaviour in the community put them in danger or because their aggressive behaviour posed a threat to others in their current placements. This group included two boys who had a history of offending, absconding and being involved in selling sex. Two girls were moved from the same children's home where their behaviour had become out of control. Finally, a ten-year-old boy frequently ran away, becoming involved in offending and placing himself at risk through drug and alcohol use. He was placed from his family home.

5. Five of the seven young people not close to secure care were boys. Four of the seven were placed from residential school at age 15, one from home and two from a children's unit. All young people in this group had gone through difficult episodes in the past, the range of problem behaviours including aggression, offending, absconding, drug use and involvement in prostitution. The level of difficult behaviour at the time of placement varied but there was no immediate risk of secure care.

At the initial stage, the local authority had parental rights in relation to five young people placed with CAPS and an application had been lodged in relation to another.

Secure sample: the young people's experience of secure care

All but two of the young people in the secure sample were currently or had recently been in secure accommodation. The other two were subject to secure authorisation, but had been maintained in residential school since no secure placement was available. Ten had had at least one prior admission to secure care, the *total* length of time spent in security varying from one to 18 months. Data from the SWSI census indicated that only 24 per cent of the overall secure population had previously been in secure care. Thus, compared with the overall secure care population, the secure sample included a higher proportion of young people who had already completed a secure placement. The breakdown of time spent in the *current* secure placement was: not in secure care (2); two months or less (9); and 5–12 months (9).

Two young people in the secure sample were already involved in the adult justice system, one being on probation, the other subject to a suspended sentence for additional charges. At the initial stage, all had been placed on the authorisation of the Children's Panel, rather than the court. The SWSI census indicated that admissions from court accounted for a quarter of the total secure population and a third of the boys, so this subgroup were not included in the study. The local authority had assumed parental rights in relation to three young people.

Previous care history

The previous care experiences of both the CAPS and secure care groups were very similar. In both samples, 14 young people had been admitted to care only once. Most of those remaining had had two admissions, though one young person in a CAPS placement had been in and out of care six times. The length of time young people had previously been accommodated ranged from a few weeks to 14 years for the secure sample and six months to 12 years for those with CAPS (Table 4.3).

Table 4.3

Length of time young people had been accommodated prior to CAPS or secure placement

Time accommodated prior to placement	CAPS	Secure
Under 2 years	7	9
2–5 years	7	6
6–14 years	6	5

The average number of previous placements was also similar for both samples, with half having had four or fewer, and half five or more. One boy in the secure sample was thought to have had around 20 previous placements but otherwise the highest number of previous placements was 12.

Apart from the fact that almost all the secure care sample had in fact been admitted to secure care, both samples had experienced a broadly similar range of placement types (Table 4.4). The only other notable difference was that, compared with the secure sample, young people placed with CAPS had on average had more foster placements (4 as opposed to 2.5). The pattern of previous care is also consistent with the results of the SWSI census which reported that 40 per cent of young people in secure care had had four or more placements in local authority care.

Table 4.4

Previous placements in care

Previous placement	Number with previous experience		Average number of placements	
	CAPS	Secure	CAPS	Secure
Foster care	9	11	4	2.5
Residential school	12	14	1.3	1.6
Residential unit	19	16	1.6	2
			Average time	*Average time*
Secure care	4	18	5 months	6 months

Behaviour difficulties

Information from records and interviews with social workers indicated that there had usually been several reasons why young people had been thought to require a secure placement. In most instances there was concern about the young person's safety and approximately half had also been involved in serious or persistent offending. As outlined in Table 4.5, a similar range of behaviours was presented by young people in the CAPS and secure samples, the main differences being that rather more of those in secure care had a history of offending.

Table 4.5
Behaviour difficulties recorded prior to placement

Recorded behaviour difficulties	CAPS	Secure
Physically aggressive at times	18	14
Alcohol misuse	12	11
Drug misuse	11	12
Absconding	11	15
Prostitution/sexual exploitation	8	7
Theft/shop-lifting offences	7	11
Other offences	7	9
Self-harming behaviour	6	7
Assault offences	6	10
Sexual behaviour presents a threat to others	3	4
Car offences	2	5

Some individual young people exhibited several of the above behaviours, with seven or more separate causes for concern having been recorded for half the CAPS sample and almost two-thirds of those in secure accommodation. While the CAPS young people had on average been charged with fewer offences, some behaviour could potentially have constituted an offence. For example, all but two of them had been aggressive to others, usually when provoked or under pressure in residential establishments. Most of the shop-lifting by young people in both samples happened during periods of absconding from home or care.

In addition to recording specific difficult behaviours, the Goodman Strengths and Difficulties Questionnaire was used to provide a standardised measure of emotional and behavioural difficulties. This comprises a small number of easy to understand questions, which make up a well-validated measure to assess whether children and young people's behavioural and emotional difficulties are within or outwith the normal range (Goodman, 1994). The scores reported here are based on the responses by carers and key workers at the first interview stage. The initial scores placed around half the young people in both samples in the "abnormal" category, while only a third fell within the "normal" range.

Table 4.6
Initial Scores: Goodman's Strengths and Difficulties Questionnaire

Categorisation by Goodman score	CAPS sample	Secure sample
Normal	7 (35%)	6 (33%)
Borderline	3 (15%)	4 (22%)
Abnormal	6 (30%)	4 (22%)
High level of difficulty	4 (20%)	4 (22%)
Total	**20**	***18**

*2 missing.

Information was therefore obtained from records and interviews on the *range of problem behaviours* and from the Goodman scale on the *level or severity of emotional and behavioural difficulties*. While both the range of behaviour problems and the Goodman scores were similar for both samples, the pattern of correspondence between these two dimensions was different for each of the two samples. For around two-thirds of the secure sample, the two scores were compatible, in that most of those who had presented a high number of behaviour difficulties also scored high on the Goodman scale and vice versa. Two-thirds of those rated as having seven problems or more were rated as abnormal or having a high level of difficulties, while all but two of the seven young people who had six behaviour problems or less came into the normal or borderline categories.

In contrast, there was correspondence between the two scores for less than half of the CAPS sample. Of the ten rated as normal or borderline on the Goodman scale, half had presented over six problem behaviours, while this applied to only four of the ten rated as abnormal. The discrepancy between the two scores is likely in part to reflect the tendency of some carers to accentuate problems, while others minimised them. However, it also highlights that, when considering the level of difficulty presented by an individual young person, it is helpful to distinguish between at least two elements: the degree of emotional harm they have suffered and how that manifests itself in challenging or self-harming behaviour.

Given this complexity, categorising young people according to their level of difficulty can only be an approximate and imperfect exercise. However, taking the range of difficulties *and* Goodman scores into account, the sample could be classified as follows:

Low difficulties	CAPS	Secure
(i.e. normal or borderline Goodman score *and* 7 problems or less)	5	5
Medium difficulties (i.e. normal or borderline Goodman score *and* 7 problems or more OR Abnormal or high level Goodman score and 7 problems or less)	11	7
High difficulties Abnormal or high level Goodman score and 7 problems or more	4	8

Taking the Goodman scores and range of problem behaviours into account, the indications were that, within the secure sample, there were more young people with severe difficulties. However, for the most part both samples presented a similar range of challenges.

Self-esteem

Virtually all young people in both samples were considered by social workers to lack confidence and have a poor opinion of themselves.

However, when asked to rate their self-esteem, many social workers said they found this difficult. This was partly because self-esteem varied depending on recent events, but also because over half the young people were described as presenting a confident exterior which, the social worker believed, masked deep-seated insecurities and a very poor self-image. For these reasons several social workers felt unable to make a reliable assessment at all.

Taking these reservations into account, only two of the 20 young people placed with CAPS and three of the 20 in secure care were assessed as having good or average self-esteem. However, even for them, social workers noted that past experiences had probably left them vulnerable to self-doubt and depression.

In addition to social workers' initial assessments of self-esteem, young people were asked to complete the Rosenberg standard measure of self-esteem. The Rosenberg measure is well validated and has the advantage of being short and easy to complete. Respondents are simply asked to record their agreement or otherwise with ten statements describing how they feel about themselves. Most young people chose to complete the form themselves but others preferred to have the questions read to them and give a verbal response.

The responses are scored to give a result from 0–6, with six indicating lowest self-esteem. For the purposes of this study, a score of 3–4 was taken to represent moderately low self-esteem, and 5–6 very low self-esteem. On this basis, the results for the first round are reported in Table 4.7.

Table 4.7
Initial assessments of self-esteem according to the Rosenberg scale

	CAPS	*Secure*
Average self-esteem	9	11
Moderately low self-esteem	4	1
Very low self-esteem	2	3
Total	**15**	**15**

These scores evidently do not correspond with the social workers' assessments that most young people had low self-esteem, though they are consistent with the view that they were able to present themselves as confident and with high self-regard. It was evidently this image which most young people presented in completing the Rosenberg scale.

On the basis of the social workers' assessments and the Rosenberg scores, there were few indications that, in relation to self-esteem, the young people in secure care differed from those placed with CAPS.

Education

School-related difficulties were common in both samples. Prior to placement, no child in the CAPS sample attended school on a regular basis without the need for additional support. Seven young people were nominally in mainstream schooling, though only two were attending regularly and they needed considerable support to sustain this. The remainder had been in specialist education, all but one in a residential setting. Eleven young people were identified as refusing to attend school and 14 presented behaviour problems while in school. Only four had no identified problems with attending school or behaviour when there, but all of these were in some kind of specialist education setting.

In the comparison sample, six young people were nominally in mainstream school prior to admission to secure care and for three of them, no specific school-related problems were cited. Ten had previously been in a residential school and one had attended a specialist unit on a day basis. Three had not been attending school at all. Of the whole secure sample, 13 young people either refused to go to school or presented significant behaviour problems when there.

One of the notable findings from the SWSI census was that almost 40 per cent of the young people were described as academically able or very able and having the potential to improve their educational performance. Similarly, four young people from each of this study's samples were described by social workers as bright, articulate and with an enquiring mind, despite having missed substantial amounts of schooling. However, neither the SWSI survey nor our assessments were based on reliable standard measures.

Family circumstances

The family circumstances of young people taking part in the project were diverse. Both samples included two or three young people for whom a grandparent or other relative had become the main carer, though there was variation in the degree to which this had become formalised. Of those placed with CAPS, only two sets of parents were still living together, while this applied to four of those in secure care. Among the majority who had separated, a variety of family arrangements had developed, with mothers continuing to have varying levels of involvement in young people's lives, either as sole carer or alongside new partners. Significant relationships were primarily with parents, though for one young woman the main carer was her grandmother, another's main contact was with her aunt and one young man spent weekends with his grandfather.

Apart from two young people whose mother had died, all those placed with CAPS maintained some contact with their mother. Approximately half saw their mother fairly regularly, though meetings were often tense and difficult. The remainder had only occasional or infrequent contact. Among those in the secure sample, the pattern of contact with mothers was broadly similar, though seven young people had no contact with their mother, three of the mothers having died. Just under half had regular contact with their mother who continued to have a significant role in their lives. In these cases the relationship was sometimes, though not always, fraught. The remaining five saw their mother occasionally.

Contact with fathers was far less common for young people in both samples. Only four young people placed with CAPS had a father or step-father who still played an active role in their life, while another three had infrequent contact. A similar picture emerged among those in secure care, with only three young people in frequent contact with their father, while 14 had no ongoing relationship at all. Both samples included four young people whose father had died.

This pattern of family relationships is similar to the profile of the overall secure population which emerged from the SWSI census. Just under a fifth of young people's parents were still living together, while a third had seldom or never seen their father.

All the young people who took part in the study had at least one brother or sister. Both samples included ten young people who had at least one brother or sister remaining in a parent's care. Approximately half the young people placed with CAPS and a third of those in secure accommodation had a sibling who was also in care. Six young people placed with CAPS and four in secure accommodation had lost contact with a brother or sister and were keen to re-establish this. Two young men in the secure sample had home leave at an older brother's home.

Whether the young person had continuing support from their own family was one important factor which influenced the nature of individual CAPS placements and shaped their significance for the young person. Both samples were closely matched in this respect, with approximately a third still in touch with a parent or other relative who was willing and considered suitable to care for them at some point in the future. This did not mean that the relationship with the parent or carer was necessarily unproblematic, but at some point in the future they were expected to play an active part in caring for the young person or providing support and accommodation until they were able to live on their own.

The remaining two-thirds were not able to rely on family support. Most still had contact with their mother but it was not planned that they should return to live with any relative, nor was much family support expected. About half had been looked after for five years or more but the others had been accommodated more recently, some within the last two years.

Given that the majority of both samples were aged 15 or older, many were faced with establishing themselves in adult life without family support. This is consistent with the SWSI census finding that many young people in secure accommodation needed to find a placement which would provide adequate support and supervision, while allowing them to take responsibility for their lives at a pace which suited them.

Both study samples and the secure care population

It is evident that the two samples included a similar range of young people in terms of care experience, level of difficulty, family circumstances and current needs. One difference was that two-fifths (8) of the secure sample were assessed as having severe difficulties, compared with one-fifth (4) of the CAPS sample. However, otherwise the range of difficulties was similar.

In most respects the characteristics of both samples were also similar to the overall secure population, for whom details were available from a census undertaken in 1998 (SWSI, 2000). This suggests that on the whole neither CAPS nor the research had made biased selections. The main differences were that rather more girls were included in the research and more young people who had been accommodated away from home for a long time. Three-quarters of the CAPS and two-thirds of the secure sample had been accommodated for more than two years prior to their current placement, but only one-quarter of the overall secure population.

These differences between the study's two samples and the overall secure population can be accounted for in part by the fact that none of those who took part in the research had been remanded or sentenced by the court. The 1998 SWSI census revealed that those on court orders, who accounted for a quarter of all young people in secure accommodation, had distinct characteristics compared with young people placed by the Children's Panel. All but one of those on court orders was male. Though they had committed serious crimes, they typically had less troubled backgrounds than those placed by panels. For many, the onset of their difficulties had been delayed until adolescence and their schooling was less disrupted. Most were still able to rely on family support, whereas the young people placed by panels often had fraught family relationships. There were of course some whose difficulties were severe, but overall the young people placed by the court were assessed as having fewer problems and more resources to help them cope on their release.

This profile of young people who have committed serious crimes is of interest because it indicates that, despite the severity of their past actions, some would be relatively easy to manage in foster care. They would potentially benefit from the reduced disruption to their education and social development which community placement might offer. It lends support to the CAPS view that young people should not be considered unsuitable for foster care solely on the grounds of their previous behaviour. Yet such young people were not referred to CAPS. Consequently it was essentially catering for emotionally damaged rather than delinquent young people, i.e. providing a childcare rather than a juvenile justice resource.

Summary

This chapter reported baseline data on the first 20 young people placed with CAPS carers, who formed the core sample for detailed investigation in this research. Thirteen of the CAPS sample came from secure care or were at imminent risk of admission to secure accommodation. Seven were "not close" to secure care, although they each presented very difficult behaviour. All the sample had experienced family separations and usually subsequent changes in the places they lived. Half had school refusal problems and the rest all needed special educational support.

This CAPS sample was compared with 20 young people in secure residential accommodation. In many respects the two samples did not differ substantially, although the CAPS sample included three nine to ten-year-olds, whereas the youngest person in the secure sample was 13. The behaviour profiles of the two samples were quite similar in type and severity, except that the secure sample included more who had committed offences and a few more with severe difficulties.

5 **Needs and expectations**

Introduction

This chapter considers what young people were thought to need from the placements and what a CAPS placement was expected to offer. Both young people and adult respondents were asked about what they thought they needed from the placements. In response they commonly referred to two dimensions:

- what the young person required (e.g. to be nurtured, to learn self-control);
- the type of input required to meet these needs.

These two components meant that responses to questions about needs revealed expectations of the placements as well as young people's initial requirements. Thus all young people on the point of starting a CAPS placement were thought to need an experience of family life, while for virtually all the secure care sample, the main identified requirement was to be kept safe and secure. Towards the end of this chapter, consideration is given to whether this reflected essentially different requirements or a shift in emphasis to fit the current plan. CAPS and secure placements are examined separately, then the similarities and differences between them are compared.

For the secure sample, the social worker's was the only adult view obtained on needs, but for those being placed with CAPS, the opinions of the social worker, carer and the CAPS senior practitioner were sought. In most instances there was broad agreement among them as to what young people required, though different individuals sometimes highlighted particular aspects. Quite often this difference of opinion reflected competing needs, for example, when young people required to develop skills to cope with independence, yet also needed to experience being cared for, entailing a degree of dependency associated more with younger children. There was no indication at this early stage that any one group of respondents was more or less likely to highlight particular kinds of needs, so, on the whole, a combined adult view of need is presented. Young people were also asked what they thought they needed from the placement and the chapter begins by reporting their views.

Young people's views of what they needed from CAPS placements

Compared with the adults, in the first interviews young people did not talk in great detail about what they needed or expected from the placements. It was nevertheless clear that they approached placements with certain expectations and that moving to a family constituted a significant experience in their lives. In only a few instances was there an obvious discrepancy between the young person's perspective and that of the carer or their social worker.

A number of young people felt they simply needed a life outside residential care but others qualified this by specifying what they needed from a family. For some, acceptance as part of the family was a priority. One young man, who had lived with somewhat detached foster carers in the past, said he would need to feel he belonged and would not be treated as an outsider. Another young man focused not so much on joining the new family but on having a "clean break" from his former family and associates. This was one case in which the young person's views were somewhat at odds with those of the carers, who were encouraging him to continue to go home for visits at weekends. At the other end of the spectrum were young people who felt they needed to retain loyalty to their own family. A few said they needed a foster family to work towards returning home. However, some who expressed this view also wished to be accepted by the foster family, anticipating a tension which would become difficult for some young people and carers to manage. A number of those who had been in residential care thought they needed to learn how to live in a family.

Besides describing what a move to a family would entail in itself, most young people talked of needing to address the current problems they were facing. One girl wanted to stop running away, others wanted to keep out of trouble. A few young people said they needed help to get in touch with brothers and sisters they had lost contact with. Others hoped to get a job, to find a house, be helped to get on better at school or college or to learn how to get on better with other people. In contrast, a few young people rejected the idea that they needed anything from the placement, other than being looked after outside a residential setting.

[I need] help to sort my head out so I stop running. I want to stop running away but I can't.

. . . to get to see my wee brothers and sisters but I don't know if [the carer] can help with that.

. . . to learn to live in a family. Just help to keep me out of trouble.

. . . just help me to get back home. Learning me how to cope in a family and how to cope with my mum and that, learning how to tidy up the house and that.

I don't really have problems. I just wanted a family cos it's more homely. Once I'm 17 or 18 I'll need help to find a house.

My problems were sorted out when I was at [residential school] but I need to learn to be independent. I need to learn to do things about the house and how to socialise with other people . . . how to get my point across, be firm but listen to other people and don't lose the plot.

Adult views of what young people needed from CAPS placements

These various elements of what young people hoped for from the placements were also evident in social workers', carers' and senior practitioners' views. These were:

positive experience of family life	20
to be supported in a school or work placement	20
stability, security, consistency	18
to learn to accept boundaries, change behaviour	13
to be helped to live in the community/reverse the effects of institutionalisation	12
to talk through or come to terms with past emotional trauma	11
to renew or develop relationship with birth parents or other relatives	10
to prepare for independent living	10

These identified needs and expectations can be grouped under two main headings: *"Positive experience of family life"* and *"Support for life outwith the family"*.

Positive experience of family life

For virtually all of the young people referred to CAPS at this early stage, both carers and social workers thought a positive experience of family life was central to catering for their needs. However, the significance of a family experience varied depending on their circumstances.

Two of the ten-year-old boys needed a long-term family placement. One was initially placed with CAPS to assess his capacity to live in a family home. The second, placed from secure care, also needed a long-term family, though in his case it was less clear whether he would remain with the CAPS carers or be helped to move on. Both children initially presented very challenging behaviour. Within CAPS they needed to be cared for, to learn to accept boundaries, and to adapt their behaviour to family life. They also needed to be supported in school.

Five young people were expected to return to live with their own parents or grandparent, three having been placed from secure care. The foster family was seen as offering an opportunity to learn to live safely in an open setting, while providing more control, support and a less emotionally charged environment than their own family could offer at that time. The remaining two young people had been close to secure care, being out of control at home, at school, and in the community. They were thought to require firm controls but also needed carers who would work with their parents and help them develop parenting skills.

In addition to these five young people for whom the plan was to return home, there were three girls for whom this was considered a possible but unlikely option. All were girls whose CAPS placement was some distance from their home.

Though the eight young people for whom return home was a possibility had had relatively recent experience of family life, for many this had been uncertain and unpredictable, often living with parents who were violent, drank excessively, or communicated in a manipulative and/or undermining manner. The young people were therefore thought to need to experience life in a stable family where people communicated in a straightforward way and were reliable. The foster families were not expected to be free of tension but to provide a model of family life which could accommodate disagreements without rejecting or hurting family members.

This kind of positive family experience was also considered a key requirement for the ten young people who were not expected to return to live with a parent or grandparent. In addition to life in their own family having been fraught, most of them had been in residential care for at least a few years. The view of social workers and carers was that they needed "tender loving care" but also to see how a family operated. This learning was viewed as preparation for when they became parents themselves. Given that the SWSI survey (SWSI, 2000) showed the majority of young people in secure care cannot rely on family support and are in the 15–16 age range, the experiences of this last group of young people would potentially highlight what CAPS was able to offer a significant proportion of the secure population.

While there was agreement among respondents about what young people required in principle, for those who would not be returning home, there was much less clarity about the role carers would play in supporting young people as they moved into adult life. A number of social workers hoped the foster carers would become life-long friends or supports, but they were not all sure whether their local authority would fund the placement over the longer term, nor whether this was consistent with the way CAPS worked. The following was typical of several responses to a question about how long the placement was expected to last:

> It's something we've never discussed. You see because I would have the view that the best thing that could happen to Tom would be to leave him with them for the duration. He would leave them in the same way as their own children. Now whether or not that's possible, I haven't a clue . . . But I would certainly view him as being there for the next year and a half minimum. Actually I think he has to stay longer but whether or not that's financed by social work would be a different matter. I don't know what the carers' view is or what CAPS' view is.

Thus uncertainty about funding, the project's role and how young people would respond to the family contributed to longer-term plans being fluid for almost half of those who would not be returning home.

The length of time placements were expected to last reflected to some extent whether CAPS was to be a stepping stone on route to home, to another family, or to provide a restorative and possibly enduring experience of family life. Details of how long placements were expected to last are outlined in Table 5.1:

Table 5.1
Expected length of placements according to the longer-term plan

Expected length of placement	*Prepare for long-term family placement*	*Planned return to a relative*	*Return home unlikely or not possible*
6–12 months	1	4	3
13–18 months	1	0	2
19–24 months	0	0	2
Unclear	0	1	6

Irrespective of how long placements were to last or the purpose of the placement, fostering was seen by the adult respondents as providing a fundamentally different experience from secure or other forms of residential care. The distinctive features they identified for fostering were its capacity to allow young people to:

- enhance emotional development;
- change specific behaviours;
- learn skills;
- be cared for safely in a non-institutional setting.

Enhancing emotional development

Given their age and the young people's previous adverse experiences, expectations of the placements were high in terms of enhancing personal growth. Social workers and carers talked of young people needing to be accepted for themselves, to learn to trust and be trusted, and to experience reliable relationships. People only seldom used the term "attachment", more frequently talking of young people needing to engage with the family, learn to trust or make a commitment. Through this kind of relationship it was hoped that young people would be able to improve their self-esteem and confidence, better manage the effects of previous abuse or rejection and so increase their control over how they lived their life. The following comments from social workers related to two young people who had spent time in secure accommodation:

> *He needs security. He hasn't had that . . . He needs to know that he will be made welcome and that he has a safe and secure place . . . to be included in their family as well, I mean this is really important, and not to feel rejection if he misbehaves. He needs to learn how to link action and consequences and he needs to develop strategies for controlling his emotions and learn other ways of dealing with things and learn to negotiate. He needs strong boundaries to be maintained but in an accepting, loving environment – that's basically it.*

> *You couldn't bring her back to that age but we needed to get her into a family where she would be able to be a child and to act like a child without losing face – it would be OK for her to have difficulties without feeling rejected . . . It was a family we wanted so that she could basically see there is another side to life . . . someone that could give the attention and intensive support she needs.*

A need for this kind of basic emotional experience was acknowledged in relation to about three-quarters of the young people. It was the predominant requirement for some who had known little consistent care or had experienced repeated rejection in the past. Most of these young people had previously been in residential care and had formed a good relationship with at least one key worker. However, family relationships were considered much more likely to foster emotional growth, mainly because they provided continuity of care and the carers were seen by young people to be making a personal commitment. On this basis, it was argued, foster carers were able to make emotional demands which, though difficult to tolerate, could be the means through which young people would learn to make the kind of close relationships which facilitate emotional development.

For some young people, particular issues were identified as barriers to emotional growth. Virtually all young people in CAPS placements had experienced significant loss and rejection in the past and for about half it was expected that the carer would have a role in helping them acknowledge and manage the resulting pain in ways which would not cause them further harm. A few were thought to need the security of a trusting relationship to explore their sexual identity or allow themselves to behave as the younger child they had never been.

This basic need to learn how to operate in close relationships applied to all ages, including teenagers who were moving towards independent living. Eight of those for whom the placement was primarily to prepare for independence were described as also needing a sense of belonging, to know how to make an attachment or to learn to trust. Social workers sometimes recognised that it would be difficult to learn closeness and trusting while in the process of growing away from adult authority but they hoped that carers would become trusted friends who could be relied on for ongoing support.

Stability, security and consistency were mentioned as key needs in relation to all but two young people. Most had experienced a lot of change and insecurity in their lives. It was hoped that carers would stick with young people to help them develop trust and, by being consistent and reliable, enable them to understand the consequences of their actions and control risky or unhelpful behaviour.

These were high expectations, the other side of which was the fear that the placements would break down, constituting yet another rejection. This concern was expressed by a few social workers but confidence in the success of the placements was generally high at the outset. Beginning a CAPS placement was viewed as emotionally risky for the young people, while also potentially conferring substantial rewards.

Changing specific behaviours

For virtually all the young people, behaviour was identified which required change or control. For just over half this was cited as a specific need by either the carer or social worker. For the others it was assumed that meeting other emotional needs would indirectly lead to improvements in behaviour.

Modifying behaviour was more often cited as a priority when it put young people at serious and immediate risk. Five young people, including one girl and two boys placed from secure care, needed to be helped to stop running away. There were particular concerns about two ten-year-old boys who indulged in drinking, drug use and offending while absent and about two teenage girls who were at risk of being sexually exploited in prostitution. Another girl placed from secure care needed support to stop self-harming which was seen as a means of manipulating adults and receiving the attention she craved.

Conversely, although offending was an issue for about a third of the young people, it was not mentioned as a specific need to be tackled in the placement. Similarly, while over half of the young people used drugs or alcohol, this was only cited as a key focus for the placement when there were fears of immediate harm. More often there was an expectation that unacceptable behaviour would be challenged and young people offered appropriate advice, but there was much more focus on the foster placement's capacity to help with underlying emotional issues. It might be argued that the risks the young people presented to themselves and others were reframed in terms of needs. This was consistent with the project's welfare-based, child-centred approach.

Several methods were mentioned by which carers were expected to help young people change their behaviour. Firm but fair boundaries were seen as crucial for most young people and of paramount importance for some. Several young people were described as skilled in manipulating adults and having a need to be in control. Social workers generally attributed this to insecurity and anxiety, while carers were more likely to see it as resulting from previous experience in institutional care where boundaries were less consistently applied. However, most recognised the importance of boundaries in terms of emotional containment as well as behavioural control. In this context carers valued their 24-hour day relationship with the young person, which would afford continuity between actions, promised rewards or punishments and consequences. It was expected that in this way young people would learn to accept responsibility for their own actions.

Other aspects of the placement expected to achieve behavioural change included carers and their own children providing a good example and involving young people in leisure activities, in order to keep them occupied and provide an enjoyable experience in a safe and legitimate setting.

Opportunities to learn

As noted above, one key perceived advantage of foster care was that it offered young people an opportunity to learn what it was like to live in a family. This was commonly talked of by workers and carers as involving learning "about" families but it also involved developing the necessary skills to operate as part of a family, e.g. consideration for others, the use of humour and sharing. Some carers saw themselves as correcting the lower standards which had been accepted in residential care, for example, in relation to hygiene or eating habits.

For about half the young people the placement was to focus on practical skills to help prepare them for independent living. These included cooking and keeping a house, but also managing money and establishing a routine of going to college or work.

Being cared for safely in a non-institutional setting

For some young people there was an urgent need to be protected from the dangers which had resulted or almost resulted in them being placed in secure accommodation. Foster care was expected to offer a different kind of protection from that provided in secure placement. In most instances it was anticipated that, by meeting their emotional needs and providing support to address specific problems, the young people would be encouraged to desist from the behaviours which had placed them at risk such as running away, involvement in prostitution, or self-harming. The emphasis was on helping young people to develop internal controls, through providing good care and helping young people to manage the stresses and risks associated with living in the community.

Support for life outwith the foster family

While relationships and interaction within the family were seen as central to meeting young people's essential needs, providing support to manage relationships and activities outwith the foster home was almost as important. Almost all needed to be supported to attend school, college or work while about half were to be helped restore or develop a relationship with a parent or other relative. Several young people preparing for independent living needed to learn how to develop and sustain friendships or to use community resources such as health services, transport, employment agencies or sports clubs. For about a third it was planned from the start to develop a specific leisure interest. Life outwith the family thus centred primarily on supporting: birth family relationships; school; health; leisure activities; and preparing for the future.

Birth family relationships

As noted previously, all the young people placed with CAPS had a history of troubled family relationships. All but two of them had experienced parental rejection or loss, either because the parent found it difficult to engage with the child (10) or because they were emotionally unavailable because of mental illness or addiction (6). One young woman's parents had died as a result of drug use and one boy's mother had died from physical illness. In the two instances where parents were not rejecting, the nature of the parent–child relationship was nevertheless seen as fraught and contributing to the young person's problems. In terms of needs in relation to the birth family, two key elements predominated: a) learning to manage contact; and b) developing a more realistic understanding of what parents were able and willing to offer. The latter encompassed understanding why the young person was not living at home.

The main ways carers were expected to cater for these needs included establishing an appropriate relationship with parents, supporting young people to talk through their feelings, and helping to facilitate contact. Where the plan was for young people to go home, the emphasis was on working alongside parents, helping them learn how to manage the young person's behaviour, while also supporting them in establishing firm boundaries. Usually the intention was that there would be fairly frequent contact, either by phone, in the foster home, or in the course of contact visits. There were plans for one set of carers to take part in more focused family work in conjunction with the statutory social worker and a worker from another voluntary project involved with the family.

Where there was no clear plan for young people to go home but parents remained involved, the emphasis was to be more on keeping them informed and supporting parents and the young person to keep in touch in ways which were least harmful to the young person. With a few young people whose parents had expressed some opposition to the placement, this promised to be a challenging task.

In virtually all instances, support in relation to family contact also potentially involved helping young people better understand and come to terms with their family situation. In relation to over half the young people, this was considered very important if they were to be freed to make choices about how to live their own lives. Carers were usually expected to work alongside social workers on these issues, but it was also anticipated that their own close and less formal involvement with the young person would provide more spontaneous opportunities to address such sensitive issues.

Important as they were, parents were not the only family members who mattered to young people. About half the young people also had brothers or sisters with whom they wanted to resume or maintain contact. Some were living with parents at home, others were adopted or being looked after elsewhere. Several of the young people not only wanted contact with their siblings but worried about them and/or felt guilty that they had somehow let them down. While social workers, carers and CAPS workers acknowledged the importance of these relationships, in some cases they also pointed out that making contact would be difficult, especially where siblings had been separated for several years. For a few young people, establishing contact was an urgent matter which they felt was central to their own needs and well-being.

School, college and work

As noted in the previous chapter, prior to placement all young people placed with CAPS had presented difficulties in relation to attendance or behaviour in school. Nevertheless, for almost half the sample, the original plan was that they would attend mainstream school, while seven needed a specialist resource and four were to move to college or work experience. All of them needed both an appropriate educational or work resource and support from the carer in order to attend and benefit from it. School and work were not only seen as important in themselves but were also the main context in which young people integrated with the community. It was for this reason that initial plans favoured mainstream rather than specialist provision.

Health

The main health needs identified for young people were to do with sexual health, psychological well-being, and the effects of drugs and alcohol. All girls but one had a gynaecological matter or recurring infection to be investigated, and it was considered that all of them would benefit from advice on safe sex and contraception. In most instances the intention was to pursue these matters with the foster carer's general practitioner.

Five girls and four boys were thought to need help from a psychologist or counsellor, though only three were receiving this kind of service, one from a Child Guidance clinic, one from a counselling service, and one from a psychiatric hospital. Young people themselves did not always agree that they needed this kind of help, so that there was not always a plan to refer to an appropriate service. Similarly, half the young people were thought likely to have long-term health needs relating to drug or alcohol use, but the suggested remedy for this was reducing the use of the substance rather than referral to specialist services. In addition, there were chronic conditions which needed attention. One boy needed to have glasses and a girl had recurring tonsillitis.

Leisure activities

The importance of introducing young people to ordinary leisure activities was mentioned in relation to seven young people at the start of placements, there being plans to introduce them to sports clubs, drama groups, cadets, choirs, line dancing and bowling. These were seen, primarily by the carers, as an important means of diverting young people from risky activities, teaching social skills, developing expertise, and improving self-confidence.

Preparing for the future

It might be argued that all aspects of the placements were geared towards preparing young people for adult life. Enhancing emotional development, helping young people control their behaviour, learning about family life and how to manage in the outside world were generally seen by respondents as enabling young people to cope with life in the future. CAPS was adopting a holistic approach, tackling the many complex dimensions of young people's lives.

Enabling young people to access services and activities in the community was valuable as a preparation for independent living, as well as for the immediate experience or benefits. For many young people who had been in residential care, this applied to everyday matters like using public transport and shopping as well as accessing services. These kind of needs were usually identified by carers early on in the placement and most of them accorded this kind of training a high priority.

One feature of the project which promised to complicate preparing young people for adult life was that most of the young people were placed 30 miles or more from their home area. As a result, networks developed in the foster carers' community would not necessarily provide support, should the young person return to live in their home area. Where young people had few contacts or family to rely on, this soon raised the question of whether their future should be in the locality of the placement. For reasons noted earlier, initial care plans did not address these longer-term issues. When these had to be managed in practice, they highlighted two important challenges for CAPS: to co-ordinate services and responsibilities across local authorities and to provide the longer-term support some young people required, without losing the project's focus on working with young people who might otherwise be placed in secure care.

Summary of needs and initial expectations of the service

The needs to be addressed by the project were multi-dimensional. They related to past and current experiences and to anticipated future require-ments. In addition, they encompassed emotional needs for positive close relationships alongside more immediate needs to address risky or unhelp-ful behaviours or learn specific skills. Identified needs focused on the inner person, managing close interpersonal relationships and coping in the outside world.

Adopting a holistic approach, the foster placement was expected to cater for almost all the identified needs. Apart from school, relatively little input was planned from services outwith the home. A few young people were receiving counselling, but otherwise most activity outside the foster home was to centre on mainstream leisure activities in the community. This was consistent with the project's emphasis on normalisation and enabling young people with exceptional needs and difficulties to live and develop in the community.

The family experience was viewed as central to achieving this. Carers, social workers and CAPS senior practitioners conveyed a strong belief in the power of "good" parenting. Whether it was providing consistent personal care, firm boundaries or good role models, carers generally saw themselves as providing something which young people had not been offered before. Their aim was to improve young people's current experience and future life chances. This was expected to encompass and integrate two broad approaches: *tasks* which involved challenging unhelpful behaviours and learning new skills, and the *process* of offering a consistent caring relationship in which young people felt valued and secure enough for the possibility of emotional development. The key components are summarised below:

Task	Process
Boundaries, consistency	Reliable, accepting and personal relationship
Joint activities, encouragement	Talking, family life
Control/change behaviour	Emotional development
Learn skills	Improving self-esteem

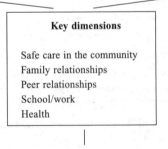

Key dimensions

Safe care in the community
Family relationships
Peer relationships
School/work
Health

Equip young person for adult life

The task elements were consistent with short-term placements, as envisaged at the start of the project. However, for most young people it was the kind of relationship carers could offer which made foster care a potential means of changing damaging behaviour and their future quality of life. Despite the fact that CAPS was set up to provide time-limited placements, there was a clear expectation that foster care's distinctive potential was to cater for longer-term, emotional needs. Social workers and carers expressed the view that the risks young people presented to themselves and others would best be addressed through catering for their long-term, underlying needs. To what extent the project's more focused remit would allow it to cater for these remained to be seen.

Needs of young people in secure placements

Whereas foster care was expected to cater for short- and long-term needs, secure accommodation was essentially considered a short-term option. Because of this it was important to distinguish between what young people required from secure care and their longer-term needs.

For the research, information on young people's needs on entry or during the secure placement was primarily used to address two questions:

- whether CAPS was catering for young people whose needs were similar to those in secure care;
- what was required of foster care, if it was to cater for young people at each stage of secure placement.

Initial needs on being admitted to secure care

Most young people in the secure units were described as having been in crisis when they arrived there. Some had been missing for several weeks, often living in what were considered dangerous situations and with some boys heavily involved in offending. Others had been transferred directly from another residential resource, usually because their self-harming and/ or aggressive behaviour could not be managed there.

On admission the primary needs identified by social workers were for:

- good basic care – food, clean clothes and care;
- physical security, prevention of running away, close supervision;
- opportunity to stop the cycle of unsafe or destructive behaviour;
- provision of external control while young person has little self-control.

Young people's essential requirements in the early stages of a secure placement were therefore to be held and cared for safely. Many had arrived hungry, tired and unkempt, so providing good physical care in a safe environment was a high priority. However, emotional holding was also important. Social workers pointed out that some young people needed the emotional security of knowing someone else would control them and their self-destructive behaviours. Coming into secure care took away choices, made few demands and introduced young people to people who cared about them. In the short term, many young people were thought to have welcomed this with relief.

Though some young people said they intensely disliked the restrictive regime of secure care from the start, others confirmed they had been pleased to arrive there. They talked of needing to be locked in and took some comfort from the fact that this had been forced upon them. None of those interviewed thought foster care would have been an option at the point when they came to the secure unit. The following were typical of comments from young people:

Sometimes you need a secure unit because you're locked up away from everything, so it's easier to get away from drugs and drink 'cos you don't have any choice.

If people are needing secure then foster care wouldn't give the kind of security that a secure unit would. You'd be able to come and go as you please. I think when you need secure, you need a secure place.

If it was me I would have just run. Foster parents cannie put bars on the windows.

These indications that secure units were good at helping young people settle after a period of crisis are consistent with evidence from the SWSI secure care survey (SWSI, 2000).

Asked whether foster carers could have provided what young people needed at this initial stage, social workers and young people were virtually unanimous that they could not. In addition to not providing physical security, foster care was seen as making too many demands, requiring young people to make a commitment in ways which they would not have coped with while in crisis. A few social workers thought that providing a foster placement at an earlier stage might well have averted the crisis but this had had little obvious impact on the few who had tried it. One young woman thought foster carers could have helped her before her drug and alcohol use became out of control, but she had not taken up the placement offered because she feared it would result in her mother completely rejecting her.

While there could be some initial relief from having little personal responsibility, social workers did not see this as being in young people's interests for long. They were clear that secure care could not just be about containment; soon young people would have to begin to address the difficulties which had resulted in the secure care placement. Secure care was expected to cater for young people's need to take stock, assess needs and plan for the future. However, if the young person's situation was to improve, they had to engage with staff and work towards this end.

Taking stock and working towards change

When social workers talked of young people needing to take stock and work towards change, they referred to what young people had to do for themselves as well as what had to be provided for them. Motivating young people to tackle the difficulties which had resulted in secure care was central to making any progress. However, young people were often described as reluctant to engage with staff in anything other than a superficial way: prepared to go along with plans which would get them out of secure care but not committed to change.

As with the young people referred to CAPS, those in secure care were considered to need help to change their behaviour, to find less destructive ways of managing emotional difficulties, and to learn how to make and sustain positive relationships with other people. Unlike CAPS, secure care was not necessarily seen as the key service through which young people would make these changes but as a mediating resource. While in secure care, young people would be assessed and encouraged to engage with appropriate services, either focusing on changing behaviour e.g. in relation to offending or alcohol, or beginning work with a psychologist or therapist. The focus was primarily cognitive, helping young people to better understand and manage their behaviour and emotions rather than establishing and learning about longer-term relationships.

However, establishing an effective relationship with the key worker and other secure care staff was sometimes seen as important, either allowing work to be done within the unit or supporting the young person to take up other services. While some social workers were very positive about the input of secure care staff, others had been disappointed in the lack of proactive work with young people. Where secure care staff did not attempt to engage with young people, the placement was considered to meet only the need for containment, not to address the difficulties which made secure care necessary.

There was more optimism among social workers about foster care being introduced at this second stage, where young people were taking stock and making future plans. In principle, the benefits of a foster placement were identified as: reducing the time young people were removed from the community; offering a new kind of experience which required young people to take some responsibility; and demonstrating that social work staff and others were serious about offering them different options. While recognising the potential value of foster care at this stage, some social workers emphasised that foster carers would need to temper their demands and be skilled in helping young people feel accepted. Otherwise the placement would simply reactivate the cycle of anxiety-driven destructive behaviour.

Some young people in secure care lent strong support to the view that they would expect to be rejected if they did not live up to foster carers' expectations and would themselves run away if they felt uncomfortable or criticised. Recognising this, some said it would be important that carers were trained to know how to handle young people, not just to make them feel at home but also to realise that young people would argue with them and misbehave:

> The foster carers would need special training, would need to know how to cope, how not to be pressured, 'cos a lot of kids would put pressure on to get their own way. They wouldn't just settle in to the family.

Several expressed fears that foster carers would be too strict and that young people would not be able to tolerate or live up to their demands:

> If you were coming in late and they were asking where you were and that – that would put a strain on the relationship.

Some people would bring a lot of hassle and that, neighbours seeing the police at their door and it's no good for them and they get sick of it and say we canny put up with this any more and there's the young person saying 'nobody wants me, what's the point?'

Longer-term needs

Given the similarities in their circumstances, it is hardly surprising that, in the longer term, the needs of young people placed in secure care were similar to those placed with CAPS. Almost all needed help to access appropriate school or work, while two-thirds could rely on little family support and over half needed help towards preparing for independence.

In relation to health, a similar range of concerns were raised about the long-terms effects of alcohol, drug and solvent abuse and at times having a very poor diet. Current physical health problems which needed attention included poor hearing, unexplained fits, unexplained limp and various gynaecological conditions. However, over a third of the young people were described as being quite fit, some making regular use of the secure unit's gym. Some form of psychological or mental health difficulties affected most young people, over half having already been in contact with a psychiatrist, and three-quarters were thought to need therapy or counselling.

Underlying their short and long-term difficulties, young people in secure care shared with their counterparts in CAPS a need for personal support which would foster their self-confidence, while also providing an opportunity to change destructive and dangerous behaviours. Despite this, foster care was not necessarily considered the most appropriate means of meeting these needs.

For many, close relationships had become associated with rejection, abuse or loss. Some had never experienced consistent care, while others had been let down by those they had trusted, often through abuse, loss or both. Neither group had much reason to trust others, while also lacking the confidence to risk further hurt. Most social workers believed young people still needed someone who would make a personal commitment to them, partly to offer the experience of a positive relationship and partly to provide ongoing, reliable practical support as young people moved towards independent living. However, the majority thought this would best be provided through a range of services, including specialist residential care, education, group work and counselling.

Foster care was seen by the social worker as appropriate to meet the needs of less than half the young people. Only two were regarded as clearly suitable for full-time foster care. Both of these were subsequently placed in fostering, one with CAPS and one with a local authority carer. It was thought that a further three would benefit from the personal commitment of foster carers through part-time or weekend care, though full-time placements would have been too demanding for carer or young person or both.

Foster care was considered potentially suitable for another four but was not offered. The reasons for this were that no family was available who would tolerate the young person's aggressive or demanding behaviour, a foster care placement would have further alienated the young person's family or the young person did not favour this option. One young man had ruled out CAPS on learning that he would probably have to move away from his home area.

These obstacles were also raised in relation to the remaining eleven young people for whom foster care was thought not a suitable option. Two had also been linked with CAPS carers but, since the placements had not worked out, were no longer considered suitable. Both had severe emotional difficulties and very negative previous experiences of family life. The most common reason for ruling out foster care was that social workers believed carers would not be able to tolerate the level of aggression, self-harming and manipulation young people would present, the likely result being that the placement would end and/or the young person would not be safe.

> *I think he would struggle to put his, I suppose, trust in carers and I think he would be very hard work. It's his constant need for attention and the physical aggression . . . he can be quite violent. He has a fascination with knives and has assaulted a lot of staff members . . . he always feels this need to protect himself. I just think he would find it really difficult to be somewhere where he felt he had to make it work.*

A second obstacle arose from fears that placement in foster care would constitute a threat to existing family relationships. This was either because the young person maintained apparently unwarranted loyalty to parents or because parents or other family members provided an important sense of identity and belonging, even if what they could offer was limited.

For a third group, foster care was considered unsuitable because of its emotional intensity and intimacy. All four of the young people to whom this assessment applied had already experienced abusive or dysfunctional family relationships. In one instance the inadvisability of family place-ment was one of the key recommendations of a psychiatric assessment. Foster care was seen to be too emotionally demanding for young people whose sense of identity was fragile, and bewildering for those who had little notion of what living in a family would entail.

Young people themselves were highly discriminating about what foster care might or might not offer and which young people might be expected to benefit. Indeed they anticipated several of the study's key findings, stressing the importance of motivation and relationships:

It depends on their frame of mind as well 'cos it's easy to make some-thing work if you really want to.

For some it might work if they'd no really had a family throughout their life and they get on with the carers it might help them, but on the other hand they just might run away and never be there.

It depends on the level of trust you build up with them. For some folk they could get on great and tell them everything but for other folk, you know, that's never had a chance to open up in their lives, that's always held things in, it could just be hard.

Foster parents would have more time for you. There is always someone there, somebody to talk to.

You'd get to know carers better than you get to know staff 'cos you'd be living there and there would only be one or two other children there. You'd have less chance of being bullied or learning bad habits from other kids that have done worse things than you.

You wouldn't get the same feeling of being locked up. It would be more homely. I'm not sure what it would be like, like would you be allowed

out or get pocket money, this kind of stuff? They seem little but at this
stage it's a big point, how much freedom you get.

Implications for foster care's potential

On the basis of these assessments it was evident that foster care was
considered to have very little to offer in the early stages of a secure care
placement when young people needed to be held and be subject to few
demands. However, it was considered in young people's interests that
this stage be kept as short as possible, allowing them to move on to
consider tackling the problems which had prompted the need for secure
care. To be helpful at the second stage, foster carers needed to be able to
manage challenging behaviour, deal effectively with a tendency to run
away at times of pressure, engage with other people in the young
person's life and regulate the emotional distance between themselves
and the young person.

Social workers considered foster care was an appropriate option for
only a minority of the young people in secure accommodation, lending
weight to the CAPS carers' view that there is a group of young people
who are unsuitable for foster care. However, social workers were basing
these views on knowledge of *local authority* foster care. A key characteristic of this, as they saw it, was that young people had to fit in with what
the family expected of them and would be rejected if their behaviour
became too demanding. In contrast, the young people were thought to
require a specialised form of care which would focus primarily on their
needs and provide stability.

CAPS' capacity to be child-centred, stick with young people and deal
with their behaviour and needs is assessed in later chapters of this report.
However, there seems to be a group of young people who need the security
and personal commitment foster care potentially offers, but find it very
difficult to live in this kind of environment. They consequently present
serious challenges to the people who care for them. It was in this context
that some social workers suggested that part-time foster care might be a
useful option, providing an element of personal engagement and positive
experience of family life but in conjunction with other services, so that
neither the carers nor the young person would become overwhelmed. This
was seen as a way of reducing the risks to young people and carers to a

more acceptable level, while also offering some of the potential benefits of foster care.

The next chapters consider what the CAPS placements provided. On this basis, an assessment can be made of the extent to which anticipated obstacles had been overcome and the high expectations of social workers placing young people with CAPS had been met.

Summary

Respondents identified two main needs that they hoped CAPS would meet for the 20 young people in the main sample:

- a positive experience of family life;
- support for life outwith the family (e.g. school, work, independent living).

Equal emphasis was placed on the enhancement of emotional well-being, through stable family experiences, as on behavioural change and skills development which have been central to most other professional fostering programmes targeting adolescents (Hazel, 1990). Apart from education, the young person's needs were to be met largely through the foster family and its neighbourhood links, reflecting CAPS' normalisation philosophy. Only occasionally were other specialist services planned.

In relation to the secure care comparison sample, social workers' appraisals of needs and placement suitability were to a considerable degree based on their knowledge of local authority foster care rather than CAPS. Nevertheless, they all thought that foster care would *not* have been a suitable option at the point of admission, on account of the severity of the young people's unsafe or destructive behaviour at that time. This study and previous work (SWSI, 1996) suggested that secure residential accommodation often provided a positive and safe response to the crisis. However, social workers thought that about a third of the secure sample might well have accepted and benefited from foster care, *once* they had settled and taken stock in secure accommodation.

6 Young people's overall experience and outcomes

Introduction

This and the following chapter report on whether placements with CAPS matched the needs and expectations identified in Chapter 5. The focus is on young people's experiences within CAPS and how these impacted on their lives during the research period. Each section begins by describing the nature of the service provided, then summarises corresponding developments in the young people's lives during the study period.

Descriptions of the CAPS service derive primarily from respondents' qualitative accounts. These also provided detailed information on young people's progress, but in addition the research sought to devise quantitative means of assessment. Indicators such as whether young people were in school or work or whether they had a stable home base on leaving CAPS provided relatively objective criteria by which to judge the impact of the service. In addition, standard measures were used to gauge developments in emotional difficulties and self-esteem.

Comparisons will be made with the secure sample primarily to highlight the distinctive contribution from CAPS. It is important to bear in mind that in each sample the outcomes did not derive entirely from the initial placement. Some young people who started off in CAPS or secure accommodation only made progress when they had moved elsewhere. For instance, one young woman who started off in secure care made great gains when she moved to a CAPS placement, whereas other young people whose placements with CAPS ended abruptly went on to do well in a residential school or unit. In relation to the CAPS sample, carers, social workers and young people each rated progress, while only social workers' assessments were obtained in relation to the secure sample. Therefore the comparative tables draw only on social workers' ratings, but in the text these are supplemented by information on the views of carers and young people as appropriate.

This evaluation of progress and outcomes reflected the distinction Parker and colleagues (1991) made between intermediate and final outcomes. The intermediate outcomes include the quality of care provided. Especially when reviewing a service for young people who would otherwise be in secure residential care, managing to sustain that person in a supportive, caring environment can be an achievement in itself. Whether they achieve better final outcomes is a separate and longer-term issue.

Assessing outcome is further complicated by the fact that there may be progress or success in one aspect of a young person's life alongside serious problems in other areas. In addition, young people may alternate between good and bad episodes. This means the reported outcome can only be an *indication* of how young people were faring *at a particular point in time.*

In the rest of this chapter there is consideration of the extent to which placements provided a positive experience of family life and helped prepare young people for the future. More specific dimensions of young people's development and the associated foster care task are examined in Chapter 7.

Providing a positive experience of family life

Nature of the service provided

The carers and foster home were by far the main component of the service offered by CAPS. They were required to operate on several levels and to undertake a wide range of tasks. Though interrelated, a distinction was made by the research between "task" and "process" elements. Task activities included teaching skills, boundary setting and changing behaviour. Process elements on the other hand were about establishing a viable personal relationship, accepting the young person and helping her or him live in a family, deal with hurt and rejection, and build up self-esteem.

Virtually all the carers blended both task and process elements, but it was clear that individual carers tended to emphasise one approach or the other. Carers presented their actions as being guided by what young people needed, but, while this was borne out to some extent, it was also evident that perceptions of needs varied, depending on the carers' perspective. This was particularly evident when young people moved between placements.

Based on interviews with young people, carers and social workers, two main orientations among carers were identified according to the emphasis on behavioural change or relationships and experience (Table 6.1). Those who were more task-oriented saw their role as experts helping young people effect change and adopt a different lifestyle. Others were more process-oriented, with the primary aim of working alongside very damaged young people to provide a positive experience of living safely in a community-based family placement.

Table 6.1
Orientation to the fostering role

Orientation	*Task-oriented*	*Process-oriented*
Role	Expert	Partner
Aim	Change behaviour	Provide a nurturant home
Style	Teaching and helping	Working alongside
Perception of the young person	Developing and having deficits to be made good	Having competence and strengths to be encouraged
Perception of the young person's needs	To learn developmentally appropriate behaviour and lifestyle	To make choices and exercise autonomy responsibly and with guidance
Approach to discipline	Limit-setting and consistent	Negotiated and flexible

These differences correspond with wider differences in adult approaches to children (Hill and Tisdall, 1997; James and Prout, 1998) and to foster care (Hazel, 1981; Downes, 1992; Triseliotis *et al*, 1995).

The differences were about emphasis rather than content. For example, all carers established some basic rules, but those who adopted the task approach tended to have more rules and to devote more attention to ensuring these were kept. They put greater store by teaching young people new ways of behaving and relating to other people, sometimes using a system of reward and punishment to effect change:

I think the majority needed, for want of a better word, "normal" family life with boundaries and responsibilities . . . basically it's coming back to parental control. There had been very little parental control in the past for the ones we've had. And they don't take too kindly to it!

Oh boundaries, it's just constant. She came in at 25 to 12 instead of 11 on Saturday. Now I know that doesn't seem a lot but for Angela, if you give her an inch, you're lost completely. She says she's sorry but . . . I say 'if you are sorry you change your behaviour'.

I don't think CAPS is about changing the young people – I don't think CAPS expects a lot of change. But we ourselves would hope to achieve more in the way of change.

You want them to move forward, move on. I mean you don't want your own kids to remain static – you want them to develop and grow – and it's the same with these kids.

Carers who primarily adopted a process approach also had rules and encouraged young people to change some negative behaviours. However, these elements did not predominate. Instead, carers in the second category saw their task as finding ways of making the placement work, thus enhancing the quality of their present experience and extending the time that could be spent in placement. This approach involved much negotiating and as far as possible making the young person responsible for their own actions, while still ensuring the carer remained in charge:

Boundaries are good and young people need boundaries, but some people need one type of boundary and another young person needs another type. So I don't talk much about boundaries because each individual needs a different set. And you have to get to know them before you know what set of boundaries they need . . . with Christine boundaries are very flexible but we have this thing when at some point I say 'right now, this is me taking over. I'm taking over' . . . but we negotiate most things.

You can't work miracles for them but what you can make it is just a wee bit easier for them. Maybe help them learn to cope with their problems a wee bit better, trying and putting them on the right road rather than going down the slippery slope – that's what we would be doing.

I don't try to get them to change really. I think if you can show the child, regardless of how much muck they're flinging at you, an acceptance, a knowledge – 'I know what you're doing is really rotten, but I can understand why you're doing it. I canny change it but maybe I can help you accept it.' And in doing that you might give them the ability to change.

I don't think you can actually change them – you just make them see it in a different light than they did. If there's any changing they have to do it themselves. You can't, I don't think, change much of how they are.

Whereas the first group of carers referred to themselves changing and controlling young people, the second group described creating the environment in which young people could change themselves. The carers in the second category tended to see young people as essentially good and sought ways of highlighting strengths, for example, through seeking to frame breaking rules in a positive light. Thus, when one girl stayed out until 2 am, her carers praised her for coming home at all, seeing this as an improvement compared with her usual pattern of running off.

There will be further reference later to how these two approaches operated in relation to specific elements of the fostering task. First, however, we consider the extent to which placements had succeeded in providing a stable and positive experience of family life.

Placement duration

Placement duration has been much used as a criterion for judging placement outcomes, but it is a complex subject. Since it was not originally the intention that placements become long term, our interest was not simply in how long placements had lasted but whether they had endured as long as was planned or as long as they were needed. Twelve placements had begun with a clear timescale being set from the start, of which two-thirds were expected to last for less than a year and a third for one to two years. For the remaining placements, plans about how long the young person should remain in the project evolved as the placement progressed.

Determining the length of time placements had actually lasted was not always easy, since some started very gradually, with young people spending increasing amounts of time in the carers' home. Three others included periods when the young person was with carers on a part-time basis. In addition, four young people had transferred once or twice to other carers within the scheme. The list below refers to time spent with the project as a whole, including introductory periods, part-time stays and transfers:

Less than 3 months	3	(all completed)
4–6 months	3	(all completed)
7–9 months	4	(all completed)
10–12 months	2	(all completed)
13–24 months	4	(two ongoing)
Over 2 years	4	(all ongoing)

By the third round of the research, six of the 20 young people were still within the scheme, all having stayed longer than the scheme originally envisaged. Fourteen *young people* had left CAPS but, taking account of moves, 20 *placements* had ended. Social workers and carers considered that only two of these completed placements had lasted as long as expected, while for a further two a clear timescale had never been established. The fact that a placement lasted as long as expected did not necessarily mean that initial plans had been realised. One younger boy who had spent the planned six to seven months in placement moved on to residential school as a result of him continually absconding and putting himself at risk. The original plan had been that he would return home. Conversely, not lasting as long as planned did not necessarily mean the placement had failed to meet young people's needs. One of the girls placed from secure care had stayed only seven months in placement, rather than a year as planned. However, she had been able to return to her parents' home and had reduced her self-harming behaviour, so that in these important respects identified needs had been met.

Thus a more critical question was whether placement duration was as long as needed. Social workers and carers agreed that only two placements did last as long as needed. In a few other instances, the placement was said to have lasted as long as it was useful, because the young person seemed to have benefited as much as they could from the placement, yet still had significant difficulties. Only one completed placement, for a young woman who had been placed as an alternative to prison, was thought to have lasted as long as planned *and* needed. She had been with the carer for 18 months, more than half on a part-time basis. The carer continued to support her through several serious crises after she moved to her own flat and planned to continue to do so indefinitely.

Placement endings

Besides the length of the placement, the way it ended was also important. Of the 20 completed placements, six had finished in a planned way, with the young person moving to another CAPS carer (3), returning to live with a parent (2) or moving on to independent living (1). Six placements finished slightly earlier than anticipated for negative reasons, because the young person became violent within the foster home (4), ran away (1) or made an allegation against the carer (1). Of the eight unplanned endings, in five instances the young person simply left the foster home and did not return. The behaviour in the community of three young people led to them making enemies so it became necessary to leave the area.

There was seldom one clear reason why placements ended. Rather, a number of interacting stresses either resulted in a decision that the placement should be brought to a close or led to a particular incident which hastened the placement's end. Despite the intensity of some of the difficulties, no placements finished because the carers decided unilaterally that they were no longer willing to care for the young person. Similarly, in no placement was it suggested that insufficient support from CAPS staff had resulted in placements ending prematurely. Some of the common reasons given for placements ending unsatisfactorily are listed below, with an indication of the number of situations in which each applied, either in a primary or contributory way. These are based on carers' and social workers' responses.

Young person's aggressive or destructive behaviour in the foster home	(9)
Young person's aggressive, destructive or criminal behaviour outwith the foster home	(9)
Lack of suitable school or work placement	(8)
Young person's loyalty to their own family or way of life	(7)

Young person running away	(7)
Young person did not want to be in the placement	(6)
Lack of therapeutic or psychological service	(6)
Poor match/relationship between the young person and carer	(3)
Poor match between two young people placed together	(2)

It is clear that young people's behaviour was often cited as prompting the end of a placement, with lack of support services being equally important. Often the two were closely interlinked. For example, lack of school or work posed a particular strain since it made young people feel under-valued and bored, while also resulting in them being at home all day, thus posing additional strains on the foster carers. When interviewed after placements had ended, most young people blamed themselves for the fact that plans had not been realised, citing their own inability to adapt or keep their temper as the major problem. Only a few blamed the carers or felt in retrospect that the placement had not been right for them, for instance, because they wanted to be with their own family.

Given our interest in what CAPS could offer as an alternative to secure care, the 13 cases were examined where young people had joined CAPS from secure care or because they were at imminent risk of admission there. Nine of such placements with CAPS had been sustained for over six months. Of the four placed directly from secure accommodation, length of placement varied from a few weeks to over a year, with contrasting implications. For example, one girl returned to secure care after four to six months, having continued to put herself at risk through absconding, but another returned to her parents' care after eight months because she was no longer self-harming and the parents were more confident in their ability to manage her behaviour. One boy left after a few weeks, but another was still in his placement when the research fieldwork ended. These contrasting immediate outcomes highlight the importance of considering how far young people were thought to have made gains as a result of the placement.

Extent to which young people had benefited

Both carers and social workers considered that all young people in the CAPS sample had benefited at least in part from the placement. On a five-point scale, both rated half the sample on the middle point and approximately a quarter on each of the top two points. None considered that the placement had helped only a little or not at all.

Adult assessments of benefit indicated a close relationship between the length of time young people had been in placement and the amount they were considered to have benefited. All but one of the ten young people rated as having benefited fully or almost fully had been in placement for at least a year. All four thought to have fully benefited from the placements had spent at least 18 months there. The fact that longer placements conferred more benefits is an important finding, in view of the recent emphasis on time-limited interventions. It also vindicates the scheme's flexibility in moving away from its original shorter time limits.

Of the 15 young people who assessed the benefits of the placements, eight thought they had benefited fully, three partly and four only a little or not at all. When asked what the benefits had been, young people talked primarily about how the carers had treated them and the times they had enjoyed with them, rather than how they had progressed. Of the eight who thought they had benefited fully from placements, only three had been with the project for more than a year.

The nature of benefits from placements

This section provides an opportunity to assess the extent to which the key requirements of stability and learning to live in a family had been achieved, while also examining whether the anticipated fears of further rejection and emotional turmoil had materialised. In order to portray the diversity of young people's experience and how they had benefited, it is helpful to consider the gains from placement mainly in terms of four subgroups, defined according to length of placement and social worker's assessment of the benefit for the young person (See Table 6.2).

Table 6.2
Four different types of CAPS experience

Subgroup	Placement duration	Benefit rating	Number of young people in group
1	18 months and over	Fully benefited (5)	3
2	12 months and over	Significantly benefited (4)	6
3	6–12 months	Partly benefited (3–4)	6
4	Less than 6 months	Partly benefited (3–4)	5

Each group encompassed a wide range of age, level of difficulty and previous experience. The groupings illustrate that, in general, benefits were greater for placements of more than a year. Young people needed time if they were to gain substantially. Equally, when there was little apparent benefit, the placement was likely to end.

1. Placements which lasted and conferred high and enduring benefits

Of these three most successful placements, two young people, both girls, had been placed as an alternative to secure care or prison. One girl, aged 13, had been persistently absconding from residential care and putting herself at risk, while the other, aged 17, was facing prison, having committed a number of offences, including an assault. The third, a boy, was not close to secure care but had a troubled childhood and was placing himself at risk in various ways. All three were highly motivated to join a new family. Two were also glad to be placed at some distance from their home community, although the third initially resented having to live beyond easy reach of her friends.

Two were still in placement by the time the field work was completed, while the third had moved on but was still in contact with the carer. They had all experienced continuity of placement in the scheme, staying with one CAPS carer throughout their time with the project. The carers were all very experienced, combining task and process as described above, but with a clear focus on helping young people find what was right for them rather than trying to impose what the carers held to be right or desirable. For example, the carer of a 17-year-old would have preferred her to spend less time at her boyfriend's than actually happened, but was able to negotiate an arrangement that sustained the young woman's willingness to stay in the scheme and accept advice.

The high level of benefit from the placement derived to a considerable extent from the fact that the young people had found carers they could rely on for support and friendship for the foreseeable future, even when the placement ended. The resulting sense of security enabled young people to confront and manage a series of difficult issues about their own drug use, self-harm, abuse, family relationships, sexuality and aggression. Placements had not been characterised by straightforward progress but by carers sticking with young people through these difficulties, adopting a problem-solving approach, and showing that they need not be overwhelmed and thrown off course when problems arose. Thus they were not just dealing with current problems but developing the confidence and skills to cope with whatever life would present.

Social workers' comments on these placements give an indication of some of the benefits and to what they attributed their success:

Young person A

She has developed a sense of maturity that she never had before. Although she will still argue with you, she will argue far more like a grown-up and will accept – eventually will accept – 'well, right, OK I'll accept what you're saying' – whereas she would have stormed off – would have screamed and shouted and stormed off. Before going to the carers, there was no negotiating with her.

I think the carer's sort of staying power was positive for her . . . [the carer] just stuck with it. It kind of gave her the message that 'You can have your tantrums and your mood swings and do whatever it is you want but I'm still going to be here and I'm not going to let you down' . . . there was one incident when she said, 'That's it. I'm going to trash your house' . . . And the carer said. 'Well, if you are going to trash my house there's not an awful lot I can do about that but you know I'm still going to be here' and she never did it. Just stormed off in a sulk then came out and apologises, which was unheard of. I think that was a first!

Young person B

It's almost like talking to two different people when you think back to who she was and who she is now, but she's very clear about who she is.

The biggest thing [the placement provided] was security and accepting her for who she was – unconditional love if you like – because she didn't get that before. To really know she was cared about – because [in her own family] she was used more than anything – [The carers] have taken her unconditionally because they knew who she was before she came in and they still wanted her, no matter what she had done. If she is lectured to or reprimanded or sent to her room it is all very civilised, you know, very rational and talking it through with her and when it is finished it is over, not brought up all the time.

Young person C

It's kept him safe, allowed him to mature, allowed him to access appropriate education and to keep in contact with his family.

It gave him stability and just the same set of faces all the time and also a feeling of being part, really being part, because it's like well 'these are our children and grandchildren' and you know, just recently there, he was really involved in preparing for a family birthday party . . . He has been able to talk to the carer about [bereavements] . . . work through the notion he had got that anyone he got close to would die . . .

[There was a very difficult situation] when he was getting into some dangerous stuff. We were having high-profile meetings with Heads of Service, etc. and that night the carer sat and spoke to him and said, 'think about it, think of what you're sacrificing, putting at risk. We can't stop you but it's in your best interests [that you stop]' and that was a breakthrough.

Each of the young people in this group talked in glowing terms of how the CAPS placement had turned around their lives. For each of them the long-standing and personal nature of the relationship with the carers was central:

She's been like a mother to me. She's done everything a teenager needs like attention, love, sitting down talking, do you know what I mean. She's really brought me out of myself.

Of the two older ones, one found her carer's support invaluable when she subsequently faced serious problems managing on her own, while the other was delighted that the carers would continue to help him out and be part of his life once he moved to his own tenancy nearby.

2. Placements which lasted over a year and conferred significant benefit

The six young people in Group 2 included one placed from secure care and two who were very close to being placed there. All were considered to have benefited considerably, but with significant drawbacks.

Nearly all (5) had experienced less stability than hoped for within CAPS, including in three instances an abrupt placement ending. The reasons for moves within CAPS related to events within and outwith placements. One young woman moved following an assault on a carer, this being a repeat of previous behaviour. A young boy was moved twice until carers were found who could manage his particular need for close supervision. In a different case, a boy moved because he had exhausted the employment and training opportunities in his first carer's home area, this resulting in considerable strain on himself and the carer.

For two of the young people in this group there had been a poor relationship between the young person and the carer. The social workers and carers thought the young people had benefited because their difficult behaviour had been tackled and they had been well cared for, but there were few indications that this had positively affected how they behaved or felt about themselves.

Despite these difficulties, most of these young people were thought by social workers to have benefited considerably from living in a family. For four of the young people in this group, the main benefit was that they had learned to cope with family life, having previously been used to group living. For some this meant that expectations of them were much higher in that the people they lived with expected them to conform to the rules of reasonable behaviour expected of everyone else, instead of making special allowances. Thus one boy had to learn that his food fads would not be catered for, so his tantrums would gain nothing. By contrast, others had learned to work within negotiated rules, as opposed to the highly structured reward system which they had become used to in residential school. Also, the close supervision afforded by family life meant that the young people were more immediately accountable for their actions. While some found this very uncomfortable and continually challenged the carers' rules and expectations, others responded to the personal approach. Many carers took the view that, having learned to take responsibility for their own behaviour, young people would be better equipped to live in families and cope in the outside world:

We feel she has matured a lot. She has been able to take decisions. You know, say how she actually feels about it, rather than listening to what someone else is saying to her.

3. Medium-term placements which conferred some benefit

In terms of their circumstances and time spent with CAPS, the experience of the six young people in this group most closely matched the original plans for the scheme. All were either placed from secure care (2) or close to being placed there (4) and spent 6–12 months in the project. Their most obvious gain was that all were able to live in the community at a time when they might otherwise have been in secure care. Their experiences were characterised by significant gains but also quite serious difficulties. It was young people in this group who most clearly demonstrated that good experiences do not necessarily lead to positive outcomes, while difficult placements could have positive consequences or be retrieved by the subsequent care arrangements.

The most striking example of this was a young boy who described one of his three CAPS placements as providing the best experiences of his life. He said he could hardly put into words how good it had felt to be living with people who liked him and cared about him. The carers had been 'like a mum and dad', teaching him about cooking and budgeting, listening to him talk about his past and treating him with respect. Fishing trips with the male carer and a Christmas spent with all the extended family stood out as 'just brilliant, the best time I've ever had'. Nevertheless, the placement ended in an unplanned way as a result of his drug use and tragically he died a few months later.

A young woman established a good relationship with her carer, made progress at school and planned to go to college. However, after consuming a high level of alcohol when in a respite placement, she decided to return to an uncertain future among her extended family, ceasing contact with her carer and social worker. Another placement was characterised by crises and ended with an assault on the carer. Even so, the young person spoke fondly of her time with CAPS and periodically kept in touch with the carers.

Two young women in this group had been placed directly from secure care. One of these was returned to secure accommodation following continued running away and eventually made good progress in a residential school. The placement experience of the second girl was fraught and the carers felt she was benefiting little from what they had to offer, so it was agreed she would return home. At the third stage of the research, some of the original difficulties remained but the girl was continuing to live safely with her mother. This was thought to have been possible only because the carers had worked closely with the parents, who became more able to challenge the girl's manipulative behaviour. Thus, the apparently unpromising placement processes had nonetheless resulted in her being able to leave secure care and return home within six months. The social worker summed it up as follows:

My overall view is that the CAPS placement was successful. Because, OK, she tried school and she found that too hard and reverted back to the attention-needing behaviour... but that was a previously entrenched pattern before she went to CAPS. But what the placement did, it focused down and down, and her flights of fantasy and manipulation of the truth and exaggeration were addressed all the time because the communication between the school, the carers, the parents and me was too tight. And that was what she started to rebel against. The other bit that was 100 per cent successful was that family contact was reestablished and built on over the time of the placement. While she was in secure, that had broken down completely, so that was another very positive feature.

The final boy in this category was aged ten when placed. After a short settled period, the placing authority moved him, for financial reasons and with little notice, to one of their own authority's carers, only to return him to the CAPS placement when he ran away. However, the social worker felt his trust had been lost and he began to put himself at risk by running away, then drinking and getting into trouble with older boys. He made it clear he wanted to be home. Eventually he moved on to a residential school where he made much better progress. By the end of the research he had not run away, nor been involved in offending, and spent each weekend and holidays at home.

4. Short-term placements which conferred some benefit

These five young people were in placement for only a few weeks or months and for the most part this appeared to have had little impact on their lives. Two placements ended when the young persons did not return after home leave, and in the other three cases, the ending was prompted by aggressive or offending behaviour.

The group was diverse, but a common feature was that the young person wanted something different from what was on offer. One had never wanted to be with a CAPS family. Two wanted a much shorter placement than their social workers planned. Another wished to stop contact with his birth family, but found that the carers insisted on him spending weekends with his family.

One of this group (the only girl) was thought to have benefited from the consistent way in which she had been treated in the placement and the fact that she had been encouraged to take responsibility for her own actions. After leaving she did well in residential care and, by the third stage of the research, was preparing to move to independent living and attend college. The longer-term outcome had been less successful for the four boys, two of whom were in prison. Nevertheless, two who were interviewed said they had enjoyed some of the times they spent with the carers and one was very keen to renew the contact by letter or phone.

These brief accounts illustrate the young people's varied and usually mixed experience in terms of benefits and outcomes. This diversity makes it difficult to assess which factors made for a positive outcome. What often seemed to matter was the degree of fit between what the carers offered and young people's needs and circumstances. That is illuminated by the ways that young people appraised living in the CAPS households, which a few described as the best experiences of their lives, while others felt disappointed or rejected.

Young people's views of family life in CAPS

It is hardly surprising that the young people who enjoyed being in the placements very much wanted to be there, whereas most of those who did particularly badly did not. It is an important principle in the project that young people commit to what it has to offer. However, in practice this did not always apply. A quarter of the young people in the sample had come into the project in an emergency situation, having had very little opportunity to say whether this was what they wanted. In addition, even though young people coming from secure care have a choice, this is not entirely free if the alternative is to remain in locked accommodation.

Once in the placements, most of the young people felt that their views were listened to and taken seriously, although some said they didn't say too much in meetings:

They listened to you and tried to work out what was best.

You get plenty chance to say what you want to.

I don't say much in meetings. I can't be bothered. I'd like to say more about not having a job but I can't be bothered.

They do listen but there's no really anything to say. I'm happy the way everything is just now.

However, a few said they had never been happy with their carers and described considerable frustration at trying to have that point of view heard. Some did not want to be with carers at all, while others would have liked a change of placement. Such moves were generally avoided within the project, partly in the interests of continuity and partly because of lack of availability. Sometimes young people's requests to end or change placements were seen as manipulative or unwarranted. In these situations there was obviously a tension between taking account of young people's wishes and providing a continuous experience through which, it was hoped, they would learn to work through difficulties and reduce their need to control situations. However, few young people who had consistently wanted to be somewhere else felt the placement had provided a good experience of family life.

Most young people felt that the level of closeness they had established with the CAPS carers suited them, indicating that distance regulation was generally well managed in the project. This applied to some who were glad to be integrated, as well as others who wanted a more distant relationship, perhaps because of strong ties to their own families. However, a few young people thought their carers had given false or confusing messages about whether they could become part of their family.

In several discussions, the young people referred directly or obliquely to the distinction between being part of a family and being cared for as part of the carers' work. It was very important to a number of young people that *their* carers went beyond what was required of them for work purposes. One girl said she knew her carers loved her as they did their own family:

Not every carer is like that. There's a certain boundary they canny pass. Do you know what I mean? But [my carers] they really love me and that. I've been quite lucky to have carers like them.

For others the indications were more modest: that the carers were prepared to take them on holiday, pay to include them in family outings or show they enjoyed the young person's company. One boy used the following example to describe how the personal element meant a fishing trip with a carer, rather than residential staff, could have quite different significance:

Because it's easy for enough for them to spend someone else's money and take you out and say, 'C'mon I'll take you fishing' or 'c'mon I'll take you swimming' because they're spending someone else's money, but he [the carer] was doing it out his own pocket and his own time. Like, when he was taking me fishing, he'd take me out and he'd buy sweeties for us and all that first, he'd buy me fags and my juice, my crisps and then we'd go out and we'd sit on the boat all day. And he was paying for the permits out his own pocket and no bothering claiming the money back. And it was like he wanted to do it, it wasn't as if he was just doing it because it was CAPS money, it was because he wanted to do it with me.

As long as this kind of personal commitment and liking was conveyed, it did not worry young people that carers were caring for them as a job. However, a few expressed resentment at carers who talked primarily in terms of work:

She was wanting to work with me and do this and do that . . . but I mean when you go to foster parents, it's supposed to be like folk who want to look after you, and, like, want you to be part of their family. But it wasn't like that.

One of the key dimensions on which young people judged the quality of their experience with the carers was how rules and boundaries were managed. Young people often talked of how "strict" carers were, but in discussion it was clear that there were several strands to how rules were set and managed and that these were more or less acceptable to most young people. The key seemed to be that the rules and how they were established took account of the individual young person's needs and wishes, rather than being set for the household. There seemed to be a preference for a few basic house rules, e.g. about having a shower every day, bringing down clothes for washing, but for other matters to be negotiated. There was a particular dislike for households which had rules set out on the kitchen wall or imposed set times for going to bed or turning off lights, irrespective of the young person's age. This, young people said, was too like a children's home.

Yet it would be wrong to suggest young people wanted carers to be lax. Bringing them into line was taken as a sign of caring and was quite acceptable, as long as they felt that the rules were in their best interests and that similar standards would apply to carers' own children. For example, certain boys spoke very fondly of female carers who ruled all the men in the house, while there was considerable resentment among the few young people who thought carers' own children were exempt from what was required of those in placement. Again it was the quality of the relationship between carer and young person which made boundary setting acceptable or not (cf. Triseliotis *et al*, 1995):

They treated you like part of the family. And you never got treated any different from anybody else but at the same time if you played the game with them, then they played it with you and their rules weren't strict. They were good rules.

On the basis of what young people themselves said, it would seem they preferred carers who adopted a partnership approach and were responsive to the young person's needs and wishes. Crucially they were more inclined to talk over personal difficulties with people who took time to listen to them and understand something of their experience, rather than impose their own view of how things should be:

But she [carer] knew how I felt and [male carer] understood how I felt – actually understood and he would actually sit and he would let me do the talking. Whereas the social workers are always doing it, he would sit and let me do the talking and he would sit and just listen to me. And that was really good because nobody had really done that with me before, it was always like the staff, it was them that was doing the talking and you weren't getting a chance. Whereas with [male carer], he would just sit and listen to you, so I actually spoke to him about things I've never told anyone before.

Underpinning many of the comments from young people were clear indications that finding themselves accepted by carers was a profoundly empowering experience which allowed some to risk believing that they just might be worthwhile people. Being "accepted" could mean different things, but key components were that they felt valued and had a special place in their carers' affections. As one carer also said:

. . . the breakthrough comes when they realise that you are actually affected by what they do, you as a person. He could not believe that we had sat up all night and been out looking for him. That's when they realise you are serious . . . when they see they matter to you like that you can start to make demands and they might think you've a right to be doing that.

In contrast, one young person said the carer and social worker 'did not deserve' to know about his life since they dismissed what he said as worthless, while a few others talked about being hurt and angry when carers conveyed a lack of respect or warmth.

Several young people described themselves as essentially "good", even though their behaviour had at times been "bad". Not surprisingly, it was empowering and reassuring for young people to find carers who could recognise and tap into their essential "goodness", while also accepting that they would sometimes be "bad".

> *I was always the person I am now but I had to put a face on, do you know what I mean, because of where I was staying and stuff like that. But when I came up here I could go the way I wanted and the carer helped me there. But I always have been me – but I've never had the chance to express it the way I wanted to.*

Correspondingly placements were painful for the few who found themselves feeling marginalised or second best.

There are therefore several indications that task elements were more effective when carried out within a relationship of mutual respect in which the young person felt cared for and valued. This is consistent with Downes's concept of alliance formation as being the basis of effective intervention with adolescents (Downes, 1992). Similarly, drawing on attachment theory, Bell argues that children will only feel secure enough to get in touch with and express their feelings in the context of a relationship based on trust. She suggests that relationships based on supportive and companionable interactions with adults are more likely to help build self-esteem and trust than those which emphasise adult domination and control and so resonate with elements of abusive relationships (Bell, 2002).

Comparison with the secure care sample

The 20 young people in the comparison sample placed in secure residential accommodation typically had shorter placements than the main CAPS sample. Approximately half spent less than three months in secure accommodation, six spent up to three to six months there, and the remaining four were still in secure accommodation by the second stage of the research.

All secure placements were thought to have lasted as long as planned and all but one as long as needed. This is a much higher proportion than in the CAPS sample. This partly reflects the greater control exerted within secure units. Another factor may well be that CAPS was at an early stage, testing out its practice and learning from experience, whereas the secure system is well established.

Three-quarters (14) of the young people who had been in secure care were thought to have benefited from the placement. On a five-point scale, these 14 were almost evenly distributed among scores of three, four and five. That left a quarter of placements thought to have conferred little or no benefit, which applied to none of the CAPS placements. The main benefits from secure placements were that young people had been kept safe and had been among people who accepted them. Some young people had also been helped to address the difficulties which had resulted in the secure care placement but around half the social workers thought the period in secure care could have been more productive. There were criticisms that some young people had simply been detained. Indeed half the placements were thought to have been detrimental in some way. Some young people had suffered anxiety at being in a locked setting, but the most common drawback was that loss of personal responsibility and withdrawal from the community resulted in young people being less well equipped to cope with life when they left.

Young people's circumstances on leaving CAPS or secure care

Young people's movements on leaving CAPS provided an indication of whether the CAPS placement had contributed to longer-term plans in the ways which had been envisaged at the start. They also reflected the extent to which the placements had helped prepare young people for their future life. This section provides a comparison with young people who had been in secure accommodation and shows that the post-placement trajectories were very different.

Only one of those who had left a CAPS placement had moved to the kind of living situation which had been planned at the start of the placement. To some extent this resulted from the unpredictability of the young people, but also from the fact that CAPS was breaking new ground, so it was difficult to know how young people would fare. In their enthusiasm, carers and social workers often started with high aspirations. By contrast, three-quarters of the secure sample moved on to the type of placement that was envisaged.

Leaving to one side whether or not the outcome was planned, a striking difference between the two samples was that many more of the CAPS young people were able to sustain some form of community living (see Table 6.3 for details). At the second stage of the study, only six young people placed with CAPS were in an institutional setting, compared with 15 of those who started in secure care. By the third stage, the numbers were down to four and seven respectively.

Table 6.3

End circumstances for young people in both samples

X denotes one young person

End circumstances	CAPS sample	Secure sample
Living with parents or another relative on a reasonably secure basis	4	3
Own tenancy or supported accommodation	1	6
Foster care	7	2
Residential care/school	2	6
Homeless accommodation/ Unsettled	4	2
Prison	2	0
Psychiatric unit	0	1
Total	**20**	**20**

One respect in which the two groups were similar was that a small number had returned home or to live with another relative. While this, in some instances, was thought to be the result of input to improve family relationships, it mostly reflected a natural progression towards young people being accepted by their families when they were no longer so dependent and the role of the social work department in their lives reduced (cf. Bullock *et al*, 1993).

A key difference between the two samples was that placement with CAPS could delay the point at which young people moved into their own tenancy or supported accommodation. While six of those who started in secure care had already moved into semi-independent living, only one of those with CAPS had yet managed this. On the positive side, this was because some carers had convinced local authorities to prolong the CAPS placements until young people were ready to cope on their own. Two young people were in the process of securing housing in the carers' home area and would thus be assured of ongoing support. This is one illustration of how being placed with the project could dramatically change the direction of young people's lives.

However, less positively, four young people who had left CAPS on an unplanned basis at age 16 or over were still in homeless or temporary accommodation by the third stage of the research. Another two whose living arrangements had been uncertain at the second round were in prison by stage three. In contrast, only two of those who started in secure care were living in homeless or temporary accommodation, while none were in prison.

Summary

The small numbers in the two samples and the diverse experiences of young people in CAPS make it hard to generalise about outcomes. Certain clear differences did emerge, though the meaning and significance of these requires careful interpretation. Six of the 20 placements in the CAPS sample were continuing at the end of the research and appeared to be providing a long-term family base for the young people. On the other hand, very few CAPS placements that had ended did so as planned (12 out of 14) or with a move to the kind of placement originally envisaged. In contrast, secure accommodation placements tended to proceed as initially expected and with a better chance of achieving supported accommodation. In the longer run, most young people placed in CAPS were able to stay out of residential care, sometimes within a supportive family, but sometimes in isolated, unsettled or risky circumstances. Furthermore, social workers were more likely to see young people as having benefited from a CAPS placement than from secure accommodation. Some of the unplanned end circumstances of CAPS placements were positive (e.g. staying on with CAPS carers or in close touch with them), whereas a few young people left under a cloud only to make good progress in a subsequent placement, like a residential school.

Compared with secure accommodation, CAPS kept more young people out of institutions not only in the short-term but also in the somewhat longer run encompassed by the research. For some this resulted from continuity of fostering and could bring great opportunities, but others encountered unpredictability and risks. The chances of living in a fairly settled family home were greater, but so were the prospects of unsupported and high-risk "independence". Secure accommodation tended to afford a quicker and more certain route to semi-independent living arrangements. (CAPS' role in preparing young people for independent living is discussed in the next chapter.)

Successful CAPS placements normally lasted at least 12 months. Young people's own accounts suggested several important factors affecting positive outcomes:

- the young person's initial commitment to CAPS;
- carers conveying respect for young people's views;
- a degree of family closeness which fitted the young person's orientation to family life;
- foster carers actively caring for and about the young person, and not treating their role as simply "work";
- rules applied in an adaptable and fair manner.

It was also evident from the overall picture obtained that it was crucial for carers and the young person to have access to adequate support, appropriate education and, when necessary, specialist services. This last point is examined more fully in the next chapter.

Overall then, it may be summarised that CAPS placements were likely to provide a good experience for young people while they were there, but after leaving the project their circumstances or quality of life were not necessarily better than those who had spent a period in secure care. The key findings from this chapter on the intermediate outcomes of the placements are summarised in Table 6.4.

Table 6.4

Overall placement effectiveness in meeting identified needs

Identified needs/expectations	Relevant findings	Factors which increased the likelihood needs would be met
Positive experience of family life	Carers and social workers agreed all young people had benefited	Placement lasted more than 18 months
	Three-quarters of young people said they had enjoyed the placement	Carers adopted a flexible partnership approach
		Young person wished to be with a family
		Young person and carers had congruent expectations of family life
Stability/continuity	Only a minority of placements lasted as long as planned or needed	Young person wished to be in family
	Two-thirds lasted over six months	Carers were willing to establish life-long links with young people
	Four young people were considered to have made a life long link with the carers' family	Carers maintained links with young person's own family
		Suitable schooling or work
Help to live in the community	Carers were able to manage very challenging behaviour	High level of support given to CAPS carers
	Of 13 young people in or close to secure care, nine were sustained in placement for at least six months	Carers expected to work with problem behaviour
		Suitable schooling or work

Identified needs/expectations	Relevant findings	Factors which increased the likelihood needs would be met
Preparation for independent living	By the third research stage, one young person had moved to independent living and a further two were preparing to move on	Placement lasted over 18 months
		Planned placement ending
	Three were in homeless accommodation	Carer formed links with the young person in his or her home area
		SWD willing to adequately support young people placed outwith their home area
		Suitable supported accommodation

7 The young people's developmental progress

Introduction

Having considered young people's overall experience with CAPS, this chapter considers how the placements helped with the specific aspects of young people's lives identified as requiring change or support. As in Chapter 6, the format is to summarise the service provided, then evaluate its impact by means of qualitative and quantitative data. In addition, a brief introduction sets each topic in context. The aspects addressed are:

- enhancing emotional well-being and development;
- changing and influencing behaviour;
- supporting aspects of young people's lives outside the placement,
  education
  family relationships
  health
  leisure activities;
- Preparing for independent living

Enhancing emotional well-being and development

Context

In the preceding chapter it was noted that, while virtually all young people were considered to have had a worthwhile experience with CAPS, outcomes were unequivocally positive for only a minority. Several carers and social workers argued that, even if the benefits were not evident from their post-placement circumstances, young people were emotionally stronger and so better equipped to cope with life in the future. The study was not long enough to test this claim, but did seek to understand as far as possible what kind of emotional support had been provided and what its impact had been. Enhancing emotional development was central to the CAPS philosophy. In virtually all placements, one goal was to increase self-esteem and/or help young people come to terms with past events involving rejection and abuse.

The service provided

CAPS placements

Carers described a host of ways through which they encouraged young people to see themselves as worthwhile people, from taking an interest in their clothes to framing reading difficulties as an acceptable kind of problem. One of the young people explained how carers' commitment and help with finding work had over time made her feel special. This in turn led her to realise that she had choices about how she behaved and did not need to follow the example of her friends. This influence, she said, was 'slipped in without you noticing it'. In other words it was built into everyday life.

This capacity to convey that young people were special was not simply a matter of individual carers' actions. Building each placement around young people's needs was one of the principles of the project. Several social workers identified this as the main difference between CAPS and other foster placements where young people had to fit in with the family's lifestyle. Inevitably, fitting in also applied to some extent with CAPS, but the process of accommodation was usually two-way, and carers were expected to be available for young people as required. The four-weekly meetings to review developments also conveyed the message that the young people mattered.

All the carers saw their role as offering a personal relationship by someone who cared about the young person enough to take them into their home and help them tackle whatever problems they faced. Through building such a relationship, it was hoped young people might take the risk to grow and change (cf. Howe *et al*, 1999). Where a level and pattern of attachment which suited carers and young people had developed, the benefits were considerable. However, carers also described some young people, a few outwith our sample, for whom the placements activated attachment needs which the carers could not meet. A few teenagers aged over 16 were described as clingy, reluctant to be separated from the female carer and/or desperate to be claimed by a family. Managing this in a time-limited setting proved difficult for several carers and young people.

The model of a reliable friend worked well for many young people while they were in placement. The key components were that carers helped them with practical matters (e.g. finding work, sorting out school), as well as being open to their distress. In our interviews, many carers described occasions when they had been able to discuss difficult and painful issues openly and honestly, while articulating them in ways which young people could understand and had found useful. As noted in the previous chapter, some young people gave similar examples from their perspective, making it clear how important it was to them to have found a trusted ally. In these circumstances, it was perhaps more appropriate to talk of forming a supportive and productive alliance rather than attachment.

The importance of carers being skilled in helping young people with emotional difficulties was reflected in the fact that a course in counselling skills was part of CAPS' core training. Several carers emphasised that good listening was essential in getting to know young people and what mattered to them. Some carers said the counselling course also helped them learn to support young people in coming to their own solutions, rather than offering advice or imposing the carers' view of what should happen. A few young people chose to talk with carers about very sensitive matters they had not shared with others, while virtually all said they found carers easy to talk to. However, one young person complained she had felt under pressure to "talk" and a few had found that their own view of their needs and situation had not been heard.

Only three young people had regular external counselling, psycho-therapeutic or psychiatric help while in placement. In each case this was established before the placement began. Another four were referred for one of these services during the placement but none of them got beyond an initial meeting. In addition, a few carers had advice from specialists, for example, in managing sexually aggressive behaviour.

The social worker's role in promoting young people's emotional development varied. While most had a productive relationship with the young person and provided continuity with people and events prior to the placement, a few played only a limited role because they were based too far away, had an acrimonious relationship, or were still getting to know the young person. Only one social worker was considered to undermine the young person's confidence through lack of interest and commitment.

Secure placements

Turning to the comparison group of young people who started in secure care, three-quarters of the young people were thought to have established a productive relationship with at least one member of residential staff. As with the foster carers, young people responded when staff took a personal interest in them and conveyed that they mattered. For some, the social worker was the main person in their lives and thus central to their emotional development. One young woman repeatedly asked the social worker she had known for many years to adopt her. In other situations social workers worked closely with the young person and residential care staff to promote self-esteem and develop emotional maturity.

More than a third of the young people also saw a psychologist, psychiatrist or professional counsellor over an extended period, so that access to specialist services was higher than among those with CAPS.

In general, secure and CAPS placements were expected to impact differently on self-esteem. Several social workers commented that loss of liberty meant admission to secure accommodation was likely to adversely affect self-esteem, though the close attention from staff which followed could convey a sense of being accepted and valued. In contrast, the child-centred focus of CAPS was expected to boost self-esteem, though most social workers suspected that the benefits were reduced when placements ended abruptly. The following section considers the assessed impact on individual young people.

Progress in relation to emotional development

Anecdotal accounts of young people's progress indicated that some from both samples had shown signs of significant maturing and development. These included taking a pride in their appearance, being able to express their views more effectively, and challenging oppressive family members or peers. For a more objective and systematic assessment of progress the research relied on two standard measures: the Goodman's Strengths and Difficulties Questionnaire (SDQ) and the Rosenberg measure of self-esteem.

The SDQ assesses whether children and young people's behavioural and emotional difficulties are within or outwith the normal range. Completed at each stage of the research, it provided a useful means of comparing the CAPS and secure samples and gauging the progress of individual young people. However, the results do need to be considered alongside other information. Despite being a well-validated measure, there were clear indications that carers' attitudes to young people affected how they completed it, with some tending to emphasise young people's difficulties and others to minimise them. Similarly, a higher score at a later stage could indicate greater awareness of difficulties rather than an actual change.

The measure was completed by carers, key workers, social workers and young people at different stages of the research. The results reported here are based on the carers' and key workers' responses for the first round, carers (CAPS) and social worker (secure) for the second round, and primarily social workers' responses for the third. Table 7:1 provides details of the results at each stage of the research, using the divisions suggested by Goodman (1994): *0–13 normal ; 13–16 borderline; 17+ abnormal*. Ten of the 20 young people in the CAPS sample were rated as "abnormal" at the start of the study, with four scoring over 25.

Table 7.1

SDQ scores for CAPS and secure samples at each stage of the research

| | Round 1 | | Round 2 | | Round 3 | |
	CAPS	Secure	CAPS	Secure	CAPS	Secure
Normal	7	6	6	5	7	6
Borderline	3	4	2	4	1	5
Abnormal	10	8	12	10	9	6
Total	**20**	**18**	**20**	**19**	**17**	**17**

At each stage the distribution of scores was very similar for both samples, with approximately half in the abnormal range. In most respects, carers assessed CAPS young people as having more difficulties than were reflected in the young people's own scores. The opposite was the case among young people in secure care, almost three-quarters of whom placed themselves in the "abnormal" category.

By comparing the first and last scores, Table 7.2 provides a profile of overall progress. In order to sharpen the profile, borderline scores were combined with the "normal" category.

Table 7.2
Overall progress as assessed by the SDQ

Development over the study period	CAPS	Secure
Improvement from abnormal to normal	4	2
Normal at start and end point	6	8
Abnormal at start and end	6	4
Deterioration from normal to abnormal	3	2
Total	**19**	**16**

Five of the six young people who had been scored as abnormal at the start of the research and normal at the end had been in CAPS placements, four from the start and one having transferred from secure care. However, three of the six had not made progress while with CAPS but had done so after leaving.

As noted in Chapter 4, initial assessments of self-esteem were somewhat contradictory in that social workers considered most young people had very low self-esteem, while most young people's scores in the Rosenberg indicated no problem in relation to self-esteem. Follow-up data from the Rosenberg scores were only available in relation to young people placed with CAPS. These indicated very little change, with only two young people obtaining a higher score and two a lower score.

Asked more directly how they felt about themselves, half the young people placed with CAPS thought they had come to feel better as a result of the CAPS placement and half thought there had been no change. No-one said that they felt worse about themselves. According to social workers' assessments, there had been some improvement in self-esteem for two-thirds of young people placed both with CAPS and in secure care.

Changing and influencing behaviour

Context

CAPS carers varied in the extent to which they explicitly focused on changing young people's behaviour, but all carers tried to influence young people's actions, since these were often central to their difficulties. In some instances, specific behavioural targets were identified in the four-weekly meetings, for example, that the young person would start to take more responsibility for his or her own laundry or would respond in a non-aggressive way when angry. However, most attempts to change behaviour were more subtle and, as with promoting self-esteem, built into everyday life. Carers repeatedly reminded us that the capacity to influence young people depended on first earning their trust and confidence. It was not simply a question of enabling the young person to learn techniques and strategies, though these could be very useful, but of inspiring young people to want to change and giving them the confidence to do so through support. Of course building up this kind of relationship took time and in the meantime, carer and young person had to strike an agreement about what would and would not be acceptable.

In the first interviews a wide range of behaviours was cited as requiring change. These included improving table manners and personal hygiene, becoming less agitated and/or aggressive, reducing temper tantrums and food fads and behaving in a less sexually provocative way. Of particular interest to the research were the behaviours which had or might have resulted in young people being placed in secure accommodation, namely offending, self-harm and absconding.

The service provided

CAPS placements

Both carers and some young people agreed that the close personal supervision foster care afforded was crucial to modifying and guiding young people's actions. In terms of controlling negative behaviour, carers were often able to anticipate difficulties and take steps to divert young people from unhelpful or destructive behaviour. On the other hand, when young people did misbehave, they had to face the carers and take responsibility for their actions, compared with perhaps having a new shift dealing with them in residential care. Some distinctive aspects of foster care were also thought to promote good behaviour. Some young people and carers described how young people viewed carers or their children as models of good behaviour and tried to emulate them. Conversely young people were not subject to negative influences from peers in ways which might occur in residential care.

Carers were asked to indicate which specific methods they used to influence or control young people's behaviour. The most common methods, used in virtually all placements, entailed talking over behaviours, considering the consequences for the young person and others, and offering advice. In addition, about a third of carers had successfully encouraged a young person to develop a new interest, for example, in fishing, sport or drama, partly as a diversion from less acceptable behaviour.

While talking to young people could be helpful, some carers emphasised that it was even more effective to use young people's current experience. For example, a young person would learn more about how to behave in work or college by attending and having support to deal with difficulties as they arose, rather than by talking about how they should behave. This was partly why it was so difficult for placements to remain productive when opportunities for work or school were not available.

In line with psychological learning theories, carers used incentives and sanctions. The main sanctions open to carers were to stop young people from going out and to curtail their use of pocket money. Pocket money could not be forfeited but part could be temporarily withheld or diverted to young people's savings. About half of the carers said they had at some point used each of these options. Other sanctions were to limit access to television and to "fine", for example, for slamming doors. Some carers involved young people in deciding what sanction would be appropriate and, where an incident had been anticipated, this could even be agreed in advance. Thus a sanction became a consequence the young person chose to incur, rather than a punishment over which they had no control.

The most contentious issue concerned whether carers were entitled physically to stop young people running away. The formal agency policy was that young people could be strongly advised not to run away but not physically stopped from doing so, for example, by carers locking doors and windows, barring their exit or removing their shoes. Several carers strongly disagreed with this, especially in relation to children aged under 14. A few had been in the position of having to let a child of that age leave their home, knowing the young person would engage in dangerous behaviour. The rules, they argued, prevented them from protecting young people and so fundamentally undermined their role as carers.

This issue evidently affected how carers were able to manage absconding, one of the behaviours which might result in secure placement. On the whole carers relied on their usual repertoire of strategies to manage this and other behaviours such as offending and self-harm. Close supervision, taking a personal interest, talking over consequences and setting clear rules and expectations were the key means through which these behaviours were tackled. However, subtle differences reflecting carers' differing approaches also emerged. For example, faced with a young woman who was staying out and putting herself at risk, one carer said:

We need to find ways of changing this because if you keep staying out I am not able to keep you safe and so cannot do my job.

Another carer's response was:

If you are not seen to be keeping to the boundaries and working with me, you will be moved to a residential school.

While one appealed to the young person's own responsibility, the other emphasised an external threat. From the subsequent behaviour of the girls in question, it seemed the former approach had been more effective.

Secure placements

The situation for young people in secure care was different in several important respects. Firstly, their behaviour was controlled primarily by being physically held, which also meant that they were not able to learn to change through making choices. In addition, adjusting to the secure environment was seen as a temporary necessity, not something which would equip them for community living.

While it might be expected that the service would place a sharp focus on addressing the specific behaviours which had resulted in secure care placement, this was not apparent for most. Only one boy had been helped with anger management, one had briefly attended a course for young people involved in car crime, and one had had extensive counselling in relation to his sexually abusive behaviour. In addition, a few girls who self-harmed had had psychiatric help.

Developments in relation to problematic behaviour

Information on developments in behaviour over the study period was obtained primarily from carers and social workers at each stage of the research. They were specifically asked to rate changes in offending and self-harm. Social workers noted at least one change in behaviour during the placement in relation to three-quarters of the young people placed with CAPS. Approximately half the young people thought they behaved somewhat differently at home or in the community since being placed with CAPS.

Very significant changes in behaviour were described in relation to some individuals placed with CAPS. For example, one boy who had repeatedly had hour-long tantrums about food quite quickly learned to control his temper, negotiate about what he wanted and eat most of what suited the rest of the family. This change was attributed to firm handling, resisting manipulation and teaching him to appreciate the give and take of a family home, rather than expect a team of staff to provide for him.

Many of the carers actively sought to reverse institutionalised practices which "made excuses" for young people and allowed them to behave in ways which were unacceptable in the wider community. The success of this approach was evidenced by one boy who was able to go on a college visit to Europe, having been barred from a trip with his residential school two years before on the grounds of poor behaviour.

While most change was evident among those who remained with CAPS longer term, some who left earlier showed indications of change. One social worker believed that a girl who had spent under six months in placement displayed less sexualised behaviour, while another was said to lose her temper less often.

Quite significant changes were also reported in relation to a few of the young people placed in secure care. This normally followed sustained input by staff who took a keen interest in the young person. One young boy had attended a project to address his sexually aggressive behaviour, while also working with an education resource, his social worker and secure care staff towards preparing for community placement. At the third stage of the research he was placed with a local authority foster carer. There had been no sexually inappropriate behaviour, he was coping in school, and managing a difficult relationship with his mother. Another 16-year-old boy significantly changed his behaviour while living in a residential school, where staff took a personal interest in his well-being. Key to their approach was to recognise his significant emotional and learning difficulties, rather than expect him to fit in with what was expected of the group as a whole. On this basis he had stopped running away and had managed to challenge some bullying, thus reversing his usual scapegoat role.

Developments in relation to running away

Approximately half the young people placed with CAPS had absconded in the past. For only five, including two ten-year-old boys, this was one of the major issues which was causing concern immediately prior to the placement. Three of these five young people stopped their running away behaviour while with CAPS. From the accounts of young people, social workers and carers, this change was due to feeling comfortable in the foster home and wanting to stay there. The two young people who persisted with their running away had strong anxieties about their birth families and wished to be with them.

By the third stage of the research, only one frequent absconder from the secure sample still ran whenever he was released. Most of the others had grown to a point where running away was unnecessary, as they could stay with friends or relatives as they chose.

Developments in relation to offending

Criminal behaviour was a common feature in both samples. All young people in the secure sample and 15 of those placed with CAPS had previously been charged with some form of offence. The types of offences they had committed included assault, theft, drug possession, vandalism and car-related offences.

Six of the 15 young people with a history of offences had reduced their offending during the CAPS placement. These were all girls. There had been an increase in offending for three and six did not change. Only young people who had stayed with CAPS for over a year sustained their improvements until the end of the research.

The secure care sample did not have the opportunity to offend for the first part of the research period. However, half the sample had also shown a reduction in offending by the third round.

Self-harming behaviour

Prior to being placed with CAPS, 13 young people had been engaged in behaviour which caused themselves harm or put them at serious risk. Seven young people had actively harmed themselves on at least one occasion, for example, by cutting themselves, overdosing or attempted hanging. An additional six young people caused themselves harm in ways which were less obviously intentional, for example, by refusing to eat, consuming excessive amounts of drugs and alcohol or becoming involved in prostitution. Among those in secure care, seven had actively harmed themselves and another seven put themselves at risk through their lifestyle, for example, by joy riding, drug use and involvement in prostitution.

Social workers' assessments suggested that the level of self-harming and risk taking reduced for most young people in both samples (Table 7.3).

Table 7.3
Developments in relation to self-harming

Progress in relation to self-harming	First round		Second round	
	CAPS	*Secure*	*CAPS*	*Secure*
Self-harming/dangerous behaviour reduced	5	6	9	9
No change	4	6	2	4
Self-harming/dangerous behaviour increased	2	2	0	0
Total	**11**	**14**	**11**	**13**

Overall, it may be concluded that both samples included young people whose behaviour improved dramatically and others who made little progress. In general, the patterns were similar. In other words, placement in the community did not lead to poorer outcomes despite the absence of physical controls on behaviour. This suggests that the focus on need did not detract significantly from CAPS' ability to manage risks.

Supporting aspects of young people's lives outside the family: education

Context

In recent years there has been increasing attention to improving the educational experiences of looked after children (Borland *et al*, 1998; Jackson, 2001). It would be difficult to overstate the importance of education in this project. It proved critical in terms of reducing carers' stress, providing a structure for young people's lives during the placement, and preparing them for the future. In Chapter 3 some of the issues in relation to accessing appropriate educational resources were highlighted. Here the focus is on young people's experience and progress.

While education was important for all young people, its significance varied, depending on whether the young person was to attend mainstream school, a specialist resource, college or work experience. Whereas attending the local school was a key element of being included in a community, specialist provision provided an opportunity for young people who had missed out on education to catch up. College or work experience was a key part of managing the transition to adult life. This section considers in turn young people's experiences and progress in each form of provision, in acknowledgement of their distinctive significance, then concludes by outlining educational or work circumstances at the end of the study.

The service provided in relation to mainstream school

Arrangements for setting up mainstream school placements varied, depending primarily on the level of difficulty and support needs of the young person. Where previous difficulties had not been too severe, the carer simply approached the local school and arranged for the young person to start. However, more often young people had significant support needs and more formal arrangements were required. These usually involved an educational psychologist from the young person's home authority. One authority paid for three afternoons of additional support activities for a secondary school pupil, a service which was thought to have been critical to sustaining the placement.

While careful assessment and negotiation prior to placement was helpful in ensuring the necessary supports were in place, they also sometimes delayed the start of school and in some instances the CAPS placements themselves. A number of carers found this frustrating and worried that it gave young people the impression that they would not be welcomed in the school. Where placements had been made in an emergency, delay in setting up schooling meant that young people could be out of school for some time. One young boy had only a few weeks schooling during a seven-month placement, which put considerable stress on himself and the carers. Indeed the carer considered that lack of schooling had contributed to the placement breaking down.

Even where professionals such as social workers and psychologists were involved in negotiating placements, carers had a key role in establishing day-to-day links with the school. In each case at least weekly contact was established between the carers and someone from the school, usually the head teacher or a member of the guidance staff. The aim was to spot and deal with difficulties early on and, in some cases, to reduce the young person's scope for creating trouble.

The role carers adopted in such meetings and negotiations varied but a key element was to facilitate communication and problem-solving between the young person and the school. At times carers told us they reminded schools of their responsibilities, encouraging them to find a way to manage a particular problem. On other occasions carers would hold the young person to account, emphasising that certain behaviours were unacceptable. Evidently carers could only be effective in this role having gained the respect and confidence of the young person and school staff. According to a number of social workers, this also called for considerable skill in negotiating and communicating in situations of conflict. In virtually every case, carers found key school staff were helpful, took an interest in the young person, and were generally committed to sustaining the placement. Inevitably some teachers were more sympathetic than others and at times, changes of teacher or timetable were organised to avoid clashes.

It was evident that, while contacts with school were important, supporting young people's education involved much more. On a practical level, carers ensured that young people got up and arrived at school suitably dressed and equipped. Emotional and social support was equally important, this encompassing the full range of strategies outlined in the previous section. Particularly important were fostering self-confidence and helping young people learn new ways with which to deal with anger, while also providing lots of opportunities to talk about incidents at school, spot the danger points and plan ways of managing them. Underpinning all of this was the message that education mattered.

Young people's comments on their experience in mainstream schools were generally positive. However, some acknowledged that transferring from a small group specialist setting had been much more difficult than they had expected, requiring them to share teachers' attention, take responsibility for themselves, and cope with unsympathetic peers and staff in ways they had not anticipated. All accepted the carers' close involvement with the school and none felt it was intrusive. This was doubtless helped by the way in which carers tried to keep the young people involved. For example, when one young woman requested to stop the individual behaviour support she received three times a week, the carer encouraged the school to agree to her wishes on a trial basis. Within a short period of time the girl changed her mind and asked for it to resume.

Mainstream school: the extent to which plans had been realised, developments and progress

The initial plan for nine of the 20 CAPS placements involved attendance in mainstream education. Despite thoughtful support from carers and school staff, three did not start or stopped within a day or two. Attendance was established for six, but only two of those arrangements had continued beyond the second stage of the research. In both instances, the young people's commitment to school was underpinned by their very strong wish to remain with their carers. In two other cases, at the third stage of the research the young person was in a different school or college after leaving CAPS. When mainstream school placements were not sustained this was usually linked to difficulties in adjusting from the more individualised approach of small group teaching in a residential or secure unit.

In terms of progress, at the second round only one of the six young people who had attended mainstream provision was considered by the social worker to have made overall educational improvements. A further three had made progress by the third round, one of whom was still with CAPS. Only two young people thought that being with CAPS had helped them do better at school.

One young woman stood out as progressing particularly well in mainstream school, despite an exceedingly troubled background. The carer, social worker and young person identified how a combination of efforts by all the relevant parties had contributed to her academic success and much improved behaviour. The school provided individual support and staff showed flexibility and support. The carer kept in regular contact with the guidance teacher and advocated on behalf of the young woman, while also supportively challenging her attitudes and behaviour. The young person brought to the situation intelligence and an ability to get on with peers. She developed in confidence and social skills. All this was supported by periodic review meetings, which included the social worker.

The service provided in relation to specialist schooling

When it came to setting up specialist school placements, the process was more formal. Social workers and educational psychologists contributed to assessment, identified an appropriate resource and secured the funding. All but one of those in specialist education were being taught in residential schools. This was usually on a day basis, though two remained resident, spending weekends and holidays with the CAPS carers.

Among the young people who were included in the study most who required specialist education had been quite readily placed. Four of the seven continued to attend their existing school, while arrangements were in place for the others before or shortly after starting the placement. All placements were considered suitable in educational terms, but four required significant daily travel with a round trip of about 60 miles to school. By the later stages of the research, it was clear that the project was finding it much more difficult to access specialist schooling. When changes of specialist resource were needed for two young people in the sample, they proved impossible to find. This put considerable strain on the foster placements, resulting in one ending.

As with mainstream schools, carers had a key role in ensuring that young people were both physically and emotionally prepared for school. In many respects arrangements for collaboration were similar too. Carers established regular contact with a specific person in the school to keep each other informed of issues or incidents likely to spill over at home or at school. There were also differences. Where the schools were not local, most contact was by phone. Another contrast was that schools had their own regular review system and would invite CAPS staff and carers to these, in addition to school staff attending the statutory review and sometimes the less formal four-weekly meeting. Some carers and young people felt that this number of meetings led to unnecessary duplication.

Compared with local school teachers, staff in residential schools expected to have a more significant role in relation to young people's welfare, while also holding particular views about what was in the young person's best interests. Some schools employed a social worker for day pupils and/or operated a key worker system. In most instances this was helpful. For example, continuing support from the key worker proved critical for one boy in getting him through a difficult start to the placement and sustaining day attendance at the school where he had previously been resident.

However, tensions did arise when the carers and school had different ideas about where the appropriate balance lay between setting boundaries and supporting young people in their own choices. As a result, some carers found the school unduly harsh and inflexible, while others felt the boundaries and expectations they themselves had set were undermined. Usually difficulties were productively aired and managed. In one case the social worker thought the carer's intervention had resulted in the school changing their previously negative perception of the young person, thus creating the scope for her to change her behaviour and make considerable progress in her studies. In another case, though, differences in viewpoint eventually led to very fraught communication between the carers and school and the school placement ended. These contrasting outcomes illustrated that carers could negotiate effectively, but also that it was difficult to influence established practices in residential schools. The need for complex interaction between foster care and residential schooling itself resulted from a dearth of educational day provision.

Specialist achooling – the extent to which plans had been realised, developments and progress

In terms of progress, at the second stage of the research five of the seven young people who attended specialist education from CAPS placements were thought to have made a clear improvement (compared with only one of the six who attended a mainstream school). Moreover, all of the three young people in the CAPS sample who were awarded Standard Grades[3] had all been taught in residential schools, two as day pupils and one as a resident.

Most specialist school placements ended as planned, but after leaving school it proved difficult to find work. By the third round of the research all but two had no education or work placement. Both those who were in college or work were still living with their CAPS family.

The experiences of the eight young people in the secure accommodation comparison sample who moved on to residential schools were very similar, with good immediate outcomes usually followed by difficulties in gaining employment or further education. The specialist school placements were nearly all stable and several obtained qualifications, but at the third stage of the research only one was in employment and the seven others were unemployed.

The service provided: work/college placements

Moving into college or work placements proved a difficult transition for most young people in CAPS. This was an issue for four young people who had already left school when starting with CAPS and for an additional four who were expected to move to college or work experience during the course of the placement. Another six reached school-leaving age in the course of the study period but had left CAPS before any plans for college or work were made.

Carers took an active part in setting up college placements, finding out about provision in their area, liaising with college staff, and helping

---

[3] The Scottish school qualification usually taken at about age 15.

young people select the most appropriate course. Sometimes this was straightforward but, despite the range of courses on offer, it could also prove very difficult. Certain courses providing the necessary supervision and support were mainly for young people with specific learning difficulties such as Down's Syndrome. These were not acceptable to young people placed with CAPS. Other specialist programmes did not have the level of support and supervision required to deal with the troubled young people placed with the project.

One carer provided a graphic written account of a placement where the young man became demoralised when repeatedly asked to leave work and college because the courses or projects were unable to manage his learning and behaviour difficulties. This undermined the significant progress the boy had made in the foster home, eventually resulting in him moving to CAPS carers in another area. There he was able to attend a more suitable local college and made good progress in reading, social skills, and preparation for independent living.

When young people started work or joined a training scheme, they did not want to be identified as different from their peers. Also the emphasis was on them adapting to the work environment, rather than having special allowances made for them. Therefore the scope for carers collaborating closely with supervisors was generally far less and their support was indirect. For example, they encouraged young people to apply for jobs or schemes, helped build their confidence, made sure they got up on time, and conveyed a clear expectation that it was not an option to stay at home and do nothing. For some young people, this level of support was enough but others found themselves in dispute with peers or superiors and the jobs ended.

The location of work or college was an additional consideration in situations where young people were placed outwith their home area. Both the young people whose college or work became established decided to remain with CAPS and to move to more independent accommodation in the carers' home area. This meant that the carers' support and familiar college or work would continue as the young person went through the process of learning to live alone. However, others returned to live in their home area, in which case any links with careers or colleges had to begin again. This was another of the gaps in continuity, which resulted from young people being placed far from their home. Some carers were keen for these difficulties to be anticipated and more actively managed, for example, by social workers taking an active role in locating further education or work in the home area and co-ordinating this with plans to move back there. Some social workers worked in this way but others were reluctant to do so, preferring to rely on what the carers' local area could offer.

Progress in relation to work or college

By the time the fieldwork ended, almost three-quarters (14) of the young people placed with CAPS had reached school-leaving age. Nine were unemployed. Five were attending work or college and in three of these cases this was associated with an extended CAPS placement, two of which were still continuing. The other two individuals had spent only a short time with CAPS and reached their college place from a residential placement. It proved no easier for young people from secure care to find work or training on reaching school-leaving age. As with CAPS, nine were out of work at the follow-up stage, while three were attending college or had a work placement.

We end this section on education by briefly comparing overall developments in relation to the young people who started off in CAPS placements and secure accommodation. One difference was that young people placed with CAPS were more likely to have an opportunity to attend mainstream school. Given the level of previous schools difficulties, this was a high-risk strategy, reflected in the fact that few of them were able to cope there for long. Thus at the second stage of the work, more than half the CAPS sample were neither at school nor working, compared with a third of the comparison sample, most of whom were still receiving specialist education. Young people from both samples found it very difficult to move into further education, training or work. However, of the eight from both samples who were in work or attending college, six had spent time in CAPS, including one young woman who began in a secure unit.

Family relationships

Context

As noted in Chapter 5, all the young people placed with CAPS had experienced troubled family relationships. Nevertheless, most young people retained a significant relationship with at least one parent. For one young woman the main carer was her grandmother, while another's main contact was with her aunt, and one young man spent weekends with his grandfather. Most had regular contact with a brother or sister, though some had less frequent meetings and six had at least one sibling with whom they had no contact at all. At the start of the research, seven young people indicated that they wanted to increase or renew contact with a brother or sister.

In interviews with young people, the significance of their parents was very clear. Some were reluctant to talk about their parents at all but most who did were very loyal, sometimes presenting an idealised view of family life which did not accord with their previous experience. A few said they had clarified before agreeing to CAPS that the carer would not try to replace their parents. They were keen to emphasise that, though their parents' way of life might be different from that of the carers, it was not inferior and was probably the one they would choose for themselves. On the other hand, a few young people did compare favourably the care they were receiving in CAPS with what their parent had offered.

In terms of Holman's (1980) distinction between exclusive and inclusive fostering, the project's approach and that of most carers was clearly inclusive. It was the project's policy to involve parents, as long as this was in the interests of the young person. This was especially important for the eight young people whose initial plan was to return home. However, helping young people manage family relationships did not necessarily mean working closely with parents. With some young people the priority was to better understand their family situation and how to manage relationships in ways which were least detrimental to themselves. This was a process which might entail coming to terms with abuse, rejection, guilt and neglect.

A number of carers talked of how important it was to gain parents' confidence and to reassure them and the young people that they were not seeking to replace them. Carers who adopted this perspective were usually sympathetic towards parents' difficulties and encouraged the young person to see their parents in the same light. Other carers were more critical of parental failings and believed these should be acknowledged with the young person. The most experienced carers were particularly skilled at judging when each approach would be most helpful for the young person. They also exercised great care before acknowledging that parents had behaved in ways which were unacceptable; aware young people could later use this against the carer in a way which might damage their relationship. Experienced carers were also able to tolerate criticism and challenges from parents of a kind which made newer carers very angry.

The research's resources did not allow for contact with all parents, but four were interviewed to provide some indication of the parental perspective. They were selected on the basis of their willingness to participate, geographical proximity and having had ongoing contact with CAPS staff and carers. Their views are incorporated in the following sections.

The service provided for the CAPS sample

Where it was envisaged that young people would go home, it was generally seen as helpful for the carers to work with the parents towards this aim. However, a number of factors limited what carers were able to offer. One obstacle to contact in person was the distance between the carers' home and where the parents lived. None of the young people had been placed within their home authority. Even a distance of 20–30 miles could make contact difficult. One mother had to take two buses to reach the carer's home and found this too much to manage. Without an opportunity to build up a relationship, phone contact became primarily about keeping parents informed.

Even where contact could be established, expectations of the carer were not always clear. One authority provided a taxi to take a parent to the carer's home but once she was there the carer was not sure what the purpose of the visit should be. They talked about managing the young person and the carer hoped to have some influence, but the parent did not acknowledge problems in her parenting and saw meeting with the young person as the main purpose of the visits. The work carers could do with parents was to some extent dependent on relevant issues having been identified in a wider forum and included in the care plan. However, there were also dangers in formalising their input too much. It was the apparently spontaneous and informal approach of carers, their separateness from social work staff, which often made what they had to offer acceptable to parents. Working with parents thus brought into focus questions about carers' authority, the nature of partnership, and the distinctiveness of their expertise.

Carers and social workers considered that positive work had been done in three of the eight cases where the initial plan was for young people to go home. These three very different situations illustrate the range of work done with parents. One set of carers had taken part in structured sessions with the whole family, alongside the social worker and staff from another NCH project. They had also maintained daily phone contact with parents, with each sometimes visiting the other's home. The social worker and carers reported that the parents had found this very helpful, but the boy was made anxious by his loss of control and set about bringing the placement to an end through behaving aggressively and destroying the carers' property. When interviewed at the follow-up stage, the boy remembered the carers fondly because, despite his behaviour, they had never "judged" him.

Another set of carers managed to gain the confidence of parents who had initially opposed the placement. The carers achieved this trust by reassuring the parents in their words and actions. They kept them well informed through daily phone calls and dealt with any tensions in a consistent and straightforward manner. In turn the parents had become more consistent and straightforward with their daughter and after about seven months they were able to live together, something which had not been possible during the previous two years. When interviewed at the second stage of the research, the girl's mother acknowledged how helpful it had been to have another couple tackling the problems she and her partner had struggled with for several years. She echoed comments made by other parents, saying it had been reassuring that carers had not found a quick solution. It seemed this had increased the parents' confidence, while also allowing them to work on managing the young person's behaviour, rather than expecting a "cure".

In both of the examples described so far, carers and parents formed an alliance to manage young people who were seen as manipulative and controlling. The young people found this threatening and both responded by behaving in such a way as to ensure the placement ended. Nevertheless, social workers and carers agreed that the experience had been worthwhile in terms of challenging established patterns in the parent–child relationship.

In a third example of positive work with a young person for whom return home was initially planned, the alliance was very much between the young person and carer. In this case the young person learned not to be manipulated by her family or feel responsible for all their troubles. As she gained in confidence, she had become able to decide when and in what circumstances it would be helpful for her to see family members. This to some extent mirrored the carers' approach which was to welcome family members to the home but apply certain conditions to ensure it worked well for the young person. These carers were careful not to criticise the family, realising this could threaten their own relationship with the girl as well as deprive her of the opportunity to work out a form of understanding which was right for her at this particular stage. Though initial plans were that this girl might go home, these were changed when it became clear that her needs would be better met in other ways.

When there were no plans for the young people to go home, the aim was sometimes to help them establish or redevelop a link with parents for the future, while others also needed help to understand why their parents had been unable or unwilling to care for them throughout their childhood. In such cases, contact between carer and parent was usually less frequent and focused primarily on practical matters such as arrangements for home leave. However, a number of carers had helped re-establish contact between parent and young person, one taking a key role in enabling a mother to express her negative feelings about her son, yet continue to remain involved in his life.

In addition to carers, the local authority social workers had a key role in supporting young people's contact with parents, while a few also encouraged parents to become more involved in their children's lives or helped young people to come to terms with their parents' absence. Some social workers were also helping parents with their own problems or with difficulties in relation to other children living at home or in another care setting. One boy and his mother relied on a social work assistant they both trusted to facilitate contact; during periods when she was withdrawn from the case, this resulted in long gaps between meetings.

Service provided for the secure care comparison sample

Of those in the secure care sample, five were expected to return to live with a parent or other relative, not necessarily straight from the secure unit but in the near future. For them there was considerable attention to ensuring that parents and other close relatives could visit. The sample divided into three almost equal groups for whom the emphasis was on:

- supporting parents or other relatives to retain contact and/or play a part in the young person's life;
- enabling young people to make sense of and cope with negative family relationships;
- supporting both young people and parents.

Some secure care staff worked directly with young people and/or their parents but their main role was to ensure that parents felt welcome and were able to meet the young person in privacy. Sometimes they also had to ensure that the young person was kept safe. Work was primarily with young people and parents separately, with very little family work being offered.

Social workers played a key role in making arrangements for parents to travel to the secure unit, sometimes taking them there by car. They were also important in terms of keeping in touch with parents and over-seeing events in young people's lives. In about a third of cases, social workers also directly addressed family relationships. Given the difficulty in engaging with young people on these issues, being able to do this depended in part on the kind of relationship the social worker had been able to establish with the young person and parents.

Developments and progress in family relationships

Contact

At the start of the placements, approximately three-quarters of the young people in both CAPS and in secure care were in regular contact with at least one relative. For the majority the link was with a birth parent, but grandparents, aunts, brothers, adoptive and foster carers also kept in regular contact and were expected to continue to do so. The remainder had no reliable family link, but all but one had sporadic contact with at least one parent. Five young people placed with CAPS spent most weekends with a parent or other relative throughout most of the placement. Four mothers became regular attenders at the four-weekly review meetings.

In recent policy, contact has almost invariably been seen as a good thing (see e.g. Cleaver, 2000). However, despite the importance of family support, high or increased family contact in this study was not necessarily a positive sign. Less contact might indicate that the young person was becoming more discriminating about what was in his or her best interests, while more contact could mean older teenagers were becoming embroiled in parental crime.

To gain an understanding of the impact of the CAPS placement on contact with parents, it was important to differentiate between the development of family contact *during* the placement and what happened *thereafter*. Details are outlined in Table 7.4.

Table 7.4

Developments in contact with parents or main carers during CAPS placements

X = one young person

Developments in contact	Initial plan was for return home	Initial plan was for independent living or new family
Contact increased during placement and remained high or increased further thereafter	1	4
Contact decreased during placement but increased thereafter	3	2
No change in contact during or after placement	2	5
Contact decreased during placements and remained low	1	2

It is evident that contact with parents or guardians increased during placement for more young people who did not plan to return home than for those who did. All five who had increased their family contact during the placement and afterwards were young people who, having left care by the time the research ended, were independently establishing patterns of support. In some instances, carers had facilitated the links with parents or other relatives during the placement, sometimes working to overcome quite entrenched resentments on the part of parents and young people.

At the other end of the spectrum, eight young people had reduced contact during the placement. For some this resulted from being placed far from home, which they resented. In other cases the placement provided an opportunity to re-evaluate whether the contact was in their best interests and the young people had been active participants in deciding to see less of their parents.

Of the seven young people who wanted to have more contact with a brother or sister, four had been able to do so at one point during the CAPS placement.

For young people in secure care it was hardly surprising that contact generally increased once they moved to open placements and were able to visit home. By the time the research ended, over half (12) had more contact than they had had at the start. All but three of these were over 16 and kept in touch with parents and siblings as it suited them.

Progress

While frequency of contact was one criterion social workers used to rate progress in family relationships, a range of others applied. These included:

- young person's capacity to have a realistic view of what their family could offer;
- quality of communication between parents and children;
- parents' willingness to show commitment to the young person;
- parents' capacity to deflect young person's manipulation;
- young person presenting less challenging behaviour to parents or carers.

Rating progress was not straightforward, especially where there had been improvement in some respects and deterioration in others. The research assessed progress primarily on the basis of social workers' ratings (see Table 7.5), because these were obtained on virtually all young people at each stage of the research.

Table 7:5
Social work assessments of developments in family relationships
(second stage assessment)   X = one young person

	CAPS	*Secure*
Improved	5	9
No change	9	8
Mixed	4	3
Deterioration	2	
Total	20	20

No characteristic distinguished the five young people out of 20 whose family relationships were regarded as having improved. They were diverse in terms of age, length of time they had been in care and whether their return to a relative's care was planned or not.

More carers than social workers thought that there had been no change (13), with only four acknowledging improvement. Young people's views were similar, with four thinking they were getting on better with members of their own family and most of the rest believing there had been no change. Approximately a quarter of the young people in CAPS placements thought the CAPS carers had helped them get on better with members of their own family, either by acting as a mediator through which contact had been re-established or by supporting them in challenging parents' control over their lives.

Improvements in family relationships between the second and third stages mostly signified changed circumstances after leaving CAPS. Three moved closer to their main relative. Of two young people who remained with CAPS, one had made continuous progress in coming to terms with and managing difficult family relationships, while the other had moved placement and started to have more family contact.

Social worker assessments for the secure comparison sample indicated a higher proportion of improvements (Table 7.5). It is possible that expectations for this group were lower and some social workers did state that the amount of change for young people in secure care was modest. Several social workers attributed these improvements primarily to the fact that the young person had become an adult who demanded less from parents and whose problem behaviour such as running away caused less distress. These developments were also noted among young people placed with CAPS, providing a good illustration that progress can result from maturation and changed circumstances rather than service input.

Health

Context

As noted in the previous chapter, two types of health needs were identified for young people in both samples. First, there were concerns about the short- and long-term effects of some aspects of their lifestyle, such as drug and alcohol misuse, poor diet and unsafe sexual behaviour, while some also suffered from one or more chronic or recurring medical condition. In addition, about three-quarters in both samples were thought to need some form of counselling or psychotherapeutic service. However, since not all young people agreed to this, it was planned for only a few.

Service provided in relation to health

Young people placed with CAPS were registered with the carer's general practitioner who provided a direct service and referred on to specialist services as required. On the whole, collaboration with general practitioners worked well in that most carers found their own doctors were helpful and interested in the young people, though some struggled to manage a range of difficult issues they had little experience of. The most common requirement was for girls to have advice on contraception and safe sex, while several also required investigation of a gynaecological condition or recurring genito-urinary infection. Virtually all of these issues were dealt with by general practitioners, though not necessarily resolved if young people did not stay in the placement for long. Another drawback of the localised nature of the service was that referrals to specialist services could be disrupted when young people moved placement. A few young people had moved by the time an appointment with a specialist was offered.

Whereas carers' role as an intermediary within education was well established, this was more complex in relation to the medical services, partly because young people often wanted and were entitled to confidentiality. In one situation the general practitioner was unwilling even to let the carer know whether the young person had consulted with him. This was of particular concern to the carer, since the girl had a history of overdosing. School medical staff and hospital services which the girl contacted interpreted confidentiality differently, being willing to co-operate with the carers to try to manage the girl's behaviour.

A few respondents expressed the view that there would be some advantages in accessing a specialist agency such as Brook Advisory for advice on contraception and sexual health. One young woman's experience also suggested that it might be advisable to refer through a specialist service for help with the emotional impact of abuse. Having plucked up the courage to ask her general practitioner to refer her to a psychiatrist, she was dismayed to find that he expected her to talk about such difficult issues without taking any time to build up trust or find out what she expected from meeting with him. As a result she was more reluctant than ever to seek professional help to deal with events in her life which continued to cause her distress.

The experience of the health service was also somewhat fragmented for young people in the secure care sample, as they moved around different placements. Thus for both groups discontinuity was an issue. It seems that an arrangement is required whereby young people who are looked after can gain reliable access to skilled and sensitive medical services, which are maintained when they move.

Progress and developments in relation to physical health

Progress in the young people's mental health overlaps with emotional development which has previously been considered, so only physical health is examined here. At both follow-up stages of the research, social workers considered that there had been no change in the physical health of the majority of young people in both samples. Most of the rest were rated as having better health. These improvements were attributed to being cared for in a settled environment as opposed to living on the streets or frequently running away. The few examples of deterioration all related to continuing drug use. Thus health changes were seen to result from the young person's lifestyle rather than the provision of specific services. Two young people still in CAPS placements had made significant gains at both stages. Among specific improvements for young people within CAPS were losing weight through taking up sport and eating a healthy diet, and persuading a young person to wear much-needed glasses. In terms of sexual health, several young men and women in both samples were thought to have become more discriminating in their choice of partners. Despite the explicit attention given to contraception, three young women with CAPS and two in the secure sample had become pregnant.

Leisure activities

Introducing young people to leisure activities was an aspect which was seldom emphasised by social workers. A number of carers, though, considered this a central element of the young person's experience. Developing new skills and joining community groups were cited as means of enhancing young people's self-esteem, helping them to mix with a range of people, taking their mind off worries, using their time productively and providing an alternative to illegal or anti-social activities.

The range of activities young people engaged in was varied. One young person joined a drama group, while others went to cadets and guides. Some attended clubs on their own, others engaged in sports or other activities along with the carers. One set of carers were keen on bowling and each young person placed with them came to share their interest. Another's interest was showing dogs, while others attended church and associated activities. More informally, a number of families enjoyed going out for meals and thought that, in addition to being enjoyable, young people learned a lot from this about how to behave in public.

Arranging or participating in these various activities called on differing kinds of input from carers. Where young people attended community groups, a decision sometimes had to be made about how much information to give to leaders, for example, that a young person might be likely to run away. When carers or members of their family also attended the group, they provided any necessary supervision themselves, while also at times intervening in interactions between the young person and others. For one young man, long fishing sessions had afforded an opportunity to talk for the first time about sensitive events in his past.

The value of such leisure activities lay primarily in the young person's enjoyment, which was most usefully assessed by the young people themselves. Most of those who had attended group activities for any length of time said they enjoyed them, some speaking in glowing terms. In contrast, others who had not enjoyed group activities had given them up. Young people who had developed a skill, for example, bowling or fishing, were proud of their achievements, while the boy who had unburdened himself to the carer conveyed a sense of complete contentment as he talked about the fishing trips.

Not all carers considered leisure activities particularly important. A few suggested that, since teenagers seldom spent their leisure time with their parents, young people should do likewise in placement thus ensuring foster care would replicate "normal family life". This was one respect in which carers varied in their understanding of what was meant by "normal family life", while also illustrating how carers' views influenced the young person's experience.

Preparing for independent living

In light of the high proportion of young people in secure accommodation who need support towards independent living, what CAPS could offer in this respect merits some attention. The difficulties care leavers face are well documented and include poverty, poor access to suitable accommodation, and unemployment (Broad, 1998). Young people who have been in care are over-represented among those who are homeless and in prison. To provide young people with the necessary support, leaving care schemes now typically seek to provide support over an extended period, ideally beginning when young people are still in care and continuing until they are established in accommodation and employment. Developing support networks is recognised as critical, acknowledging that "independence" does not mean coping alone but in the context of formal and informal supports. Nor is the move towards "independence" linear. Instead young people ideally need to be able to return at times when their circumstances require it (Broad, 1998). Where young people remain living or in contact with foster carers, the provision of this kind of flexible support is potentially very valuable (Wade, 1997).

Virtually all the input described so far was geared at least partly towards helping young people cope as adults. In addition, carers focused on specific skills such as managing money, shopping and housekeeping. For some young people a programme was devised through which, under the supervision of the carer, they increasingly took on responsibility for their own shopping, cooking and laundry. One of the issues raised by several carers was that the generous pocket money allowance provided by CAPS ill-prepared young people for managing on the benefit level income many would have when they left. From having £15 per week for pocket money and £60 per month for clothing, young people would have to learn to survive on around £40 per week. Several carers would have favoured a scheme whereby carers could place some of the young people's CAPS allowance in a savings account which they could access after leaving the project.

Since adequate income, availability of housing and social support are central to a successful transition towards independent living, previously reported findings on young people's employment status and accommodation arrangements provide an indication of how well equipped they were to cope. As noted earlier in this chapter, few from either sample who had left school had obtained educational qualifications or were in employment or education. The accommodation circumstances at the time the research ended of those moving towards independent living were more often poor than good. On the positive side, three had moved or were in the process of moving from a CAPS placement to their own accommodation with carer support. However, six were in temporary homeless accommodation, living in unsettled situations with relatives or in prison. In contrast, six young people who had started in secure care were coping in their own tenancy or supported accommodation, albeit with some difficulties in certain instances. Only one was in homeless accommodation and none were in prison, though two were still held in secure accommodation.

Thus moving to a CAPS placement in preparation for independent living entailed both opportunities and risks. A few benefited from the wide-ranging support carers provided throughout placements and from the fact that some carers continued to support young people when they moved on. This was associated with placements lasting a reasonable length of time and then young people choosing to settle in the carers' home area. Conversely, risks were associated with unplanned endings and the dislocation from their home area, which most placements involved.

While moving out of their home area allowed some young people a welcome "fresh start", it also presented some difficulties in building up supports which could be sustained after leaving the placement. For example, contacts at college or work, leisure activities and friendships developed in the carers' locale were not directly transferable to the young person's home area, where there might be equally important family and professional support networks. For some young people, this presented a difficult choice which could be underpinned by considerations of whether to try to opt for the carers' rather than their own family's lifestyle.

Distance also reduced the scope for CAPS carers to support young people who returned to their own communities. One carer had managed to support a young woman who chose to return to a tenancy in her home area, 20 miles from where the carer lived, providing a relationship which proved crucial to helping the young person get through a series of serious personal crises. However, given the demands of current placements, it was not envisaged that this could become normal practice.

These findings highlight the importance of projects like CAPS paying very close attention to young people's future support networks. Several carers thought the project should develop their own Throughcare provision, since, having removed young people from the system and their home environment, the project had a responsibility to support them through to adulthood.

Overall assessment of outcomes

CAPS placement outcomes

The evidence presented in this and the preceding chapter indicates that outcomes were multi-dimensional and could be assessed from a range of perspectives. It was important to distinguish between the immediate impact of the placement and what happened thereafter. In addition, it was acknowledged that it could be an achievement for such vulnerable and damaged young people to manage to live in a family, so that outcomes had to take account of the quality of their *experience* as well as their *post-placement circumstances.*

In order to reflect both these dimensions, a summary measure of overall outcome was adopted, using four criteria which related to both the young people's *experience* in CAPS and *circumstances* at the final stage of the research. The four criteria were:

Experience:	social worker's assessment of benefit from the placement;
	whether the placement ending had been planned or unplanned
End Circumstances:	whether in stable and secure accommodation;
	whether in school or work.

The social worker's assessment of benefit from the placement was selected as a criterion since this was obtained in relation to all young people at each stage of the research. Whether or not placement endings were planned was selected as a key indicator of the quality of the young person's overall experience since the potential significance of further rejection or disruption was highlighted by social workers at each stage of the research. It was also a matter on which a relatively objective assessment could be made. Stable and secure accommodation and availability of education or work are associated with better future life chances.

Young people who scored positively in three or four of these criteria were considered to have had a good outcome, while those who scored two were rated as moderately successful, and outcomes for those scoring one or zero were assessed as poor. On this basis the overall outcome was as follows:

- good   8
- moderate   5
- poor   7

Four of those who had a positive outcome were still in placement while the remaining four had spent from six weeks to a year with the carers. Each of the three groupings encompassed a wide range of young people and placement circumstances.

Comparison with outcomes for young people in secure accommodation

The same criteria cannot be used to assess overall outcomes for young people in secure care, primarily since the placement ending criterion was less applicable. However, taking the other three dimensions into account, a clear picture emerges that secure placements were considered to have provided a poorer *experience* but that *outcomes* for young people who had spent time there were similar or better than for those placed with CAPS. While social workers considered that all the CAPS sample had benefited from their time with the project, this applied to only three-quarters of placements in secure accommodation. In terms of educational or work outcomes, attainment was similar for both samples and approximately the same proportion had no education or work by the time the research ended. However, compared with those who had been with CAPS, more of the secure sample had made the transition to a relatively stable independent living situation.

In addition to these broad outcomes, throughout this chapter it has been evident that progress in specific aspects of young people's lives was assessed as similar for those in secure accommodation. While research tools and methods may not always be sophisticated enough to reflect the complexities and nuances of young people's experience, a consistent picture emerges that, at least in the short term, similar outcomes were achieved for both samples.

Inevitably the general picture masks the fact that, for some young people with CAPS, the outcomes were extremely good. There was agreement among all concerned that some young people's lives had been transformed, primarily because they could expect to rely on the support of their carers indefinitely. This long-term, personal input could not be provided by secure care which is essentially a short, time-limited service.

Summary

This chapter has reviewed evidence on how the CAPS sample fared with respect to key emotional, educational and social dimensions of their lives. CAPS' philosophy and most carers' daily practice stressed the importance of supporting emotional growth, although the abrupt endings of half the placements did not assist this. Overall, improvements in emotional development and self-esteem were similar for the CAPS and comparison samples. Few of those in CAPS placements were linked to psychiatric, psychological or specialist counselling services. Access to medical care was often difficult or fragmented.

Three-quarters of the young people placed with CAPS and all those in the secure sample had previously been involved in offending. At the follow-up stage, a quarter of previous offenders placed with CAPS and a third of the secure sample had reduced their level of offending. Where absconding was an issue for a young person in CAPS, this sometimes remained a problem and contributed to placement endings. However, some young people had learned to face difficulties which would previously have prompted them to run away. There were reductions in self-harming behaviour, in both CAPS and secure accommodation.

It was originally planned that almost half the CAPS sample would attend mainstream school but placements proved difficult to sustain and at the follow-up stage only two young people were currently attending. College and work experience placements proved equally difficult to sustain and only one of eight young people who had left school by the follow-up stage was in work or training. Specialist placements, mostly within residential schools, had proved stable and resulted in three young people obtaining Standard Grades. Social workers considered that between research interviews more young people in secure care than with CAPS had improved in education or work.

Significant sustained improvement in family relationships was not common in either sample. Involving the young person in local recreational activities was seen by some carers as a crucial component of the normal-ising benefits of family placement, but was not a priority for others.

Some young people had received crucial support from carers in the move towards independent living. However, circumstances and distance meant that this could not always be provided. When placements ended abruptly, suitable alternatives were seldom readily available.

Using a composite assessment, eight of the 20 young people in the CAPS sample had "good" outcomes overall, four in completed and four in ongoing placements. Outcomes were similar for young people in both samples, though in general, CAPS placements provided a more positive experience. That similar results could be achieved with challenging young people and without the expense and loss of freedom associated with secure care constitutes notable success.

8 Stakeholders' evaluation of CAPS

Introduction

We have noted throughout this book that the project could be evaluated according to different criteria and perspectives. From the young people's perspective, there was a distinction between the experience of living in the placement and whether they achieved good outcomes. As CAPS' paying customers, the local authorities' perspectives were evidently crucial. This chapter considers the extent to which CAPS met local authorities' requirements and expectations by considering:

- whether CAPS could cater for the young people they wished to place;
- whether CAPS provided a high-quality service;
- whether CAPS offered value for money.

These questions were addressed in interviews with the social workers who placed young people in the scheme. In addition, we put them to senior managers in three authorities which had made extensive use of the scheme. They were interviewed as stakeholders and had an overview of their agency's use of the scheme.

Senior staff from NCH and representatives of their fostering panel were also interviewed to provide an assessment of the project's progress by those participating in its development.

Capacity to provide the placements local authorities required

We noted in Chapter 2 that authorities looked for CAPS to provide placements for three broad groups of young people:

- currently in secure care and able to leave earlier if an alternative placement in a family was available;
- behaving in ways which were likely to result in secure care;
- currently in residential care but would benefit from a family experience with carers who could manage their significant difficulties.

Social workers and managers who had direct experience of working with CAPS expressed confidence that the scheme's carers were able to offer a high-quality service for some young people in each of these three groups. However, as it was a relatively small scheme, young people might wait some time for a suitable placement to become available. Some managers had found that CAPS made every effort to accommodate young people who were at the point of secure care placement but this had not always been possible.

Most social workers and managers expected CAPS placements to be of short or intermediate duration, i.e. lasting one to two years at the most. Their view was that CAPS could be relied on to provide an excellent service for these young people, but it became expensive if required over several years. However, a few were willing to pay for CAPS on a long-term basis for children with very serious difficulties who needed a high level of support to sustain family and community life.

Usually local authorities' formal policy was to use CAPS solely for teenagers with severe difficulties who were close to secure care. However, in practice several had extended their use of the scheme to include young people who were challenging but not necessarily at the point of secure placement. One authority's representative thought their own foster carers could have managed some of the children they referred, had it been possible to allow them the luxury of a singleton placement. In these instances, CAPS was compensating for a gap in the local authority service, rather than extending the range of young people who could be offered a family placement. A number of local authorities would have liked to have had the resources to develop their own foster care service along the lines of CAPS but others preferred to continue to buy in CAPS for the small number of young people who would need such intensive support in a family setting. Thus some authorities viewed specialist foster care as an extension of mainstream fostering services, while others considered it quite distinct in terms of the young people it could cater for and the level of skill carers required.

Quality of the service

Social workers and managers were very positive about what CAPS offered. Many described staff and carers as very professional with a sound understanding of young people and their needs, and a skilled approach to assessment, training and carer support. Some social workers said they learned a lot from working with CAPS staff and appreciated opportunities to talk over professional issues with them. In terms of organisation, the four-weekly meetings were cited as particularly helpful, both to facilitate close co-operation between all concerned and to ensure that plans were carried through.

Turning to the carers themselves, there was virtually universal praise for their perseverance and skill. Carers' willingness to stick with young people through very difficult behaviour was recognised and appreciated. Where placements had ended, it was acknowledged that this had been unavoidable or in the interests of the young person. Indeed in some situations, social workers thought that carers had continued for too long with young people whose behaviour indicated little commitment to the placement and/or put the carers at risk:

> I think it's the degree of tolerance that the carer has. We've got some good foster parents here who put up with a lot but there would be lines where they would say 'no, I'm not putting up with that any more'. And I think [the CAPS carer] carried it further than that. I mean there have been times when I've thought, 'I don't know how you put up with that, – maybe you shouldn't put up with that' – but no, she's prepared to do that. I think maybe because it's seen as a job.

Other ways in which social workers differentiated between carers within the scheme and other foster carers were that the former expected to cater for the child's individual needs, rather than expecting them to fit in with their own family routine:

> It's the bit about them kind of fitting round her rather than like a lot of normal foster placements, where children are going in and are expected to fit into a normal family routine that they've not been part of . . . Obviously it can't be totally geared towards the young person's wants and needs but the fact that she has an identified carer – and

the carer does go out his way to do that – does make a difference.

Another frequently mentioned characteristic was that carers expected difficulties and were able to handle angry or abuse behaviour effectively because they did not take it personally:

> *The carer took on board the fact that if [the young person] was acting out or being abusive towards her, this was not personal at all.*

> *CAPS placement was more professional than ordinary foster care. They didn't take slights and tantrums personally. The didn't feel personally wounded by it and that meant they were able to respond more constructively to help with the inappropriate behaviours.*

In addition to their commitment, insight and understanding, a number of social workers commented on how skilled carers were in communicating with children:

> *The communication is excellent, – that's got to be said. The communication with any child – one boy I had with them was nine, so they are obviously used to young and old. But it's the open discussion, the non-threatening way they can put things across. Even when things are difficult the communication skills are excellent and that's not easy. Not a lot of people can do that.*

> *I think it's just their down-to-earth approach. They don't panic about things, they just sit down and tell her like it is. It's not the threats about 'if you keep doing this you're out of here'. But by the same token they're not making it acceptable. So it's finding the balance.*

All of the above were identified as key components of professionalism, as was the carers' ability to make decisions and manage day-to-day difficulties without constantly involving the social worker:

> *The professional bit is there in that she is prepared to do things like contacting the school, handling anything that comes up. Again, most foster parents would be on the phone to us if we were in contact with the school. It would be us that would be making the contact a lot of the time and feeding back to them whereas it's the other way round – [the carer] does that and feeds back to me.*

The majority view among social workers was that the scheme's carers did offer a distinctive service, which in several respects was different from non-specialised family placements. However, a few social workers had expected carers to take on a wider range of tasks or be better informed, for example, about the criminal justice system or welfare benefits for care leavers.

In general, CAPS carers were considered able to provide a more intensive and skilled service because they had access to extensive support and training, while as paid professionals they expected to work with difficult situations. The importance of 24-hour support was often mentioned by social workers as an essential component of CAPS. From their point of view it meant that the CAPS project dealt with most emergencies themselves, involving the social worker or stand-by service only to keep them informed. One exception was that local authority stand-by teams would often become involved in returning young people who had run away. Some social workers told us that managing this was difficult, partly because they often had little information about the young person and partly because carers varied in how they responded in such situations. While some would come to collect the young person and talk over the implications of the absconding, others expected the stand-by service to arrange for the young person to be returned to them. A need was identified for better information sharing and clarity about the carers' role in these situations. Concerns were also voiced about some young people who repeatedly ran away, thus continuing to put themselves at risk.

When asked to identify aspects which had been problematic or which the project could improve, social workers most frequently mentioned communication. It had sometimes been difficult to contact senior practitioners. Also a number of social workers had not been kept informed or consulted about matters affecting the young person, for example, arrangements for respite, when another young person was joining the placement, or in terms of planning future placements. Echoing the range of opinions among carers, some social work staff considered it essential for young people with such severe difficulties to have singleton placements, while others identified potential benefits from sharing. Several social workers would have liked to have been more involved in the matching process. A few felt that their knowledge of the young person had been somewhat undervalued at the start, leaving them unsure of their role in the placement. However, others were happy to leave decisions about matching to project staff and carers. Perhaps inevitably, more dissatisfaction was expressed when placements did not work out as well as had been hoped for. Nevertheless, lack of success in placements was usually attributed to the severity of the young people's difficulties, rather than the quality of service CAPS provided. Social workers and managers also highlighted that lack of appropriate schooling restricted the potential of some placements, while the cost to the local authority increased considerably when arrangements were made for young people to attend a school at some distance from the carers' home.

Views of senior staff and members of CAPS' fostering panel

Staff participating in the development of the project expressed considerable satisfaction with its progress. While changes to the original partnership arrangements had resulted in temporary financial uncertainty for the project, accepting referrals from a wide range of authorities was considered to have proved an effective way of working. There was pride in the fact that NCH was at the forefront of extending professional foster care in Scotland and confidence that CAPS had been well managed and implemented. The financial risk involved in providing the start-up funding from voluntary funds was acknowledged and one suggestion for future projects was that initial core funding should be available from a statutory source. The only other thought on how CAPS might have been developed differently was that the manager's workload had been underestimated and had become excessive, until a depute was appointed in the third year. Despite this, the management of the project was considered to have been excellent, facilitating the professional development of staff and carers and managing with skill and confidence the inherent tensions which delivering a service of this kind entails.

Those interviewed were confident that the project was providing high-quality care for young people who would not previously or otherwise have been offered foster care. They believed that, despite some widening of referral criteria, the project had retained its commitment to providing an alternative to secure care and was catering for some of the most challenging young people in Scotland. The project was described as providing a much needed service, while also highlighting what foster care can achieve when carers receive appropriate support, recognition and reward.

Costs and value for money

Initial plans were to provide detailed information on the cost of each placement to the two partner local authorities, but these were revised when the project started to provide a national service and to provide more diverse placements. In these circumstances, it was agreed that the research would concentrate on identifying the range of costs for individual placements, key factors which affected these and whether placements were considered by stakeholders to have provided value for money in comparison with other options. It was not part of the research brief to obtain details of the costs of secure placements.

When asked whether they thought CAPS provided value for money, both social workers and managers took into account the quality of the service, what the alternatives might have been, and what the experience had been for the young person. In situations where a young person would otherwise have been in secure care, they believed the savings were clear. However, CAPS was as expensive as residential care and more expensive than mainstream foster placements, which led some managers to express frustration that so much money was being spent on a few children rather than being used to develop their own services. Social workers found judgements about value for money difficult when there really was no alternative for the young person concerned. Only a few social workers or managers necessarily looked for good outcomes when making judgements about value. More often they talked about the young person having been supported through a very difficult time and having a unique experience which they considered very valuable.

At the time the research was completed, the standard cost of a CAPS placement to local authorities was £850 per week. This comprised:

- carer's fee (£454);
- respite (£166);

- management costs (£110);
- maintenance (£100 or £120 depending on age).

In addition, there was a linking fee of £750 and three one-off charges per year for birthday (£100), Christmas (£100) and extra expenses associated with the summer (£200).

Though the basic fee of £850 constituted the total cost of a few placements, most also incurred additional expenses. Information on additional costs for each placement was obtained primarily from social workers, supplemented when necessary through contact with clerical staff in local authorities, educational psychologists and independent educational establishments. This indicated that costs varied widely. For example, some young people required money to cover sports or leisure interests, while placements were more expensive if young people needed additional respite. However, the main additional costs were for travel and specialist education, so that the factors which most influenced costs were:

- whether young people were in specialist education;
- how far the school was from the placement;
- the distance of the placement from the placing authority.

If young people were in specialist schooling, the authority had to pay for the education and for transport to and from the school. For one boy this amounted to £430 for the school place and £200 per week for travel by taxi, resulting in a total cost of £1,400 per week for CAPS and education combined. Even without the extensive travel costs which applied in this case, the combined charge would typically be in excess of £1,000, which is approximately comparable with the average weekly cost of a residential school placement. Neither of these include a costing of social worker time and travel, which would obviously vary depending on the distance between the placement and the social worker's office and the particular requirements of the young person. It follows that if the alternative is residential school, placement decisions for individual young people can be based on what is right for them rather than financial considerations.

An alternative arrangement was to provide behaviour or learning support within mainstream school. The provision of individual support three half-days a week had been critical in sustaining one school placement. The cost to the local authority was approximately £170 per week.

The distance between the placement and the child's authority added to the costs mainly because of travel expenses for young people to keep in touch with members of their family and for social work staff to attend meetings and visit the foster home. The most expensive placements from this point of view were those from an island authority, where an air fare of over £200 per person was required for each round trip. In addition, young people and carers were sometimes accommodated in a local hotel when meetings and contacts with family were arranged over a few days together. More typical examples of travel costs were £60–100 per month. These would be incurred in social work visits to the foster home, to transport young people to counselling sessions or to facilitate access. Obviously these costs would not apply in future projects if it was possible to provide more localised placements. Because they were idiosyncratic, costs for travel associated with the island authorities were not included in the overall assessment of CAPS placements reported below.

The research did not cost social work time but details were obtained from social workers of how many hours they devoted to supporting the CAPS placement. Most estimated that keeping in touch with the young person and carers and attending meetings took up around 10–12 hours per month. Inevitably the exact amount of time varied, depending on how long it took to travel to the foster home and the level of contact required at any particular time in the placement. However, most social workers did *not* find that the young person took up more of their time than had been the case prior to their placement with CAPS. Several commented that most of the time they devoted to the young person in the context of a CAPS placement was productive, rather than simply responding to crises as had previously been the case. In addition to the social work time, several young people had had some input from other social work personnel, most often homemakers and Throughcare staff.

Thus the total direct cost for a CAPS placement normally ranged from £850 to £1,400 per week. This is significantly cheaper than secure placements which at the time of the research cost around £2,500 per week. The costs reported here included care, education and access to appropriate leisure activities but not the costs of social worker time. However, the fact that CAPS placements on average lasted longer than those in secure care meant that the total cost to local authorities would not always be less. Compared with residential options other than secure, CAPS costs are roughly comparable. This supports other evidence that good-quality foster care is not necessarily cheaper but can provide added value for many young people (Knapp and Fenyo, 1989). It follows that more value will be derived from foster care if there is clarity about what any specific programme is able to offer and greater discrimination about which young people are most likely to benefit from this or other options. The final chapter concentrates on what can be learned from this research to further this process.

Summary

During the course of the study, CAPS built up a reputation among local authorities for providing an intensive, high-quality service and this was reflected in the views of key stakeholders interviewed by the research team. However, while positive, their enthusiasm was qualified compared with that of senior management and others who had participated in CAPS' development. NCH management underplayed emerging difficulties, emphasising instead the innovative nature of what was on offer and its achievements. Stakeholders, while praising many aspects of the scheme, also identified a number of limitations. On the positive side, the commitment of carers and the professionalism of staff were recognised and highly valued. The approach to assessment, preparation, training and support of staff was considered to exemplify good practice, while it was acknowledged that local authority staff could learn a lot from working alongside project staff. On the other hand, stakeholders recognised that not all placements turned out well for the young person. Distance from the young person's home area and difficulties in securing education sometimes added to young people's stress and to the placement's cost. A gap was apparent between councils' wish to minimise the duration of this expensive service and the research evidence that most of the more successful placements lasted at least a year.

The typical direct costs of a CAPS placement were around £1,000 per week, so it was clearly not a cheap option. In addition to the standard fees, expenditure was usually also required for specialist schooling and travel. The input of time from social work staff was at least as high as with alternative placements, though in the eyes of some it was more productive. Many local authority respondents thought that CAPS either offered good value for money or represented the only option, but some wondered if the sums could be better used for more young people.

9 Towards the limits of foster care?

Introduction

As highlighted in the introductory chapters, and as the title of the book suggests, CAPS was in some respects "testing the limits" of what high-quality foster care could offer some of the most challenging young people in our society. Confident that they were creating a service qualitatively different from existing foster care, CAPS managers were keen that the service should be independently evaluated in order to maximise what could be learned from the project's innovative work. The specific aims of the evaluation were to describe the project's development and how the first young people placed with the project had fared, compared with a similar group who had been placed in secure accommodation at around the same time. The study also set out to examine the foster care task when working with young people who would severely test the limits of individual families' capacities to cope and contain their behaviour. On this basis the research hoped to increase understanding of professional foster care's potential as an alternative to secure accommodation. In this concluding chapter we highlight key findings and consider their implications.

Having read through the preceding chapters, the reader will be aware that drawing together the findings of this study presents something of a challenge. Indeed perhaps the strongest message from CAPS and its evaluation is that this kind of fostering service is characterised by tensions, competing demands and paradoxes, within and across each aspect of its operation. In addition, as argued in Chapter 1, the work of the project and opportunities for young people were crucially shaped and influenced by elements of the current child welfare system and social climate. As we review the main findings and consider their implications, it is our intention to highlight some of these underpinning tensions and dynamics. Through this we hope to do justice to the complex challenges CAPS staff, carers and young people faced on a daily basis. Inevitably it is more difficult to convey the passion, commitment and at times humour with which they tackled these challenges, though for projects planning to replicate CAPS, these would presumably be equally important ingredients.

Movement away from original intentions and operating requirements is a common feature of social programmes. Typically the first few years of a project are characterised by change, trial and error before organisational stability is attained. Much effort is required to gain legitimacy among key stakeholders:

> *Scholarship has focused on the conceptual underpinnings of interventions along with evidence of their outcomes but has given less credence to the consideration of the messy challenges of putting these ideas into practice.* (Cameron et al, 2001, p 327)

In the rest of the chapter, key findings are reported in relation to:
- developing a service;
- defining professional foster care;
- young people's experience in placement and outcomes;
- foster care's potential as an alternative to secure accommodation.

Under each section key findings are summarised and their implications considered, both generally and for projects planning to replicate the service.

Developing a service

Partnership arrangements and funding

CAPS was set up to provide foster placements for young people who would otherwise be in secure care. Initial funding was provided by NCH. Original plans to operate in conjunction with two local authorities did not materialise, largely because of financial considerations within the authorities concerned. This meant referrals were slow in the early stages, resulting in temporary concerns about the financial viability of the project. Nevertheless, in the first three years CAPS expanded to provide a service for two-thirds of Scottish local authorities, with a capacity of 36 placements. The view of project staff and managers was that the revised arrangements worked well. At the same time, the wider geographical coverage had implications for inter-agency communication and the distance between placements and children's home communities. Also the failure to obtain funding for an educational support worker as originally planned proved to be a major omission.

Operating in a market economy meant CAPS had to widen its operation to ensure financial viability. This made it difficult to retain an exclusive focus on providing an alternative to secure care. Through its expansion CAPS showed that there is a demand for an intensive fostering service for very troubled young people.

CAPS' experience demonstrated that this kind of project requires significant core funding in the early stages and that partnership arrangements should be agreed in detail before a scheme of this kind is established.

Placement length

The original plan was that placements would last approximately six months, though it soon became clear that this was too short a period in which to help young people with long-standing difficulties, so the expected time-scale was revised upwards to 12–18 months. In practice it also proved difficult even to operate within this longer timescale, largely because there was a lack of placements for young people to move on to, especially long-term families for the younger age group and Throughcare provision with intensive support for care leavers. In addition, most young people were thought to need security and reliability, so there was a reluctance to move some on once they had begun to establish a degree of trust with the carers. For these reasons some CAPS placements became quasi permanent. Though this diverged from initial planning, the research indicated that longer placements were among the most successful. While some young people derived considerable benefit from short placements, those who achieved best outcomes had remained at least 18 months in the project and established what they expected to be a life-long link with the carers. This highlights the capacity of some young people to establish significant new attachments, even at this relatively late stage in their troubled childhoods.

The shift from short time-limited placements to providing quasi permanent care is important and can be understood in different ways. CAPS evidently came to fill gaps in wider service provision, perhaps indicating that it is difficult to focus exclusively on extending intensive foster care, when mainstream placements are in short supply. Since a need for young people to experience reliable and consistent personal relationships was commonly identified, the move to longer placements might also indicate that the project became essentially needs-led. This observation would be uncontroversial, except for the fact that eligibility for the scheme was based on risk.

As argued in Chapter 1, risk has become the dominant concept in child welfare. This means entitlement to resources is determined by risk rather than need, with high-risk cases gaining access to more expensive and specialised services. In addition, there is a preference for short- rather than long-term interventions, since these are thought to encourage self-sufficiency, while also reducing costs. CAPS' original plans to provide a time-limited community alternative to (expensive) secure accommodation fitted well with this approach, the idea being that CAPS would provide an intensive placement at a point of high risk, thus enabling young people to move on to (less expensive) mainstream provision. However, in practice young people needed specialised support over a longer period, and, since the relationship with individual carers became important, they could not easily be moved on. Local authorities therefore found themselves funding expensive placements long after the high level of risk had subsided, with the result that cost savings were less evident.

During the research period, few local authorities moved young people simply for cost reasons, indicating that there was a general commitment to promote young people's best interests. However, most were reluctant to guarantee funding in the longer term, preferring to periodically review whether the young person continued to warrant such an expensive resource. This resulted in uncertainty for some young people who were keen to remain with their carers. This was an example of how the interplay of needs and risk considerations permeated CAPS.

While it seems reasonable to conclude that future projects should consider in advance the implications of providing short- or long-term placements, CAPS' experience indicates that some key influences on practice are beyond the control of individual projects. It also highlighted that that it is over-optimistic to expect young people with serious difficulties to make significant gains within a few months.

Education

In the original plans it was expected that one of the partner authorities would fund an educational support worker, but since the partnership arrangements changed, this did not materialise. The scheme still hoped to create such a post to liaise with schools and colleges and in order to provide temporary part-time teaching when young people had no school placement. However, well beyond the point when the research ended, it had still not been possible to fund this. Securing educational placements proved difficult, especially when young people required specialist education and moved outwith their own area, since receiving authorities gave priority to local children. As a result, some young people had little or no education for several months which, in addition to compounding their educational disadvantage, added considerably to the stress in placements. In principle and where appropriate, the project encouraged young people to attend mainstream school, though some had difficulty sustaining this and most needed additional support. Any extra services were usually paid for by the placing authority and in some instances, coupled with close collaboration with carers, these enabled very challenging young people to remain in school and make progress.

In the current climate it is not surprising that accessing appropriate education proved difficult. Present policies encourage inclusion in mainstream provision, so specialist resources are scarce. Since specialist education is often an important component of strategies to avoid residential schooling, local authorities are keen to keep the places available for children from their own area, partly because the authority would be responsible for the cost of residential placements, should this be required. As local authorities and independent fostering agencies increasingly place across authority boundaries, it may be that interagency agreements on cross-border school placements should be developed.

In his recent survey of independent fostering schemes, Sellick reported that most incorporated some educational provision (Sellick and Connolly, 2001). Certainly lack of education provision was a serious problem within CAPS, suggesting that similar projects would be well advised to consider in advance how the complex needs of the young people placed would be catered for, either within or outwith the scheme. Equally, local authorities commissioning such a service need to act corporately so that not only social work services are committed to providing resources for the child.

Carer recruitment

In terms of recruitment, CAPS exceeded its original targets in that by the end of its third year there were 28 carer households: 23 couples and five single women. Among couples, five men were main carers, while their partner continued to work outside the home. Carers were recruited across Scotland's central belt. Over half of those recruited had not previously been local authority foster carers, but had relevant experience, for example, in nursing or residential care. Three-quarters of the carers joined CAPS as an alternative to paid employment. Their level of remuneration was comparable with that of senior residential workers. At the point when the research ended no carers had left the scheme. Carers and project staff agreed that effective recruitment and retention depended on a "support package" which included high rate of pay, 24-hour support, regular respite and access to training.

The project demonstrated that professional foster care schemes can add to the supply of foster carers by attracting people who would not otherwise consider becoming foster carers. In deciding to work for CAPS, carers weighed up potential gains against the demands of the job. The same kind of calculative approach applied when working in the scheme in that carers debated what level of disruption and risk should be tolerated to warrant the payment of a "professional fee".

CAPS carers encompassed a wide range of family and work arrangements, reflecting the more flexible life patterns which characterise present-day society. Projects offering fees which equate to a professional salary can thus expect to recruit a more diverse group of carers, with varying expectations of what the carer role should entail.

Defining professional foster care

Although the payment of significant fees in itself meant the scheme could be described as "professional", defining the professional foster care role and task was not so straightforward. From the start it was expected that carers would be required to complete certificated courses in counselling and managing challenging behaviour, with further training provided as required. In addition, carers met regularly with senior practitioners to review their work and development. With this level of training and support it was expected that carers would be equipped to provide a service qualitatively different from traditional foster care. In practice the role and expectations of professional foster carers were gradually worked out during the scheme's first three years, through discussion, practice and changing administrative arrangements. Three key dimensions were:

- equality, autonomy and accountability;
- extending and developing expertise;
- relationship between work and family life.

Equality, autonomy and accountability

In the early stages of the project, considerable emphasis was laid on the fact that carers would enjoy parity of status with CAPS staff. However, in practice senior practitioners were responsible for monitoring and developing carers' practice, so that in terms of accountability they were higher in the organisation's hierarchy. In time this was recognised and senior practitioners came to be seen as carers' line managers. Arrangements for supervision became more formalised, with carers working to a development plan. A significant minority of carers preferred the earlier less formal and more collegiate approach, but most carers responded readily to these developments and by the end of the study a system of line management had become established. This was seen by staff as an essential means of allocating responsibility, ensuring a high-quality service was developed and maintained, and managing risk within the organisation.

Underpinning these developments were competing perspectives on the professional status of foster carers. On the one hand being "professional" meant that carers' expertise was recognised, and given expression in increased carer autonomy. Carers expected and were required to make a wide range of everyday decisions, drawing on their own discretion and judgement. In some situations where other foster carers would have required the approval of the social worker, CAPS carers had the scope to decide what was appropriate and inform the social worker later. In this respect carers were arguably more "professional" than social workers whose scope for independent judgement has been considerably curtailed in recent years. Instead social workers operate according to a managerialist model, especially in situations involving risk. This requirement for increased monitoring and accountability inevitably impacted on carers too. Indeed becoming professional also meant being treated more like a social work employee, as reflected in the introduction of supervision, standard recording requirements and a line management system. Thus "professionalism" both augmented and restricted carers' autonomy, constituting a tension which was also reflected in their contractual status as self-employed but deriving their formal authority to care for children through the scheme.

The high level of autonomy carers enjoyed was somewhat anomalous in the present service context, especially in light of its preoccupation with risk. This therefore prompts questions about a) how carers came to be trusted to operate safely and b) the implications for how risk was managed.

In the permanency planning field it is widely accepted that substitute carers need a degree of autonomy in order to exercise parental authority. Since an experience of family life was an important part of what CAPS offered, similar arguments applied. Thus carers were arguably trusted because they drew on parental authority, common sense and detailed understanding of the individual child, in contrast to professionals whose more general competence and knowledge are increasingly viewed as suspect. Paradoxically, it might therefore be argued that it is carers' quasi-parental status, albeit informed by additional training, knowledge and skills, which allows them such scope within the present system. The practical nature of the fostering task also means a degree of autonomy is essential, especially when carers work in their own home. Being located in a private home also makes the management of risk less visible.

Although carers were accorded considerable autonomy in situations of *potential* risk, when dangers were explicitly identified in terms of child protection these were managed within the formal social work system. Within the latter, the needs and circumstances of the individual child were still important but decisions and actions were strongly guided by more general principles and by agency procedures for managing risk. As a result, carers could find their own strategies for managing risk were curtailed, as for example when carers were instructed not to physically stop young people from running away. In some respects the two systems operating in tandem helped keep young people safe. Another perspective would be that while the carers' discretion-based approach was concerned primarily with the welfare of the individual child, the more formal system was also concerned with the more abstract management of risk within the organisation. In Houston's terms it might be argued that while the first approach focused on the young person as subject, they were objectified within the formal system (Houston, 2001).

Straddling two approaches was sometimes frustrating for carers, especially in situations where they found their autonomy restricted but doubted the capacity of the formal system to protect the child. This duality also potentially made carers vulnerable themselves. While trusted to routinely manage potential risk, this only became visible when something went wrong. Thus, as a number of carers anticipated, they would be subject to close scrutiny or censure, should someone in their care seriously harm themselves or someone else.

CAPS' experience indicated that managing projects of this kind calls for considerable expertise in balancing carer autonomy and accountability. In their own and young people's interests, it was important for carers to know the limits of their own expertise and in what situations they should seek advice from their line manager or the child's social worker. Those planning future projects should therefore be aware that professional foster care requires new and distinctive forms of management, which regard the foster carers as respected workers with considerable day-to-day discretion, but who are line managed by project staff. Competent and skilled project management is essential to ensure standards are maintained, while also valuing carers' diverse approaches and personal commitment. Carers' somewhat ambiguous status allows them to adopt a child-centred, needs-led approach within a system which prioritises risk considerations. However, it may also leave carers vulnerable, especially in projects setting out to manage risk in the community.

Carers' ambiguous status was also highlighted when a child made an allegation against them. Whereas in most respects the scheme tended to treat carers as trusted workers, those subject to an allegation found themselves suddenly investigated in broadly the same way as would apply to ordinary families in the community. This was distressing and potentially undermined carers' professional confidence. CAPS' experience indicated that it would be helpful for future projects to agree procedures for responding to allegations against carers with local authorities in advance, and that these should incorporate independent support and representation for carers.

Extending and developing expertise

An important dimension of professionalism was that carers were expected to extend their expertise to encompass traditional social work skills such as report writing and carrying out written assessments. Most carers welcomed this broadening of their role, but a minority worried that diversifying too much might result in the core fostering task being under-valued. For the latter group fostering was essentially about providing something akin to "ordinary" family life for young people whose previous experience and needs were far from ordinary and who required nurturing care. To them, professional fostering was about being able to accommo-date greater demands and needs within the home.

From the start there was debate about the level of demands and risk professional carers would be expected to work with. The project's policy was to accept referrals on all young people who met its criteria and consider whether a carer could safely manage and meet their needs. Some carers accepted this and, with support, had extended the range of beha-viours they were willing to manage. However, others would have liked reassurance that young people with a history of certain types of aggressive behaviour would not be considered for fostering. In addition to con-sidering their own and their family's safety, some carers felt they had a responsibility to the wider community. Carers varied in the level of risk they were prepared to accommodate and in their understanding of CAPS' expectations of them as professionals. Some also questioned whether young people who were very damaged or needed constant supervision could benefit from the emotional intensity and informality of family life.

These considerations are evidently central to determining the limits of foster care. If the distinguishing contribution of foster care is its capacity to provide something akin to "ordinary family life" within the community, then it will be less effective, even undermined, if asked to work in ways which might threaten family or community life. In a similar vein, Kirton argues that, irrespective of payment levels, the extent to which pro-fessional carers can tolerate difficulties is limited because of their location within the private sphere of the family (Kirton, 2001). Corrick (1999) suggests that it is a tall order for carers to take on the tasks of professional foster care while also running a family home. Combining the two becomes even more difficult in the face of community scrutiny or antagonism, so that this is an important factor in determining the level of risk and disruption which can be managed within foster care. Jordan highlights the point that, in contrast to the rhetoric of present policy which views "the community" as a benign resource, most communities reflect current punitive attitudes towards young people (Jordan, 1999).

CAPS' experience suggests that similar projects should develop a means of exploring and agreeing these complex issues with carers, both in relation to individual young people referred for placement and with a view to establishing broad principles to guide policy and practice.

Relationship between work and family life

It was expected that, compared with traditional fostering, a somewhat different balance would be achieved between work and family life within a professional service. The key difference was that the young person's specific needs should be addressed and accommodated, rather than expecting him or her to fit into existing family routines and practices. Social workers considered this was essential if foster care was to cater for young people with entrenched and complex difficulties. There were indications that, as the project progressed, carers were expected to make increasing space for CAPS work in their family life. For example, carers who had regular visits from their grandchildren were initially confident that this in itself would excuse them from working with young people who presented a risk of abuse. However, over time, and as carers' skills developed, the expectation was that these visits would be curtailed or supervised to allow the carers to extend the range of young people they were able to accommodate. Similarly, though some carers strongly resisted this, at least one household had made provisional arrangements for their own children to be temporarily cared for elsewhere, at times when the child placed was in crisis or making excessive demands.

It therefore seemed that as carers' skills developed and they were more able to cope with more risky and demanding placements, the work increasingly encroached on their family life. Nevertheless, carers retained considerable discretion over which young people they accepted and how they ran their own home. In this context too, the balance between carer autonomy and agency requirements was constantly negotiated to find a mutually acceptable position. However, this again raises the broader question of whether there is a point at which work demands and the adjustments necessary to accommodate them mean the household no longer offers an experience of "ordinary family life".

From the young person's perspective, combining work and family life raised issues about whether they were valued and accepted for themselves or simply as part of the carer's job. For several young people who committed to placements, it was crucially important that their carers cared about them personally, not just as a "placement". Carers' entitlement to respite highlighted that the relationship was in fact contractually based, especially if provided by a series of carers rather than a member of the extended family. Whereas regular respite fitted well with the original plan for short-term placements focusing on specific tasks, it was somewhat at odds with catering for longer-term needs for consistency and acceptance.

Creative tensions or irreconcilable demands?

This section has highlighted some of the tensions and competing demands which are inherent in the professional foster carer's role and everyday practice, especially in work with young people who may present a risk to themselves or others. In other chapters we have described in some detail how, despite these, CAPS staff and carers managed to provide some highly skilled and committed care. Therefore our intention is not to be unduly negative or pessimistic but to unpack tensions and make them more visible. CAPS' thriving operation is evidence in itself that, with skilled management and practice, these very complex processes *can* be held together. Whether the energy entailed is well spent to some extent depends on how much young people can benefit, a topic to which we now turn.

Young people's experience in placement and outcomes

In considering whether young people had benefited, it was important to distinguish between the quality of their experience with CAPS and whether they had made progress. The overall conclusion was that for most young people the CAPS placement had provided a valuable experience but that, within the period covered by the research, this had not necessarily resulted in improved life circumstances. Social workers considered that all young people had derived benefit from the placements, this being greatest for those who had remained in placement for 18 months or more and had established what they expected to be life-long links with carers. However, few completed placements had lasted as long as planned or needed. After two years, overall outcomes for CAPS placements were in most respects no better and no worse than outcomes for a comparison secure care sample.

Broad outcomes were assessed in terms of young people's accommodation arrangements and education or work circumstances at the time the research ended. After leaving CAPS some young people found themselves in unsuitable accommodation or homeless, an outcome which was less common among young people who moved to independence from secure or residential care. Thus moving into foster care had entailed a degree of risk, especially for those whose placements ended abruptly and before other placement options could be put in place. On the other hand, compared with those who started in secure accommodation, slightly more young people who had been with CAPS were in work or training by the time the research ended. However, finding and sustaining employment had been very difficult for everyone and more than half of those who had left school were unemployed. In addition, progress was assessed in relation to emotional and behavioural difficulties, family contact, school/work and health, with both samples making similar progress in each.

In light of the small sample size and its diversity, no statistical association could be established between particular factors and positive or negative outcomes. However, certain features and circumstances were present in more or less effective placements.

Central to a good experience was that the young person felt valued and cared for. Young people described many ways in which carers conveyed that they mattered, for example, listening to them, showing they worried about them, enjoying their company, taking them on outings or on holiday and, in everyday conversation and interaction, subtly challenging their sense of low self-worth. While this did not guarantee changed behaviour, it made young people feel good about themselves and without it there was little hope of progress. Several social workers also highlighted carers' personal acceptance and commitment as key to some small, but as they saw it highly significant, changes in young people's behaviour, such as showing genuine affection, being able to apologise, to listen to both sides of an argument, and to make less use of sexualised behaviour to gain attention. In the short term this did not necessarily result in changes in young people's wider circumstances or lifestyle, but there were indications that the experience of being valued had begun to tentatively open up their capacity to live a fuller life.

In addition effective caring involved establishing clear boundaries. Young people acknowledged the need for rules and clear expectations but preferred and felt more at ease with carers who worked alongside them in a spirit of partnership rather than assuming the role of an expert adviser.

Not surprisingly, young people's motivation to be in a family appeared to be necessary for placements to be sustained, while those who were anxious about or felt disloyal to their birth family often found the placements difficult. Some were helped to manage these feelings, but others remained unhappy and in some instances repeatedly ran away. These findings support the established view that foster care is less likely to be effective if young people do not want to be placed with a family. In addition, it was important that expectations of family life and appropriate emotional distance were mutual.

The influence of the placements on the kind of behaviours which might result in young people being placed in secure care varied. The project was generally effective in reducing self-harming and helped some young people stop running away. However, when young people continued to abscond, this caused serious concern for their safety and resulted in the placement ending. There were indications that help to modify anxiety about relationships with other family members helped reduce absconding. Apart from one boy whose placement lasted only a few weeks, persistent offending was not the *major* concern for any of the young people in the CAPS sample.

The provision of appropriate schooling or work experience was central to a good experience in placement and better outcomes in terms of obtaining formal qualifications and/or employment. Conversely, lack of schooling meant young people missed out and placed considerable strain on the young person and carers. Similarly, lack of specialist help with serious emotional difficulties was thought to have undermined a number of placements. It was difficult for some young people who had been badly hurt emotionally to make progress without skilled professional help to face and manage the pain. Potential sources of appropriate help were suitably skilled social workers, psychologists, psychiatrists and counsellors.

Being placed some distance from their home base worked well for young people who wanted a "fresh start" in a new area, particularly if they were placed with carers who were willing to maintain life-long contact. However, there were also disadvantages in that it became more difficult to access education or maintain family contact. There were particular problems for young people who were planning to move on to independent living and needed to develop local support networks. Nurturing informal supports is evidently important, in light of the poor circumstances of some young people after leaving CAPS.

Based on a composite variable which encompassed aspects of the placement experience and end circumstances, outcomes were rated as follows: good (8); moderate (5); poor (7). This is consistent with the qualititative evidence that a CAPS placement could confer considerable benefits but also entailed a degree of risk. Whereas some young people were enabled to turn their lives around and make progress, others found themselves somewhat at sea, especially when placements intended to support them towards independent living ended abruptly. Fostering's capacity to offer experiences and outcomes at each end of the spectrum has been long recognised, so these findings are not peculiar to CAPS (Triseliotis et al, 1995a).

Implications of the findings on how young people fared

With intensive personal support over time, CAPS placements helped some young people learn something of how to sustain mutually rewarding relationships and survive in school, college or work in the community. In light of most young people's previous experiences and the lack of other services such as education, this was a considerable achievement. However, changes in young people's life circumstances were more modest than had originally been hoped for. Some carers and staff viewed CAPS in terms of giving young people "choices" through showing them a different way of life from the one they had been used to. The outcome findings suggest it is important to distinguish between increasing young people's *awareness* of other lifestyles and *facilitating access* to them. Sociological research which draws attention to the underpinning dynamics which perpetuate disadvantage also suggests that their invisibility means people blame themselves for apparent failure (Bourdieu, 1987; Furlong and Cartmel, 1997; Skeggs, 1997). Thus an emphasis on giving choice, though consistent with current ideology, is not necessarily accurate or in young people's interests.

Whether these results are grounds for developing or replicating the project is largely a question of values. We noted in Chapter 1 that there had been a shift in policy ethos, from liberal principles which emphasise the intrinsic worth of human beings and promotion of social welfare to neo-liberal ideas which assert the moral superiority of self-sufficiency and are concerned with the management of risk (Howe, 1994). According to the liberal outlook, CAPS would be highly valued for its capacity to prevent loss of liberty, while offering the possibility of a personally enriching experience and better life. On the other hand, there would be concern that the risks for some young people were high, while lack of education and other specialist services reduced their life chances. Thus the appropriateness of replicating the project might depend on whether aspects of CAPS' own service and wider resource provision might be developed in such a way as to increase the likelihood of a positive outcome.

The priorities in the current neo-liberal climate are somewhat different, with a predominant focus on achieving observable, measurable results, value for money and enabling people to become self-sufficient. By these standards, CAPS would be seen as worth replicating on the grounds that it had the capacity to effectively care for a number of young people who might otherwise have been in secure accommodation and to achieve similar outcomes, without the associated loss of liberty and high costs. However, CAPS' experience highlighted that short behaviour-focused interventions were not sufficient for young people with serious difficulties, some of whom would require significant levels of support into their adult life. Longer placements meant that potential cost savings were not as obvious as originally envisaged. Perhaps most crucially, the study's findings indicated that young people made more progress when they were able to feel valued and accepted for themselves.

Whereas carers could work at finding ways of conveying acceptance and inclusion within the foster home, a somewhat different message was received when needs for other services could not be catered for. The dearth of suitable placements for education and work experience had a profoundly negative effect on young people's progress, since they missed out on opportunities to learn, while also receiving the underlying message that there was no place for them in the world of work. Similarly a lack of specialist help to resolve serious emotional and behavioural difficulties arguably implied that their well-being was of little value and that they should continue to find their own ways to manage the pain, even if that sometimes put themselves and others at risk. This equipped them to be neither self-sufficient nor safe, while also undermining carers' work towards helping young people become independent, responsible citizens. Thus, paradoxically, it might be argued that certain aspects of the current social climate made it more difficult for young people to conform to current expectations of citizenship.

Howe argues that a social work system based on neo-liberal values will in time be found wanting, prompting a return to "depth" social work which takes account of the whole person, is concerned with process, and addresses why people have difficulties, rather than being concerned primarily with managing "surface" manifestations (Howe, 1996). CAPS' experience arguably lends support to this view in that a reliable, accepting relationship proved central to helping young people address behaviours which caused problems for themselves and society.

What foster care can offer as an alternative to secure accommodation

Having reviewed findings on the potential and limitations of foster care, in this concluding section we consider what professional foster care can offer as an alternative to secure care and identify what ingredients contribute to its effectiveness. The following are discussed:

- aspects of secure care for which foster care might provide an alternative;

- foster care as part of an integrated service;
- the advantages of local and national schemes;
- costs.

Aspects of secure care for which foster care might provide an alternative

Understanding what foster can offer as an 'alternative to secure accommodation' concerns not only the efficacy of foster care but in what sense it is expected to substitute for secure placement. It is evident from this study and the wider Social Work Services Inspectorate survey (SWSI, 2000, p 341) that most young people who come into secure care have immediate needs to be held, kept safe and helped to take stock of their lives. In addition, they have longer-term needs for stability, security and emotional support. The evidence from this research and the SWSI survey is that secure care itself can hold young people safely and meet their short-term needs fairly well, while being ill-equipped to cater for longer-term requirements. In contrast young people were not always able to be held or kept safe in foster care, but could have an emotionally rich experience and in some cases achieve good results over the longer term.

This profile of the secure population prompts a fundamental question about the sense in which a proposed foster care service is to constitute an alternative to secure care. One option is to provide a direct alternative by replacing secure care at the point it is required and catering for the needs to be addressed there in a more benign setting. A quite different aim is to provide a broader service which caters for the immediate and longer-term needs of young people who have been in secure accommodation or whose behaviour has met or is likely to meet the criteria for secure placement. These alternative approaches broadly corresponded with two groups identified in the SWSI secure care survey as potentially able to benefit from foster care.

The first were young people who began to have difficulties in their teens and quickly went through a range of placements, sometimes reaching secure care within a year of first coming to the attention of social work services. Most of them were girls and they typically were academically able and could rely on continuing family support. Few were regular offenders. In most instances they had been placed in secure care because of frequently absconding or self-harming. Most were assessed as needing community placements where they could be supported to address personal and family difficulties, while resuming attendance at mainstream school where possible. CAPS worked successfully with some young people who fitted this profile but others continued to run away, so the placements eventually ended. The research suggested success was more likely if young people were motivated to join a family, were subject to few demands in the initial stages of the placement and were actively helped by the social worker and carer to address the issues which fuelled their anxiety and caused them to run away.

The second group identified in the SWSI survey had spent much longer in care and typically lacked family support. Many had had poor experiences in school and their difficulties included minor offending, absconding from care, and in some instances self-harm. Most were boys. This group of young people were considered to need intensive support and nurturing to help them move on to independent living. Several young people in this category responded well to the personal support and encouragement CAPS offered. However, a number of them found it too difficult to make the transition to the kind of life the family offered and left of their own accord. The young people whose end circumstances were least propitious nearly all belonged in this category. One of the difficulties in catering for this group was that they needed specialist education and very supportive college or work experience placements, neither of which were readily available.

CAPS set out to provide an alternative to secure care at any stage of the process, based on a belief that family placement was almost invariably better than secure care or other residential provision. The research did not bear out this unqualified faith in foster care but indicated that family placement could be extremely effective if provided in appropriate circumstances and in collaboration with other services.

Specialist foster care as part of an integrated service

From the outset it was recognised that CAPS' success would rely on effective co-operation with other services. Two key forms of service were identified:

- services provided during the placement, notably social work support,

education and psychological or psychiatric input;
* alternative and complementary care provision.

Services provided during the placement

From the carers' perspective, effective local authority social work support contributed significantly to placement effectiveness. In some of the most successful placements, carers cited the commitment of the social worker and placing authority as an important advantage, while in other situations lack of social work time had prevented planned family work being undertaken or plans for the young person to move to independent living being progressed. Thus local authorities should recognise that placement outcome will at least in part reflect the level of support they are able to provide.

Educational support and co-operation were seen by CAPS and NCH as crucial at the outset, but proved difficult to achieve. A number of mainstream school arrangements did not work out well. Long waits to obtain additional support or special placements not only interrupted the young person's academic career, but also placed strain on relationships in the foster home. The appointment of an education support worker would be a high priority for future projects which seek to provide a similar service. Also the impetus to corporate responsibility for children given by the Children (Scotland) Act 1995 and subsequent government initiatives need to ensure that all departments respond to the needs of looked after children, not only within but between different councils.

Many of the young people were also thought to require ongoing psychological or psychiatric assistance, but hardly any received this, whereas it was more readily accessed in some secure units. It was common for young people to refuse to be referred to this kind of service, while some also had to wait a considerable time for appointments and/or had moved by the time these were offered. Several carers would at times have valued access to a psychiatrist or psychologist for advice on how to manage certain young people. Future projects might usefully consider how best to make this kind of expertise available to young people and carers, possibly through engaging the services of a psychologist or psychiatrist on a consultancy basis. In addition, local health authorities should seek to ensure that access to specialist services is not reduced for young people who are looked after and move across agency boundaries.

The research has highlighted that what foster care can offer and who it can effectively cater for depends crucially on the nature and availability of support services.

Alternative and complementary care provision

Some social workers of young people in the comparison sample suggested that foster care might be extended to a wider range of the secure population if it could be offered on a part-time basis. In this way it would serve young people who would benefit from an opportunity to develop personal relationships and experience family life but were considered too demanding for foster care and/or unable to cope with the emotional intensity of family life on a full-time basis. Some young people in both samples made considerable progress at residential school, lending support to the idea that combining this with weekend foster care might work well for some young people who have serious difficulties and lack a family base. Another suggested role for part-time placement was to support older teenagers with significant difficulties cope with the move towards independent living.

The research included too few examples of part-time placements to be able to assess their effectiveness reliably. However, the experience of the four young people who had experienced part-time care indicated that it had worked well for the two who moved on to independent living, while sharing care with a residential school had mixed results. In the latter arrangement, success had depended on carers and staff communicating effectively, understanding each other's role and reaching agreement on how the young person should be cared for.

A number of carers opposed the idea of part-time placements on the grounds that it would be more difficult to help young people unlearn institutionalised behaviour which, as they saw it, was a key part of the fostering task. Some also suggested that much of the value of foster care derived from being accepted by a family on a full-time basis. This belief in the distinctiveness of foster care had contributed to the abandonment of the project's original plans for some respite to be provided in residential accommodation.

These arguments reflect questions about the purpose of foster care schemes for young people in or close to secure care which future projects would do well to consider in advance whether:

- the aim is simply to reduce time spent in secure care OR also to provide a longer-term service to young people whose serious difficulties have resulted in secure care placement in the past or are likely to do so in the future;
- the value of foster care lies simply in providing a more benign and less restrictive care setting than secure OR whether it is also expected to open up possibilities for young people to develop emotionally and be better equipped to cope with life;
- foster care can supplement open residential care OR provides a fundamentally different experience based on full-time family care.

The research findings support the view that young people can benefit from both foster and residential care, and that their interests will be best served when the two work in tandem. The potentially high benefits from foster care did not apply to all young people, yet most found the experience beneficial, even when placements were short-lived. These findings accord with arguments in favour of broadening access to foster care alongside residential provision. Many young people in secure care have entrenched problems with which they require professional help, while also being unaccustomed to the emotional intensity of family life. This adds to the case for foster care potentially having a useful role in preparing them for living in the community by providing long-term personal support, possibly on a part-time basis. It is also important that young people have access to safe, residential alternatives, should the family placement option prove too emotionally challenging. For some a period of residential care in a supportive setting may indeed provide welcome respite. The provision of respite itself highlights the limitations and tensions at the heart of professional fostering. On the one hand, respite responds to carers' needs as people carrying out a stressful task and their rights as professionals. On the other hand, it risks subverting young people's needs for belonging and acceptance, and may undermine the quasi-normal family experience which is meant to differentiate foster care from residential care.

The advantages of local or national schemes

One of the main ways in which CAPS deviated from its original plans was to make its service available to all authorities rather than work in partnership with only two. With some local authorities indicating their intention to recruit a few "CAPS-style" carers in the future, it is worth considering the respective merits of local and national schemes. Organisational issues are considered first, then how distance affected young people's placements and experience.

Organisational issues

The research results might be used to support arguments for both local and national provision. On the one hand, national projects are able to recruit a wider range of carers, thus increasing opportunities for skilled matching which proved critical to placement success. If local schemes were also smaller, it might be difficult to provide the range of carers necessary to cater for young people's diverse needs and preferences. On the other hand, operating across authorities reduced opportunities for CAPS staff to systematically identify young people who might benefit from a placement in the scheme and work closely with field, residential and secure care staff towards this. Instead project staff relied primarily on referrals from field social workers and found themselves under pressure to compensate for the general lack of family placements across Scotland. Together these developments lessened CAPS' capacity to focus specifically on catering for young people in or close to secure accommodation.

Distance between the carers and the young person's home area

Partly because of becoming a national service but also because of where carers happened to live, one of the distinctive features of CAPS was that most young people were placed outwith their home area, typically about 30 miles away. Some carers and young people welcomed this because it allowed for a fresh start, away from the unhelpful influences of friends and family. However, there were also less helpful consequences. The cost to the local authority of providing social work support increased, while in some instances additional expenditure was also required to purchase or support mainstream or specialist school placements within the carers' authority. However, the most important consideration was the inevitable disjunction between the young person's schooling and social contacts in placement and both prior and future supportive relationships. Continuity is vital for most young people, who will, in one way or another, return to their original communities (Bullock *et al*, 1993; Marsh and Peel, 1999). Only a minority may make a fresh start in the carers' neighbourhood, so the interests of most are served by helping develop support networks which will continue after the placement ends.

Continuity of support networks was particularly important for young people moving on to independent living, so that, where possible, it was helpful for young people to work towards independence in the area where they expected to be housed. For some young people, moving outwith the system of care and local resources could present a high risk, in that when CAPS placements broke down, they found themselves homeless or living in very uncertain situations. This suggests that if community alternatives are to be developed for young people approaching independence, greater attention is needed to the potential risks as well as the opportunities. Maximising continuity and support networks are ways of reducing risk and fostering resilience. This would be helped by increasing opportunities for young people to be placed with carers in their local area, nurturing all aspects of the young person's support network, and building in opportunities and resources for carers to offer part-time and after care support.

The research evidence suggests that local projects which can be inclusive of existing networks and maximise complementary working across resources might have much to commend them, particularly to young people close to independent living who make up a significant proportion of the secure care population.

Costs

In terms of cost, CAPS placements were considerably less expensive than secure accommodation. At the time the research was carried out the basic cost was £850 per week. However, local authorities could incur up to £550 per week in additional costs if young people also required specialist education and/or a substantial amount of travelling to get to school or to keep in touch with their home area. In addition, the research indicated that the best outcomes occurred when young people stayed with carers for a year or more. Consequently, to achieve the best outcomes, local authorities may need to be prepared to make the financial commitment over a much longer period than most young people would spend in secure care. On the basis of the findings presented here, it is for local authorities to weigh up whether a significant investment in a troubled young person is likely to pay off in terms of both finance and quality of life.

Concluding remarks

The study has confirmed that, with appropriate remuneration and support, foster carers are willing and able to care for young people whose behaviour is very challenging and may present a risk to themselves or others. CAPS' ability to recruit and retain a diverse group of carers suggested that they had correctly identified the key ingredients of effective support from the start. These were fees equivalent to a professional salary, 24-hour emergency support and advice, regular respite, and high levels of professional development and training. Each young person in the study was thought to have benefited from being in the scheme, with overall outcomes rated as "good" for over a third. These findings are evidence that foster care can in certain circumstances provide an effective alternative to secure accommodation.

However, the study results also urge a degree of caution, or at least thoughtful consideration, before future schemes of this kind are developed. It is anomalous in the present context that the care of young people who present a risk to themselves or others is entrusted to private households. The paradox is to some extent managed through carers' ambiguous status which combines elements of the independent professional, the employee, and the authoritative parent. Combining a high level of skill with personal commitment emerged as key to foster care's potential effectiveness. However, questions were raised about:
a) the level of challenging behaviour and risk carers are able to accommo-
    date, while still remaining an "ordinary" family in the community; and
b) carers' vulnerability when working with a high level of risk in a relatively unregulated setting.

CAPS placements also involved risks for young people, especially when placements ended abruptly after they had reached 16 and suitable alternative accommodation was not readily available. Some young people also continued to run away, putting themselves at risk. A less obvious but important risk was that young people would blame themselves when placements did not work out, thus adding to their sense of worthlessness and failure.

The study has implications not just for CAPS and any comparable fostering service. The comparison study bore out the conclusions of earlier work (Triseliotis *et al*, 1995; SWSI, 1996) that secure accommodation should not be demonised. In an ideal world it would not be necessary to lock up young people, but a number of residents, who are typically admitted during an extreme crisis following long-standing severe problems, are enabled by the present provision to remain safe and begin to take stock of their lives. Similarly, certain young people who did not stay long with CAPS went on to make considerable progress in residential school placements.

The study suggests that future projects should give prior consideration to which section(s) of the secure care population they wish to provide for, at what stage, and the type of family placement they would require. Funding and partnerships arrangements, geographical location and recruitment of carers should be determined on this basis. The research has demonstrated that high-quality foster care is cheaper than secure care but not necessarily cheaper than other residential options. It is therefore important that to achieve good value, foster care and other options are as effectively targeted as possible.

Family placements cannot provide a complete answer for all the kinds of young people with serious behaviour and personal difficulties who have up to now been placed in secure residential units. However, the CAPS scheme has shown that a considerable number can be placed in foster care and some can be helped to turn their lives around in a major way. A positive outcome was more likely when young people were able to feel accepted and valued. Aspects of the current social climate which demonise young people and restrict access to specialist support services make it more difficult for those with serious difficulties to be accommodated in the community and improve the quality of their lives. Thus, in a more tolerant and generous social and policy context, skilled foster care might be expected to achieve more and possibly to extend its limits even further.

References

Aldgate J, Maluccio A and Reeves C (eds) (1989) *Adolescents in Foster Families*, London: Bastford.

Almeida M C and Hawkins R P *et al* (1989) 'Evaluation of foster-family based treatment in comparison with other programs', in J Hudson and B Galaway (eds) *The State as Parent*, Dordrecht: Kluwer.

Audit Commission (1994). *Seen but not Heard – Co-ordinating community child health and social services for children in need*, London: HMSO.

Barnardo's (2001) *Outcomes for Children No 3: Family placement services*, Edinburgh: Barnardo's Scotland.

Beck U (1992) *Risk Society: Towards a new modernity*, London: Sage.

Bell E (2002) 'Promoting children's rights through the use of relationship', *Child and Family Social Work* 7:1, pp 1–11.

Berridge D and Cleaver H (1987) *Foster Home Breakdown*, Oxford: Blackwell.

Biehal N and Wade J (1999) 'Taking a chance: the risks associated with going missing from substitute care', *Child Abuse Review* 8, pp 366–76.

Blyth E (2001) 'The impact of the first term of the new Labour Government on social work in Britain: the interface between education policy and social work', *British Journal of Social Work* 31:4, pp 563–578.

Borland M, Pearson C, Hill M, Tisdall K and Bloomfield I (1998) *Education and Care Away from Home: A review of research, policy and practice*, Edinburgh: Scottish Council for Research in Education.

Bourdieu P (1987) 'What makes a social class? On the theoretical and practical existence of groups', *Berkeley Journal of Sociology*, pp 1–17.

Brearley C P (1982) *Risk and Social Work*, London: Routledge & Kegan Paul.

Broad B (1998) *Young People Leaving Care: Life After the Children Act 1989*, London: Jessica Kingsley.

Bullock R, Little M and Milham S (1993) *Going Home*, Aldershot: Dartmouth.

225

Bullock R, Little M and Milham S (1998) *Secure Care Outcomes*, Aldershot: Ashgate.

Byrne S (1997) 'Risks in adoption and fostering', in H Kemshall and J Pritchard, *Good Practice in Risk Assessment Vol. 2*, London: Jessica Kingsley.

Cameron G and Kerbanow J *et al* (2001) 'Program implementation and diffusion', in I Prilleltensky, G Nelson and L Peirson (eds) *Promoting Family Wellness and Preventing Child Maltreatment*, Toronto: University of Toronto Press.

Cash S J (2001) 'Risk assessment in child welfare: the art and science', *Children and Youth Services Review* 23:11, pp 811–30.

Chamberlain, P and Weinrott, M (1990) 'Specialised foster care: treating seriously emotionally disturbed children', *Children Today* 19, pp 24–27.

Chamberlain P (1990) 'Comparative evaluation of a specialised foster care program for seriously delinquent youths: a first step', *Community Alternatives* 2:2, pp 21–36.

Chamberlain P and Reid J B (1998) 'Comparison of two community alternatives to incarceration for chronic juvenile offenders', *Journal of Consulting and Clinical Psychology* 66, pp 642–33.

Clark H B and Prange M E *et al* (1994) 'Improving adjustment outcomes for foster children with emotional and behavioural disorders: early findings from a controlled study on individualized services', *Journal of Emotional and Behavioural Disorders* 2:4, pp 207–18.

Cleaver H and Freeman P (1995) *Parental Perspectives in Cases of Suspected Child Abuse*, London: HMSO.

Cleaver H, Unell I and Aldgate J (1999) *Children's Needs – Parenting Capacity: The impact of parental mental illness, problem alcohol use and drug use and domestic violence on children's development*, London: The Stationery Office.

Cleveland (1988) *Report of the Inquiry into Child Abuse in Cleveland, Cmnd 412*, London: HMSO.

Clyde (1992) *The Report of the Inquiry into the Removal of Children from Orkney in February 1991. Return to an address of the Honourable House of Commons, 27 October 1992*, Edinburgh: HMSO.

Colton M and Williams M (eds) (1997) *The World of Foster Care*, Aldershot: Arena.

Colton M (2002) 'Abuse in residential care institutions', *Children & Society* 16:1, pp 33–44.

Colton M and Drury C *et al* (1995) *Children in Need: Family support under the Children Act 1989*, Aldershot: Avebury.

Cooper A and Hetherington R (1999) 'Negotiation', in C Wattam and N Parton, *Child Sexual Abuse Responding to the Experiences of Children*, Chichester: Wiley.

Corrick H (1999) 'The professionalisation of foster care', in A Wheal, *The Companion to Foster Care*, Lyme Regis: Russell House Publishing.

Culpitt I (1992) *Welfare and Citizenship: Beyond the crisis of the welfare state*, London: Sage.

Culpitt I (1999) *Social Policy and Risk*, London: Sage.

Curtis P A, Alexander G and Lunghofer L A (2001) 'A literature review comparing the outcomes of residential group care and therapeutic foster care', *Child and Adolescent Social Work Journal* 18, pp 377–92.

Dalrymple J (2001) 'Safeguarding young people through confidential advocacy services', *Child & Family Social Work* 6:2, pp 149–60.

Dartington (1995) *Child Protection: Messages from Research*, London: HMSO.

Dean M (1999) 'Risk calculable and incalculable', in D Lupton, *Risk and Sociocultural Theory: New directions and perspectives*, Cambridge: Cambridge University Press.

Department of Health (2000) *Framework for the Assessment of Children in Need and their Families*, London: HMSO.

Dore M M (1994) *Guidelines for Placement Decision-making*, New York: Child Welfare Administration of the City of New York.

Douglas M (1992) *Risk and Blame: Essays in Cultural Theory*, London: Routledge.

Downes C (1992) *Separation Revisited*, Aldershot: Ashgate.

Earle R and Newburn T (2002) 'Creative tensions? Young offenders, restorative justice and the introduction of referral orders', *Youth Justice* 1:3, pp 5–13.

Farmer E and Pollock S (1998) *Sexually Abused and Abusing Children in Substitute Care*, Chichester: Wiley.

Fenyo A and Knapp M *et al* (1989) *Foster Care Breakdown: A study of a special teenager fostering scheme*, Canterbury: PSSRU University of Kent.

Field S (1992) 'Young Offender Community Support Scheme', *Community Alternatives* 4:2, pp 77–96.

Fonaghy P and Steele H *et al* (1994) 'The theory and practice of resilience', *Journal of Child Psychology* 35:2, pp 231–57.

Furlong A and Cartmel F (1997) *Young People and Social Change*, Buckingham: Open University Press.

Gabarino J and Sherman D (1980) 'High-risk neighbourhoods and high-risk families: the human ecology of child maltreatment', *Child Development* 51, pp 88–98.

Gabor P and Charles G (1994) 'The evaluation of specialist foster care', in B McKenzie (ed) (1994) *Current Perspectives on Foster Family Care for Children and Youth*, Toronto: Wall & Emerson.

Galaway B (1990) 'The place of specialist foster family care in a system of child welfare services', in B Galaway, D Maglajlic, J Hudson, P Harmon and J McLagan (eds) *International Perspectives on Specialist Foster Family Care*, St Paul: Human Service Associates.

Gambrill E and Shlonsky A (2000) 'Risk assessment in context', *Children and Youth Services Review* 22:11/12, pp 813–37.

Gilligan R (1997) 'Beyond permanence? – the importance of resilience in child placement practice and planning', *Adoption & Fostering* 21, pp 12–20.

Gilligan R (1999) 'Enhancing the resilience of children and young people in public care by mentoring their talents and interests', *Child & Family Social Work* 4:3, pp 187–96.

Goldson B (2000) ' "Children in need" or "young offenders"? Hardening attitudes, organisational change and new challenges for social work with children in trouble', *Child & Family Social Work* 5:3, pp 255–65.

Goodman R (1994) 'A modified version of the Rutter Parent Questionnaire including extra items on children's strengths – A Research Note', *Journal of Child Psychology and Psychiatry* 35:8, pp 1483–94.

Graham J and Hazel N *et al* (1992) 'Foster family care for homeless young people', *Community Alternatives* 4:2, pp 27–42.

Green L and Masson H (2002) 'Adolescents who sexually abuse and residential accommodation: issues of risk and vulnerability', *British Journal of Social Work* 32, pp 149–68.

Harris R and Timms N (1993a) 'The lost key: secure accommodation and juvenile crime: an English and Welsh perspective', *Australia and New Zealand Journal of Criminology* 26, pp 219–31.

Harris R and Timms N (1993b) *Secure Accommodation in Child Care: Between hospital and prison or thereabouts*, London: Routledge.

Hazel N (1981) *A Bridge to Independence*, Oxford: Blackwell.

Hazel N (1990) 'The development of specialist foster care for adolescents: policy and practice', in B Galaway, D Maglajlic, J Hudson, P Harmon and J McLagan (eds) *International Perspectives on Specialist Foster Care*, St Paul: Human Services Associates.

Hicks C and Nixon S (1991) 'Unfounded allegations of child abuse in the UK: a survey of foster parents' reactions to investigative procedures', *Child and Youth Services Review* 15:2, pp 249–60.

Hill M (1990) 'The manifest and latent lessons of child abuse enquiries', *British Journal of Social Work* 20:3, pp 197–213.

Hill M and Nutter R *et al* (1993) 'A comparative survey of specialist fostering schemes in the UK and North America', *Adoption & Fostering* 17:2, pp 17–22.

Hill M, Laybourn A and Brown J (1996) 'Children whose parents misuse alcohol: a study of services and needs', *Child and Family Social Work* 1:3, pp 158–67.

Hill M and Tisdall K (1997) *Children and Society*, London: Longman.

Holman B (1988) *Putting Families First: Prevention and child care*, Basingstoke: Macmillan.

Holman B (1998) 'Neighbourhoods and exclusion', in M Barry and C Hallet (eds) *Social Exclusion and Social Work*, Lyme Regis: Russell House Publishing.

Houston S (2001) 'Transcending the fissure in risk theory', *Child & Family Social Work* 6:3, pp 219–28.

Houston S (2000) 'Pathways to change: the application of solution-focused brief therapy to foster care', in G Kelly and R Gilligan (eds) *Issues in Foster Care*, London: Jessica Kingsley.

Houston S and Griffiths H (2000) 'Risk in child protection: time for a paradigm shift', *Child & Family Social Work* 5:1, pp 1–10.

Howe D (1994) 'Modernity, post-modernity and social work', *British Journal of Social Work* 24, pp 513–32.

Howe D (1996) 'Surface and depth in social work practice', in N Parton, *Social Theory, Social Change and Social Work*, London: Routledge.

Howe D, Brandon M, Hinings D and Schofield G (1999) *Attachment Theory, Child Maltreatment and Family Support: A practice and assessment model*, Basingstoke: Macmillan.

Jackson S (ed) (2001) *Nobody Ever Told Us School Mattered*, London: BAAF.

James A and Prout A (1997) *Constructing and Reconstructing Childhood*, London: Falmer Press.

Jenks C (1996) *Childhood*, London: Routledge.

Jones C (2001) 'Voices from the front line: state social workers and New Labour', *British Journal of Social Work* 31:4, pp 547–62.

Jordan B (1999) 'Child sexual abuse and the community', in C Wattam and N Parton (eds) *Child Sexual Abuse Responding to the Experiences of Children in the Community*, Chichester: Wiley.

Jordan B (2001) 'Tough love: social exclusion, social work and the third way', *British Journal of Social Work* 31:4, pp 527–46.

Kelly B (1992) *Children Inside: A study of secure provision*, London: Routledge.

Kemshall H (1996) *Reviewing Risk: A review of research on the assessment and management of risk and dangerousness: implications for policy and practice in the probation service*, Croydon: Home Office.

Kendrick A (1997) *Safeguarding Children Living Away from Home from Abuse: Children's Safeguards Review*, Edinburgh: The Stationery Office.

Kirton D (2001) 'Love and money: payment, motivation and the fostering task,' *Child & Family Social Work* 6:3, pp 199–208.

Knapp M and Fenyo A (1989) *Efficiency in Foster Care:Proceeding with Caution*, State Intervention on behalf of Children and Youth, Conference: Aquafredda di Maretea: Italy.

Kosonen M (1993) *Evaluation of Foster and Adoptive Care Services in Tayside*, Dundee: Tayside Regional Council.

Lowe K (1990) *Teenagers in Foster Care*, London: NFCA.

Lupton D (1999) *Risk*, London: Routledge.

Macdonald K I and Macdonald G M (1999) 'Perceptions of risk', in P Parsloe (ed) *Risk Assessment in Social Care and Social Work*, London: Jessica Kingsley.

McKenzie B (ed) (1994) *Current Perspectives on Foster Family Care for Children and Youth*, Toronto: Wall and Emerson.

Marshall K (1997) *Children's Rights in the Balance: The participation – protection debate*, Edinburgh: The Stationery Office.

Marsh P and Peel M (1999) *Leaving Care in Partnership: Family involvement with care leavers*, London: The Stationery Office.

McFadden E J and Ryan P (1991) 'Maltreatment in family foster homes: dynamics and dimensions', *Child and Youth Services Review* 15:2, pp 209–31.

Millar S (2000) 'The foster barons cash in on misery', *The Observer*, 16 July 2000.

Morris S and Wheatley H (1994) *Time to Listen: The experiences of young people in foster and residential care*, London: ChildLine.

Muncie J (2002a) 'A new deal for youth? Early intervention and correctionalism', in G Hughes, E McLaughlin and R Muncie (eds) *Crime Prevention and Community Safety: New directions*, Buckingham: Open University Press.

Muncie J (2002b) 'Policy transfers and "What works": some reflections on comparative youth justice,' *Youth Justice* 1:3, pp 27–35.

NFCA (1994) *Choosing to Foster: The challenge to care*, London: NFCA.

NFCA (1996) *Child Abuse: Accusations against foster carers*, London: NFCA.

Nixon S and Verity P (1996) 'Allegations against foster families', *Foster Care*, January 1996, pp 11–14.

Nutter R W, Hudson J, Galaway B and Hill M (1995) 'Specialist foster care program standards in relation to costs, client characteristics and outcomes', in J Hudson and B Galway (eds) *Child Welfare in Canada*, Toronto: Thompson Educational.

O'Neill T (2001) *Children in Secure Accommodation*, London: Jessica Kingsley.

Parker R, Ward H, Jackson S, Aldgate J and Wedge P (1991) *Assessing Outcomes in Child Care*, London: HMSO.

Parton N (1985) *The Politics of Child Abuse*, London: Macmillan.

Parton N (1996a) 'Child protection, family support and social work', *Child & Family Social Work* 1, pp 3–11.

Parton N (1996b) 'Social work, risk and the blaming system', in N Parton (ed) *Social Theory, Social Change and Social Work*, London: Routledge.

Parton N (1997) 'Child protection and family support: current debates and future prospects', in N Parton, *Child Protection and Family Support*, London: Routledge.

Parton N (1998) 'Risk, advanced liberalism and child welfare: the need to rediscover uncertainty and ambiguity', *British Journal of Social Work* 28, pp 5–27.

Parton N and Wattam C *et al* (1997) *Child Protection, Risk and the Moral Order*, London: Routledge.

Pine B and Jacobs M (1989) 'The training of foster parents for work with adolescents', in J Aldgate, A Maluccio and C Reeves (eds) *Adolescents in Foster Families*, London: Batsford.

Power S A W G (1999) 'New Labour's education policy: first, second or third way?', *Journal of Education Policy* 14:5.

Reddy L A and Pfeifer S I (1997) 'Effectiveness of treatment foster care with children and adolescents: A review of outcome studies,' *Journal of the American Academy of Child and Adolescent Psychiatry* 36:5, pp 581–88.

Rose N (1989) *Governing the Soul: The shaping of the private self*, London: Routledge.

Rosenberg M (1979) *Conceiving the Self*, New York: Basic Books.

Rosenthal J, Edmonson D and Groze V (1991) 'A descriptive study of abuse and neglect in out-of-home placement', *Child Abuse and Neglect* 15, pp 249–60.

Rowe J, Hundleby M and Garnett L (1989) *Child Care Now: A survey of placement patterns*, London: BAAF.

Scottish Executive (2001) *For Scotland's Children: Report: Better integrated children's services*, Edinburgh: Scottish Executive.

Scottish Executive (2002) *National Care Standards: Care homes for children and young people*, Edinburgh: Scottish Executive.

Sellick C and Connolly J (2001) *National Survey of Independent Fostering Agencies*, Norwich: University of East Anglia.

Shaw M and Hipgrave T (1983) *Specialist Fostering*, London: Batsford.

Shaw M and Hipgrave T (1989) 'Specialist fostering 1988 – a research study', *Adoption & Fostering* 13:4, pp 17–21.

Skeggs B (1997) *Formations of Class and Gender*, London: Sage.

Smith P M (1986) 'Evaluation of Kent placements', *Adoption & Fostering* 10:1, pp 29–33.

Social Exclusion Unit (1999) *Bridging the Gap: New Opportunities for 16–18-year-olds not in education, employment or training*, Parliamentary Report.

Social Exclusion Unit (2001) *A New Commitment to Neighburhood Renewal: National Strategy Action Plan*, London: Cabinet Office.

Spratt T (2001) 'The influence of child protection orientation on child welfare', *British Journal of Social Work* 31, pp 933–54.

SWSI (1996) *A Secure Remedy*, Edinburgh: Social Work Services Inspectorate for Scotland.

SWSI (2000) *Secure Care Survey Report*, Unpublished: Scottish Executive.

Testa M F and Rolock N (1999) 'Professional foster care: a future worth pursuing?' *Child Welfare* 78, pp 108–24.

The Scottish Office (1992) *Another Kind of Home: A review of residential child care*, Edinburgh: SWSI.

Triseliotis J, Borland M, Hill M and Lambert L (1995a) *Teenagers and the Social Work Services*, London: HMSO.

Triseliotis J, Sellick C and Short C (1995b) *Foster Care: Theory and practice*, London: Batsford.

Triseliotis J, Borland M and Hill M (2000) *Delivering Foster Care*, London: BAAF.

Tunstill J (1996) 'Implementing the family support clauses of the 1989 Children Act: legislative, professional and organisational obstacles', in N Parton (ed) *Child Protection and Family Support: Tensions, contradictions and possibilities*, London: Routledge.

Wade J (1997) 'Developing leaving care services: tapping the potential of foster carers', *Adoption & Fostering* 21:3, pp 40–9.

Waiton S (2001) *Scared of the Kids? Curfews, crime and the regulation of young people*, Sheffield: Sheffield Hallam University Press.

Wald M and Woolverton M (1990) 'Risk assessment: the Emperor's New Clothes?' *Child Welfare* LXIX, pp 483–511.

Ward H (1995) *Looking After Children: Research into practice*, London: HMSO.

Williams F (1998) 'Agency and structure revisited', in M Barry and C Hallet (eds) *Social Exclusion and Social Work*, Lyme Regis: Russell House Publishing.

Yelloly M (1979) *Independent Evaluation of Twenty-five Placements in the Kent Family Project*, Maidstone: Kent County Council.

INDEX

Abuse
   physical, 15
   sexual, 15–16, 48, 72
agreements, 9, 65, 202
allowances, 49, 135, 167
anger management, 158
A Secure Remedy report, 1
assessment, 17–18, 20, 33, 36, 41,
   46–49, 83, 92–93, 119–120,
   121–122, 130, 152, 154, 160,
   162, 164, 176–177, 182–183,
   186–187, 189, 195–196, 207
attachments, 200

behaviour problems, 3, 5, 86, 90,
   93, 97, 134, 189
boys, 7–8, 15, 36–40, 59, 67, 73,
   84–88, 101, 105, 108, 110, 113,
   127, 129, 131, 134–137,
   139–140, 158–159, 162, 165,
   167, 171, 173, 180, 190, 194,
   211, 216
breakdown of placements, 221
brothers and sisters, 15, 58, 94–95,
   99–100, 109, 169, 175

CAPS
   development of the scheme,
     10–11, 23, 31
   staff, 36, 51, 68, 72, 74, 128,
     165, 170, 189, 198, 204, 209,
     220

children's hearings system, 7
college, 99, 107, 109, 136–137,
   156, 158, 161, 163, 166–168,
   182, 185, 212, 216
communication, 49, 136, 162, 165,
   175, 190–191, 199
community, 1–3, 6–7, 12, 16,
   22–26, 28–29, 35, 42–45, 54,
   67, 70–71, 86, 96, 100–101, 107,
   109, 111–112, 116, 124, 128,
   131, 135, 143–144, 147,
   157–159, 161, 179, 188, 201,
   206–207, 212, 216, 219,
   221–223
comparison sample, 26, 84, 93, 121,
   142, 166, 168, 173, 177, 218
confidentiality, 178
conflict, 43, 65, 80, 162
costs, 2, 4, 24, 26–27, 31, 41, 43,
   63, 65, 192–196, 201–202, 213,
   215, 220–221
counselling, 8, 48–49, 110–111,
   117–118, 151, 158, 177, 185,
   195, 203

decision-making, 13, 190
development
   of CAPS, *see* CAPS,
     development of the scheme
   of young people, 123
diaries, 42, 74
disabilities, 16, 20, 36

prison, 41, 85, 128, 131, 137,
144–145, 180–181
professional fostering, 2, 26, 45–46,
49, 51, 54, 83, 121, 192,
198–199, 203, 206–209, 214,
219
profiles, 97
psychiatrists, 117, 152, 178, 212,
217

referrals, 12, 27, 31–33, 35–40,
42–43, 56, 71, 86, 110, 177, 192,
199, 207, 220
rejection, 25, 29, 65, 104–105, 108,
117, 123, 130, 149, 169, 183
relationships, 9–10, 28, 35, 94,
103–105, 107, 109, 111–112,
115, 117, 119, 124, 142, 169,
176, 200, 211–212, 217–218,
221
remand fostering, 3
replication, 180, 198–199
residential care, 1, 15–16, 23–24,
32, 34, 37, 39, 99, 102–104, 107,
111, 118, 123, 131, 137,
144–145, 152, 156, 187, 193,
203, 210, 219
resilience, 10, 11, 221
respite care, 83
reviews, 13, 62
rights, 7, 10, 21, 24, 47, 49, 61, 66,
73, 75–76, 78–79, 83, 87, 219
risk, 2, 6–9, 11–21, 23–25, 29–30,
32, 41–43, 47, 51, 55, 63, 65–66,
69–72, 74–75, 78–79, 81–82, 86,
97, 105, 107, 117, 127, 129, 131,

133, 137, 141, 146, 150, 157,
160, 168, 189, 191–192, 201,
203–210, 212–214, 221–223
risk assessment, 15, 17, 71
Rosenberg scale, 27, 92–93
rules, 124–126, 134, 140–141, 146,
157, 211
running away, 6, 99–100, 106–107,
113, 129, 136–137, 156, 159,
177, 179, 205, 211

Scottish Executive, 13, 21
secure accommodation, 6–10, 20,
28, 32, 36, 40, 43, 85, 87, 89,
95–97, 104, 107, 113, 120–122,
129, 136, 142–143, 145–146,
152, 155, 166, 168, 180–181,
183–185, 198–199, 201, 210,
213–215, 220–223
self harming, 6, 8, 27, 40–41, 89,
91, 106–107, 113, 118, 127, 129,
160, 185, 211, 216
social workers, 5, 8, 13, 18, 23, 27,
35, 46, 50–51, 54, 56, 59–60, 62,
64–65, 67, 71, 78, 85, 89, 91–93,
98–103, 105–106, 108–109,
112–118, 120–122, 124, 127–130,
132, 134, 136–137, 141, 143–145,
147, 149, 150–154, 158–160,
162, 164–165, 168, 171–173,
175–179, 183–185, 187–191,
193–195, 204, 206, 208, 210–212,
216–218, 220
specialist fostering, 1–6, 28, 50
specialist services, 8, 110, 121, 146,
152, 177, 213, 217

238